# Sex & the Paranormal

Paul Deane

DR PAUL DEANE grew up on the Channel Island of Jersey, before studying geology and palaeontology in London. He worked as an academic researcher before moving to the BBC, where he spent several years working as a researcher and Assistant Producer in the Science Unit; currently he is the Development Producer for a London-based independent television company. Dr Deane has had a lifelong fascination with the paranormal and has been active within a number of organisations, including the Society for Psychical Research and the Association for the Scientific Study of Anomalous Phenomena. He is the author of five full-length books, as well as numerous short articles for magazines and newspapers. He is married and lives in Hertfordshire.

# Sex & the Paranormal

Paul Deane

vega

First published by Blandford in 1999
© Vega 2003
Text © Paul Chambers 1999

All rights reserved. No part of this book may be reproduced, stored in a retrieval system or transmitted in any form or by any means, electronic, mechanical, photocopying, recording or otherwise, without the prior permission in writing of the copyright owners.

ISBN 1-84333-706-1

A catalogue record for this book is available from the British Library

Published in 2003 by
Vega
64 Brewery Road
London, N7 9NT


A member of **Chrysalis** Books plc

Visit our website at www.chrysalisbooks.co.uk

Jacket design: Grade Design Consultants
Managing Editor: Laurence Henderson
Production: Susan Sutterby

Printed by
St. Edmundsbury Press,
Bury St. Edmunds, Suffolk.

# Contents

Introduction     7

### Part one: Supernatural sexual assault

1. Spectral sex, old hags and sleep paralysis     11
2. Succubi and incubi: sexual demons with a pedigree     29
3. The queen of demons     47

### Part two: Sex for use with worship

4. Worshipping the phallus     57
5. Sex to honour the gods     64
6. Witchcraft, the devil and the Middle Ages     73
7. The power of lust     94

### Part three: Orgies, scares and panics

8. Satanism in the suburbs     109
9. A history of supernatural orgies     128
10. The invasion of the penis-snatchers     147

### Part four: Extraterrestrial sex

| | | |
|---|---|---|
| 11 | Amorous aliens | 169 |
| 12 | Aliens stole my virginity! | 178 |
| | *Notes* | 205 |
| | *Bibliography* | 210 |
| | *Acknowledgements* | 220 |
| | *Index* | 221 |

# INTRODUCTION

The subjects of sex and sexuality are strange enough on their own. When they are combined with the extraordinary world of the paranormal, however, the results are truly bizarre. In 1994, a woman in Liverpool, England, claimed that over a period of months an invisible ghost was visiting her in bed at night and molesting her. She said that she could feel its breath upon her face, hear it moving under the duvet and feel its weight on her body. She is not unique. Hundreds of similar cases of ghost rape have been recorded over the years. In the Middle Ages stories of supernatural sexual assault were blamed on demons. If it could be proved that the human victim was a willing participant in the sexual liaison with the demon, they could be tried as a witch and sentenced to death.

In 1996, three men were hanged by a lynch mob in Cameroon after it was claimed that they had magically stolen the penises of nearby villagers. Similar allegations were repeated across west Africa, leaving scores of dead and injured in their wake. Strangely, similar outbreaks of penis-snatching were reported in Singapore in 1967, in India in 1983 and in China in 1990. In November 1989, a woman claimed to have been kidnapped by aliens from her twelfth-storey apartment – over 20 people are said to have witnessed it. Such victims of alien abduction claim that their eggs or sperm are wanted for genetic experiments, the ultimate aim of which is to cross-breed extraterrestrials and humans.

This book explores the whole area of human sexuality and its relationship to that range of inexplicable phenomena that we call the paranormal. Its central focus is on the thousands of reports of human sexual encounters with supernatural beings that have occurred over the years. These encounters are startlingly common, with people claiming to have had sexual relations with, among others, ghosts, aliens, demons, witches, the devil, poltergeists, old hags, angels and gods. They also claim to have been abducted and sexually abused by Satanists, extraterrestrials, various religious groups, fairies and witches. In addition, there are the strange examples of the penis-snatching epidemics, the worship of ancient gods with sexual intercourse and phallic symbolism, the outbreaks of sexual mass hysteria and the belief in secret supernatural orgies taking place 'under the noses' of the authorities.

Some of these cases go back to Biblical times; others were only weeks old when this book was finished; still others were collected firsthand by the author. The wealth of stories is amazing and the experiences and phenomena they purport to describe are almost beyond belief. Although the range of phenomena discussed in this book might seem to be diverse and unconnected, there are common themes. It is my objective to examine all the branches of human sexual encounters with the paranormal in order to find and analyse these themes. Why, for example, are so many reports of sexual encounters with ghosts and demons, despite being taken from different parts of the world and even from hundreds of years apart, so similar? Is it because the same sexually active supernatural being is at work, or does the answer lie deeper than that?

This book, in addition to providing an entertaining account of sex and the paranormal, attempts to explain the strange phenomena with which it deals. Such an approach to the whole area of sexuality and the paranormal has never been taken before. Indeed, many of the cases discussed here are receiving their first-ever popular airing, having spent years lying ignored inside specialist journals or in the casebooks of psychic investigators.

# Part one

## SUPERNATURAL SEXUAL ASSAULT

# 1

## SPECTRAL SEX, OLD HAGS AND SLEEP PARALYSIS

*T*ales of supernatural assault are rarely to be found inside newspapers, particularly broadsheets, but in the autumn of 1995 *The Guardian* newspaper carried an article about the east African island of Zanzibar which caught my eye. The article, written by Chris McGreal, told of a scare story circulating around Zanzibar in which a monstrous demon, known locally as the 'Popobawa', was paralysing and then sexually assaulting men during the night.

The Popobawa derives its name from the Swahili for 'bat and wing', and is described as having a small dwarfish body, one central eye, pointed ears, bat-like wings and sharp claws or talons. It is reported to manifest itself in the bedrooms of Zanzibar villagers at night and then rape them while they are paralysed. The Popobawa is reported to attack men more than women and is especially prone to interfere with those who are sceptical about its existence.

One eyewitness, farmer Mjaka Hamad, described himself as a disbeliever in the Popobawa until one night when he awoke to find himself paralysed. He said: 'At first I thought I was having a dream. Then I could feel it. Something pressing on me. I could not imagine what sort of thing was happening to me. You feel as if you are screaming with no voice. It was just like having a dream but then I was thinking it was this Popobawa and he had come to do something terrible to me, something sexual. It is [much] worse than what he does to women.'[1] Mr Hamad was clearly distressed by his Popobawa experience and he was, according to the article, only one of a large number of Popobawa victims to have come forward since the 1970s. Some of them were even reported to have turned up in hospital with scratches, bruises and broken ribs as a result of their encounters.

The story of the Popobawa reminded me of a another story about a sexually active demon that I had read of a few years earlier. In March 1990, a panic swept through Thailand, Singapore and Malaysia when a spate of apparently healthy men were found dead in their beds with their lungs full of blood. A health survey by the Thai government discovered that over the previous three decades nearly 800 southeast Asian men had been found dead under similar circumstances in countries as far apart as Saudi Arabia, China and the USA. The condition was given the name 'Sudden Unexpected Nocturnal Death Syndrome' (SUNDS) and was thought most likely to be related to some form of virus.

In northeast Thailand, however, villagers came up with their own explanation. They believed that the deaths were related to a pre-Buddhist spirit called Pi, which was reputed to be a sex-starved widow who would go out looking for new husbands at night. When Pi found a new victim she would paralyse and then rape him; sometimes she would take the victim's genitals as a trophy, and sometimes the victim would allegedly die of fright. Panic swept the region, with men reportedly dressing as women and putting on make-up in the hope of fooling Pi. Others hung huge phallic effigies outside their homes and temples in the hope of warding off the evil spirit.

It is likely that the story of Pi was created or adapted from folklore to explain the untimely deaths of the victims of the medical condition SUNDS. The use of supernatural entities to explain medical misfortunes is a common pattern. For example, the Jewish sexual demon Lilith, whom we shall encounter in Chapter 3, is commonly blamed for cases of child cot-death (sudden infant death syndrome) and many modern evangelical Christians claim to heal people by exorcizing their demons. The secondary reports of Pi being able to paralyse and rape her male victims, however, are of more interest. This paralysis links the case to that of the Zanzibar Popobawa, which also immobilizes its victims before sexually assaulting them. Could it be that the two demons are in fact one and the same thing, even though the cases occurred on opposite sides of the Indian Ocean?

One of the greatest problems with studying the paranormal is the frustrating way in which so many of the phenomena in which we are interested are restricted to certain parts of the world or even certain cultures. Sightings of the Blessed Virgin Mary are, for example, almost always found in Catholic communities, as it is within this branch of Christianity that she is most revered. Such 'cultural-based phenomena', as they are known, are frustrating to those of us trying to make sense of the world of strange and apparently impossible happenings. Does the fact that some of these supernatural events are restricted to certain parts of the world or are connected with certain religious beliefs mean that they are simply a creation of the community in which they arose? Sceptics would say yes; occultists would say no.

With the cases of the Popobawa and Pi, however, we have an apparently very similar phenomenon occurring in two different parts of the world, in two communities that are not culturally linked. It is possible that the Thailand and Zanzibar cases are simply a coincidence, but I have found reference to a 'grey ghost' in Vietnam that similarly paralyses its sleeping victims and tries to suffocate them. There is also a Hong Kong phenomenon known as 'ghost oppression' with exactly the same symptoms that were traditionally blamed on supernatural beings.

These cases seem to prove that paralysing and raping demons are not just a cultural-based phenomenon that has sprung up independently in different parts of the world. In order to prove this conclusively, more examples of the phenomenon are needed, preferably ones from outside Asia and Africa. Such cases have proved to be remarkably easy to find.

## Spectral sex

The above cases of supernatural beings committing sexual assault are restricted to far-flung parts of the globe, and have mostly come from badly detailed reports that have been through many hands before they end up in print. If this is a global phenomenon that is represented in every culture, then it must logically also be found in the more urbanized regions of the world, particularly Europe and North America. Belief in demons is not great in these parts of the world, and superstition and the supernatural do not intrude into people's lives in the same way as in the more rural populations of Asia and Africa. There are, however, certain supernatural beliefs that are very strong in developed countries, one of which concerns ghosts and haunted houses.

Since the 1970s, there has been a great number of individual accounts of people in Europe and America, mostly women, being raped at night by ghosts. I used, out of interest, to keep the reports of these attacks in a file. After re-reading this file, I was struck by the extraordinary similarity between these individual cases and those of the Pi and Popobawa. As in the Asian and African examples, the ghost arrives at night, paralyses the victim, frequently sits on their chest, and then sexually assaults them. There are hundreds of examples of spectral sex in print, so much so that the *Fortean Times* nicknamed the phenomenon 'spectrophilia'.

For example, ex-nurse Gill Philipson from Liverpool, England, claimed to have been sexually molested by a ghost for a period of ten years between 1984 and 1994. She said that the attacks occurred at night and that she would wake up paralysed to find a hooded figure, with grey wrinkled skin, on top of her. She felt the figure pressing down on her and was unable even to scream to attract the attention of her husband sleeping next to her. On the advice of two 'paranormal investigators', she took a relaxation course and found that the attacks became less frequent until, eventually, they disappeared altogether.

Another case, also in 1994, involved Jill Cook from Blackpool, England, who reported being repeatedly raped by an invisible entity over a period of four months. She said that the entity would speak to her, and she would feel it pushing down on top of her; it would then touch her genitals before finally raping her. Psychics involved in trying to remove the raping ghost told Miss Cook that she was being attacked by an incubus demon and suggested that she should fill the room with electrical goods so that it blocked 'the mental signals' from the demon. We are not told of the outcome of this.

Similar tales of ghosts sexually molesting people abound. There was the woman who was trying to develop her psychic powers and who woke up to find that she was '... completely paralysed ... slowly suffocating and unable to do anything'. She was aware of an invisible being in bed with her but could not move enough to attract the attention of her husband.

Some of the most famous hauntings even make mention of them. The so-called 'Smurl poltergeist haunting' in Pennsylvania during the late 1980s had claims of a man being pinned down, paralysed and then raped by a hideous female demon, while one of his daughters was apparently attacked by what has been described as an ancient male demon known as an incubus (see Chapter 2). The tabloid press describes them as 'randy' ghosts, or similar, while New Age psychics and Christians call them demons.

Such cases have sometimes jumped the barrier from print into film. The horror film *The Entity* is about a woman who is subjected to a series of sexual assaults by an invisible ghost (this is supposedly based on a true story). Films have also been made of the Smurl poltergeist haunting. In this uninhibited celluloid age, there are many other horror films that link ghosts and sexuality.

Most cases of ghost rape have almost identical characteristics. The victim is in bed and is normally, but not always, a woman who is alone at night. (This is not to say that men are not also attacked, but that they do not normally come forward with their stories. The reverse seems to be true in the Asian and African cases, where it is only the men who come forward.) The woman wakes with a start and is aware of a presence in the room; she may hear footsteps or the sound of somebody moving in the room. She finds herself paralysed. The woman is then aware of the ghost getting into bed with her and will often describe the feeling of having its weight pressing down on top of her, and/or that she is being suffocated. It is at this point that the ghost starts to touch or feel the victim, sometimes leading to a fully fledged sexual assault. In rare cases, the victim actually feels the breath of the ghost, smells the ghost, or even sees it during the assault. These characteristics have much in common with the reports of attacks by both the Pi and the Popobawa, and suggest that there is a strong link between these cases.

The important factor about ghost rape is that it is a distinctly American and European phenomenon centred on the western tradition of ghosts as spirits of the dead. Put together with the Pi and Popobawa cases, this extends the geographical coverage of modern supernatural rape of this kind to every inhabited continent on Earth. The commonality of symptoms (paralysis, weight on the chest, nocturnal attack and sexual assault) suggests that the cause of the Pi, Popobawa and ghost rapes is the same. But could there be a genuine supernatural entity, capable of striking a man or a woman at any point on the globe, at work here?

The fact that these attacks have alternatively been blamed on a bat-winged creature, a sex-starved demon widow, succubi, incubi, poltergeists and various types of ghost suggests that, although people are undergoing essentially the same experience, the cause of it is being interpreted according to the cultural or personal beliefs of the victim concerned. Neither east Asia nor east Africa has a tradition of ghosts (in the western sense of the term), so the experience is blamed on a demon that is more in line with traditional cultural beliefs. The reverse is true in the west, where belief in demons and supernatural evil beings is relatively low but belief in ghosts, spirits and poltergeists is high. This could explain why these experiences are being given different names in different parts of the world, but does little to shed light on what it is that people are experiencing in the first place. Such an explanation is forthcoming, and it was discovered largely because of the work of one person, namely David Hufford.

## Old hags

In the early 1970s, David Hufford was a young researcher who had recently joined the Folklore Department of the Memorial University on the island of Newfoundland in Canada. At that time, Newfoundland was very much isolated from the Canadian mainland and had a small population that was, as Hufford noted, highly superstitious with a strong belief in the supernatural. Soon after his arrival, he became aware of a folklore tradition known locally as 'the old hag', in which both men and women were attacked at night by a supernatural being which paralysed them and then either attempted to strangle them or, more rarely, sexually assaulted them.

Hufford's interest was immediate and he set about investigating this apparently common experience. He collected hundreds of examples of old-hag attacks, all of which shared the same basic features. The following, from a student of his, is typical: 'You are dreaming and you feel as if someone is holding you down. You can do nothing, only cry out. People believe that you will die if you are not awakened.'[2]

The term 'old hag' was derived from the belief that it was a witch, or a similar old and ugly woman, that magically paralysed the victim and then sat on the victim's chest, suffocating them. The attacks were almost always at night and, at least within Newfoundland itself, widespread and greatly feared.

When Hufford set about investigating the old hag, he thought that it would take him 'a few months'. It was in fact to take him the best part of ten years. The results of his research, on which this section is largely based, were later published as the book *The Terror that Comes in the Night*, which is one of the finest and most thorough pieces of folklore research ever done. Hufford collected together hundreds of examples of old-hag attacks from Newfoundland and, later, from around the world. He did surveys and historical research into the topic until, by the time he had finished, the phenomenon that is the old hag had been documented in every way possible. His results provide the key to the cases of sexually assaulting demons and ghosts that we have dealt with so far in this chapter.

Hufford defines an old-hag attack as involving:

1. awakening (or an experience immediately preceding sleep);
2. hearing and/or seeing something come into the room and approach the bed;
3. being pressed on the chest and strangled;
4. the inability to move or cry out until either being brought out of the state by someone else or breaking through the feeling of paralysis on one's own.[3]

Hufford noted that, in addition to blaming the attacks on supernatural beings, the Newfoundlanders also blamed the condition on indigestion, poor blood circulation or a combination of the two. In his book Hufford provides a great many firsthand cases of old-hag attacks, many volunteered by embarrassed or shy people who had previously kept the experience to themselves. The following case is a classic example from an interview he did with 'Pat', a 24-year-old woman:

> I was in my bed. It was late at night. I was on my back and I heard a 'snurling' sound ... whatever it was I thought it was male. And ... I just felt an incredible weight upon my chest as if somebody [had] put a large boulder there ... and somebody had their hand up against my throat ... and I remember that it was dark and it had red eyes ... .[4]

Similarly, the following account comes from 'Carol', a young student living in what she later thought was a haunted house:

> I was ... in bed [and] the light was out in the room, but it was on in the hallway. And the door opened. The door knob jiggled and I thought it was the wind from the windows ... and then the door opened ... and I didn't see anyone come in. But then I looked back at the doorway and there was this bright shimmering substance, you know. Like, this very vaporous-looking thing. And as soon as I saw it I was just scared *stiff*. And I couldn't move. I was s-s-scared stiff. Paralysed! And it just sort of floats over to the foot of the bed. And I heard this 'hhhhhhhh-hhhhhhhh' heavy breathing, and I thought 'Oh, my God!' And I'm rationalizing, I'm saying, 'It's a dog! It's a dog! It's me! It's *me* breathing!' And so I held my breath and the breathing continued. And then it abruptly stopped. And whatever it was came around to the side of the bed and walked behind my back. And I'm straining my eyes to see it, but I can't move my head, because I knew as soon as I did I was just going to be this close to it, and I couldn't stand the thought. Well, I just – I couldn't move![5]

The similarities between the old-hag cases that Hufford was dealing with and the earlier examples of ghost rape and the Pi and Popobawa are obvious. All the cases involve the victim waking in the night paralysed and being aware of a presence in the room with them. The majority of people see, hear or smell what are described as supernatural creatures and some even have these creatures climbing into bed with them, sitting on their chest and touching them, sometimes sexually.

Where firsthand accounts are given, such as in the Popobawa case and some of the ghost-rape cases, the witness testimony differs little from that of Hufford's own interviewees. For example, one of the Popobawa victims described 'waking up paralysed ... then I could feel it. Something pressing on me.' In another ghost-rape case, a victim who was in bed is described as having heard:

> ... heavy footsteps on the wooden stairs ... the bedroom door opened ... the same footsteps walk over towards her bed ... she could see nobody, but sensed a presence in the room. She then felt hot breath on her face, as an invisible something slipped under the duvet beside her. She then felt a weight on top of her, feeling the hot breath in her mouth ... she could not make a sound and was rendered speechless through fear ... its breathing became quicker and quicker. Sally was disgusted at its pawing and groping of her body.[6]

Neither of these descriptions would be out of place among Hufford's testimonies of old-hag attacks, and there is little doubt in my mind that Hufford's old hag is identical to these other experiences and shows exactly how geographically widespread and common the phenomenon is.

In fact, as part of his research Hufford did a survey of people in regard to old-hag experiences and found that 15 per cent of those surveyed had experienced the classic symptoms of one, even if they had not recognized it at the time. This figure means that approximately one in six people has had an old-hag or ghost-rape experience, which is far more than the number of people claiming to have seen ghosts, UFOs or lake monsters, or to have experienced any paranormal phenomena other than telepathy.

Having established the commonality and characteristics of these apparent cases of supernatural assault, the next obvious thing to do is attempt to find a cause for it. The large number of identical cases from different cultures around the world and the fact that many individuals are not aware of others going through a similar experience suggest that these incidents are not drug-induced, hoaxed or imagined; indeed, they are very real to the victims concerned. They are also unlikely to be culturally generated in the same way as some paranormal phenomena are (such as visions of the Blessed Virgin Mary) since they occur across many cultures and have a good historical record (see Chapter 2).

Given the reality of these experiences, the real question, therefore, is whether they are caused by a genuine supernatural entity that inhabits every part of the world, or whether there is another, non-paranormal, explanation. The evidence in favour of old-hag and other nocturnal supernatural assaults being caused by a spiritual entity is actually quite thin. The 'creatures' described in the various reports around the world vary greatly. More importantly, the being that is usually sensed seems to reflect the cultural fear within the society that the victim is a part of. For example, people in Newfoundland have an old hag, while those in America and Europe have ghosts, and those in Africa a fierce hybrid demon. This suggests that the choice of supernatural creature involved in the attack is a subconscious expression of personal or cultural fears and beliefs. People in the west are frightened by ghosts, so they experience ghost attacks; those in Africa are scared of demons, so they have the Popobawa. Also, as we shall see later, in the past old-hag experiences have been mistaken for vampires, witches, the devil and other feared superstitions of the day. This reflection of inner fears suggests a psychological origin for the whole type of old-hag experience.

In addition to this, there has never been any physical or forensic evidence given for a case of supernatural rape. This could be because no cases have, as far as I know, ever been taken to the courts (how would you prosecute a ghost for sexual assault, let alone imprison it?). Equally, however, none of the cases I have read about offer any independently verified physical proof. There is no evidence of sexual penetration on either men or women, genital or bodily bruising or other common signs of physical or sexual assault. Could it therefore be that, with the close tie between cultural belief and the type of attack encountered, a more psychological explanation is needed?

## Sleep paralysis and hypnopompic hallucinations

Seeking for psychological explanations for supernatural phenomena is a risky business that often ends in controversy because, while many psychologists can see comparisons between strange phenomena and known mental processes, there are always significant exceptions that allow doubt to creep in. Therefore, in order to explain old-hag experiences and other parallel cases of supernatural assault adequately, it is necessary to find studied examples of psychological phenomena that exactly match the characteristics of an old-hag attack.

It should be remembered that an old-hag experience or ghost rape (as described earlier) is not a snatched or rare event but a fully fledged sensory experience that can last for a few minutes. Eventually, the victim is able to move or cry out and, once this happens, the attack stops. The most natural explanation is that the victim is dreaming, but, given the similarity in descriptions between cases, it is unlikely that the exact same dream is being shared by thousands of people. Also, most victims, including many that I have interviewed, are at pains to point out that they were awake and not dreaming. The whole experience is undoubtedly very realistic to its victims, and many people stay awake for hours afterwards, afraid to go to sleep for fear of being molested again.

A clue as to what may be going on comes from an experience that occurred to writer Peter Huston. At the time, he and his wife were living in Taiwan and Huston was experiencing a lot of work-related stress. He was particularly anxious about the recent installation of a telephone by his wife that had placed a financial strain on the family. For a while, he had been waking in the night to find himself unable to move and feeling a pressure on his chest, both classic symptoms of an old-hag attack. On one particular night he:

> ... awoke unable to move and finding that the telephone cord had somehow became draped over my body and was in the process of electrocuting me. In time it was over. I was able to move again, but was quite confused and upset. I was thoroughly agitated and very angry with my wife for not noticing that I'd been shaking and suffering from this terrible experience. I was even more confused to discover that the telephone cord was far on the other side of the room, and it was physically impossible for it to have become draped over my body, even if someone had been inclined to pick it up and put it there.[7]

Here we find the same characteristics as a demon-rape attack, and yet it was not a supernatural entity that was attacking Huston but an inanimate object that could not, under any circumstances, have reached him. We know from his article that he was under considerable stress and anxious about the cost of the telephone rental before the attack, which suggests that what he experienced was some form of panic attack of the sort that most of us have experienced before sitting exams or starting a new job. This suggests that old-hag attacks are heavily linked to the person's state of mind – but can the whole experience really be explained in terms of a purely mental process?

Hufford believed that the answer lay with what were, at the time of his Newfoundland research, two little-studied and little-understood sleep disorders called sleep paralysis and hypnagogic hallucination. In the two decades since the publication of Hufford's Newfoundland research, much more has become known about these two sleep disorders, and many parapsychologists and other paranormal commentators, myself included, are convinced that Hufford is correct in his identification of old-hag attacks with them.

The first clinical diagnosis of sleep paralysis was given by Silas Weir Mitchell in 1876, but its effects must have been known and talked about for some time prior to this, as is reflected in a number of nineteenth-century texts including, most surprisingly, the book *Moby Dick*, written in 1851, which describes a classic case of sleep paralysis on the character Ishmael, including the stresses leading up to it. The clinical definition of sleep paralysis is of a person who wakes up to find themselves temporarily unable to move any part of their body except the eyes. The person can remain paralysed from a few seconds to several minutes, and will only be able to move after making an effort to twitch a small muscle. Once this is achieved, the state of paralysis is broken and the person can move once more.

This correlates very well with the description of the state of paralysis experienced in the majority of cases of old-hag attacks, ghost rape and, of course, the bat-winged Popobawa demon from Zanzibar. To understand what it is that causes sleep-paralysis attacks, and how they relate to the supernatural sexual-assault tradition, one must first understand something of the complex nature of sleep in humans.

Although it is still not really known why humans need to sleep, we are likely to suffer if we do not get between four and ten hours of it a night. The rock star Keith Moon once claimed to have stayed awake for over eight days during one of his periodic rock-'n'-roll binges. I have only ever managed to go for one night without sleep and that was not a pleasant experience, so I dread to think what state Keith Moon was in by the end of his eighth sleep-deprived day.

Not only do we need a full night's sleep, but while we are asleep we also need to have a balance between certain types of sleep. Although we are not aware of it, a full night's sleep is divided into a series of different stages that repeat themselves cyclically during the night. For the purposes of what we are interested in, it can be said that there are two main types of sleep: REM and non-REM. REM stands for 'rapid eye movement', a term that was coined in the 1950s to describe the visible side-to-side twitching that occurs in the eyes of somebody in the REM sleep phase. Non-REM sleep is a passive state that occurs while the brain goes through several levels of unconsciousness from shallow to deep sleep; this type does not concern us greatly. REM sleep, however, is a much more curious and fascinating state and its role within the sleep process is central to the whole experience of supernatural rape.

Early laboratory experiments, in which sleeping subjects were woken during various stages of the sleep process, soon established that the bulk of what we call dreaming occurs during REM sleep. Wake up a person during a REM sleep cycle and they will give vivid descriptions of dreams they were having, while those woken in non-REM sleep will normally only be able to give vague half-descriptions of dreams they may or may not have been having. In a normal night's sleep, we can expect to undergo approximately four REM sleep cycles, separated by about 90 minutes. REM sleep is very closely related to the experience of sleep paralysis.

The relationship between REM sleep and cases of supernatural rape has, in the first place, to do with a self-protective bodily function that becomes enacted during dreaming. While the process of dreaming occurs, a chemical inhibitor is released by the brain which effectively paralyses the body's muscles. Although it is not certain why the body should need to be paralysed during REM sleep, the likely explanation is that, by stopping the body from moving, it will be unable to damage itself or others by acting out the dreams. In cases where this brain inhibitor fails to work, people may get up and sleep-walk or they may even flail about in bed. In very rare cases, people have been known to punch or even strangle their partners while asleep.

When sleep paralysis occurs, the reverse is happening – instead of the paralysis mechanism not working at all, it is in fact working for too long, with the person returning to consciousness before his or her brain has allowed the muscles to move again. Thus, the helpless victim finds themselves awake but paralysed – a terrifying situation that I have experienced myself on one occasion. This, in essence, is sleep paralysis, which is no more than the brain's REM sleep cycle accidentally overlapping into the waking brain's state. Laboratory descriptions of sleep paralysis perfectly match those states of paralysis that victims of supernatural assault report.

This is not, however, the solution to the whole old-hag experience. Many people have experienced sleep paralysis but have not seen, heard or felt any of the other sensations, such as a supernatural being in the room, that form a part of old-hag and similar attacks. There is clearly another dimension to sleep paralysis that is needed to explain the sounds, sights, smells and tactile feelings that accompany the state of being unable to move. This is where the sleep disorder known as 'hypnopompic hallucination' comes into play.

Hypnopompic hallucination is an unusual and disturbing sleep disorder that, to one degree or another, affects us all during the course of our night's sleep. The term 'hypnopompic' refers to the brief period of disorientation that we all experience in the few moments after waking up. The waking process normally only takes a few tens of seconds at the most and so that fluffy, blurry and unreal feeling that we all experience is very short-lived. While we are in the hypnopompic state, however, our brains are still in the no man's land that exists between being asleep and being fully conscious. It is therefore sometimes possible for the sleep state sometimes to intrude into, and become confused with, our waking experience.

Put simply, this means that our dreams can enter our own reality and become confused with real-life experience. In the same way that sleep paralysis occurs because the brain forgets to (or cannot) turn off the body's REM sleep-paralysis mechanism, so the dream state of the brain can persist after waking up, producing sights, sounds, feelings and smells that are not really there. I have woken up many times believing that I can hear the telephone ringing or that my partner has spoken to me. I have also, on a number of occasions, awoken to see a strange bright light hovering over the bed that slowly fades over a period of 20 seconds or so. All these experiences are the results of my dream state overlapping into my waking world, causing me to believe that what I was seeing and hearing were real when they were in fact no more than hypnopompic hallucinations.

Hypnopompic hallucinations can be associated with practically any stage of sleep from falling asleep (when they are technically called hypnagogic hallucinations) through all the various deeper and lighter stages in the sleep cycle. Sleep paralysis is, however, extensively linked to the REM sleep cycle, and so it is the type and style of hypnopompic hallucinations that are produced during this phase of sleep that are of most interest to those of us seeking an explanation for the old-hag experience.

REM sleep, as stated earlier, is the part of sleep when the brain does most of its dreaming, and so one would expect that anybody waking from a dream would experience more vivid and intense hypnopompic hallucinations than those waking from a non-dream (i.e. non-REM) phase of sleep. This does indeed seem to be the case. Laboratory experiments have found that people who have been woken from a dream state (i.e. REM sleep) report intense feelings of anxiety, of not being alone in the room, of hearing noises and even, more rarely, of seeing people or objects that were not there. Many parapsychologists have noted the similarity between common descriptions of hypnopompic hallucinations and other paranormal experiences, including out-of-body experiences, bedside ghosts, UFO sightings at night and the common poltergeist experience of being thrown out of bed. There are also remarkable similarities to the old-hag and other supernatural assault experiences.

The feelings of anxiety and the sense that there is somebody else in the room equate well with the first stages of an old-hag attack. Because hypnopompic hallucinations are a form of waking dream, the content of which is enhanced by the senses and thoughts of the individual, the feeling of paralysis in an old-hag attack would only serve to intensify the hallucination. We know that the nature of the attack is defined by the personal beliefs and concerns of the individual, which is why Peter Huston was attacked by a telephone cord, Europeans are attacked by ghosts and Africans by demons. If a person wakes up paralysed and believing that there is an invisible being in the room, then the cultural belief of the individual will ensure that this invisible being in fact becomes their worst nightmare, be it a ghost, demon or hag. When paralysed, another common fear, of both men and women, is the possibility of being physically assaulted without being able to defend themselves. It is this anxiety, combined with the feeling of pressure on the chest, that leads to the hypnopompic hallucination producing a sensation of a being getting into bed with the person, or of them sitting on the chest.

In other words, the hypnopompic hallucinations, in conjunction with sleep paralysis, are reflecting the very common fear of somebody else being in the room with you at night. As children, most of us feared that there was a creature living under the bed or in the cupboard. These childhood fears are reflected in adulthood as anxiety about intruders breaking into the building while we are asleep, or as a genuine fear of the dark or of ghosts or other unseen horrors. In the semi-reality that is the hypnopompic hallucination, these fears become all too real, first as a belief that there is somebody else in the room with you and then as a belief that this person has come to attack you. The supernatural element probably comes from a mixture of personal belief and an attempt to explain how it is possible for an apparently invisible being to attack you. It is a very short step from imagining that there is somebody else in the room with you to believing that they have got into bed with you, or that they are sitting on your chest. The sensations of hearing footsteps, seeing hooded figures and being touched or breathed upon would then simply be hallucinations produced by a brain that still has one part in the dream state of sleep.

This strange mixture of sleep paralysis and hypnopompic hallucination can explain all the known aspects of supernatural assaults. It can explain the association of the experience with waking from sleep, and why every human society has its own version of the old hag. It can account for the reports of paralysis and the feeling of suffocation and of having a weight on the victim's chest. The hallucinations, fuelled by anxiety, are a common reflection of the individual's fears, which are, in turn, based on their cultural beliefs.

All the above is not just speculation or a meaningless attempt to explain the apparently supernatural in a scientific way. For not only do sleep paralysis and hypnopompic hallucinations unquestionably produce the same sensations as found in old-hag attacks, but they have also been induced in the laboratory. The ability to induce both sleep paralysis and hypnopompic hallucinations strengthens the link between these disorders and the experience of supernatural assault. Sleep paralysis and hypnopompic hallucinations have both been induced in people by shortening the REM-sleep cycles (i.e. shortening the length of time they dream for) and have been found to be inhibited by the use of drugs, especially fluoxetine. This underlines the belief that they are psychologically explainable (and inducible) and capable of being stopped using pharmaceuticals. Like many sleep disorders, both are also far more common in those people of a nervous or anxious disposition and in those who are undergoing stress. Hypnopompic hallucinations that have been later interpreted as a supernatural experience have also been found to be far more common among those of a fantasy-prone nature or who have a strong pre-existing belief in the supernatural phenomenon which they have reportedly experienced.

Surveys in North America have revealed that 21–62 per cent of people claim to have experienced at least one episode of sleep paralysis; of these, 98 per cent also claim to have had an associated hallucinatory experience. Hufford's Newfoundland research found that approximately 15 per cent of people there have experienced the old hag, while a study of Hong Kong undergraduates found that 37 per cent had suffered from 'ghost oppression'. There was no difference in the numbers of men and women reporting the attacks and, among the Hong Kong students, the age of the first attack was found to be 17–19 years. If you combine these figures, you realize that this experience is not the rarity that it perhaps looks at first.

There are many who strongly disagree with the sleep-disorder explanation of these experiences, but the similarities are far too close to be explained in any other way. This is one of those rare cases in the field of the paranormal where science not only verifies that people are undergoing an apparently supernatural experience but can also explain it.

## Explaining the impossible

With old hags, ghost rape and other supernatural experiences, we are now in the rare and privileged situation of being able not only to verify that people do believe they are being raped by supernatural beings but also that this is explicable in terms of known sleep disorders. There are few other areas of the paranormal where such a good and convincing explanation can be found.

So far, we have used sleep paralysis and hypnopompic hallucinations to explain the old-hag, ghost-rape. Pi and Popobawa attacks. Once you become aware of the characteristics of these attacks, however, you can start to find parallels with a lot of experiences that have hitherto been attributed to paranormal forces. This is particularly so with historical reports of attacks by supernatural beings.

The Reverend Montague Summers, in his book *The Vampire in Europe*, describes two cases that are certain to have been based on sleep-paralysis incidents. One involves a Romanian boy who had a '... thing which he could not see, but which he could plainly feel, [come] to him every night about 12 o'clock and settle upon his chest, drawing all life out of him, so that he became paralysed for the time being and could neither call nor cry out.' The second occurred in the eastern European province of Silesia in 1591 when the vampire of a suicide troubled a village: '... those that were waking it would strike, pull or press, lying heavy upon them like an *Ephialtes* ... [The vampire would] sometimes cast itself upon the midst of their beds, would lie close to them, and would so strike and pinch them.'[8]

The more you look for symptoms of sleep paralysis and hypnopompic hallucinations, the more cases just seem to tumble out of the air at you. There is the German fairy tale about the miner who went out and was captured by witches. 'One of the witches came down, turned the miner over, whether he wanted to or not, and mounted him. Then away they went through the air ... he could barely breathe, and the witch was so heavy that she nearly broke his bones ...'[9]

Such experiences clearly had a deep impact in the psyche of people and parallels can be seen practically everywhere. The witchcraft practice of 'trucken', where a pregnant woman, or one who had recently given birth, feels a 'pressing down' on her or her child, is another candidate. Two classic examples of the trucken come from 1670 in Germany. 'George Schmetzer's wife complained of feeling that something was coming to her at night, lying on her and pressing her so that she suffered from pain ... . She suspected the lying-in maid [a sort of medieval nanny] [of coming] to her bed in the evening and lying on top of her.' Similarly, Anna Maria Cramer ' ... believed a witch was coming to her at night and lying on her, pressing on her pregnant body'.[10]

If such cases are recognizable in ancient stories that undoubtedly have been rewritten or exaggerated over the years, they are positively obvious in more modern accounts. In a letter to *Ghostwatch* magazine, Michael John Marshall related an experience that happened to him in 1956, when he was 21: '... I was awakened by a high-pitched hum unlike anything I have heard before ... I then found, to my horror, that I was virtually pinned to the bed and couldn't raise my arms ... The whole episode lasted about seven minutes.'[11]

Another classic old-hag attack was related to Peter Huston by a friend who said that he '... would wake in a paralysed state and find himself forced to watch as an old hag entered the room, floating as she came. She would then alight on his bed and proceed to sit on his chest. He would feel a palpable wave of terror, her weight bearing down and pinning him in place, and sometimes he would experience her putrid breath as she lurched over his face. Finally, after a period of unimaginable terror, she would leave; and he would find himself able to rise and move.'[12]

Possibly the greatest modern reflection of sleep-paralysis attacks occurs in the large number of alien-abduction stories that are currently being reported in the western world. These are discussed in greater detail in Chapter 12.

As well as explaining these experiences in the history of western society, the sleep-paralysis phenomenon is also firmly embedded in our cultural heritage. The traditional definition of a 'nightmare' is based on the symptoms of an old-hag experience. For example, Lewis Spence defines a nightmare as being: 'A disorder of the digestive functions during sleep, inducing the temporary belief that some animal or demon is sitting on the chest.'[13] Keysler similarly says that '*Nachtmar* ... is from *Mair*, an old woman, because the spectre which appears to press upon the breast and impede the action of the lungs is generally in that form'.[14] Hufford notes that Pliny's description of a nightmare as being *suppressio nocturna* also hints at the old hag.

One of the greatest testimonies to the power that old-hag experiences have had on our society comes in Fuseli's 1781 painting *The Nightmare*, which depicts a woman lying on her back asleep, while sitting on her chest is a red and grumpy-looking troll. This was used as the illustration to Hufford's *The Terror that Comes in the Night* and nicely sums up the features of an old-hag experience.

# 2

# SUCCUBI AND INCUBI: SEXUAL DEMONS WITH A PEDIGREE

Of all the supernatural beings credited with the ability to have sex with humans, the most notorious must surely be these demons known as *succubi* and *incubi* (singular = *succubus* and *incubus*). For nearly a millennium, belief in the ability of these demons to have sex with people has been strong, particularly among Christian communities. During the Middle Ages, so closely were they associated with devil-worship and witchcraft that many people were tortured and put to death because it was thought that they had willingly copulated with a succubus or incubus. Although this no longer happens, belief in these demons is strong within the more evangelical Christian sects, and there are still occasional reports of people being attacked by these demons.

## Origins of the demons

Traditionally, each of these two types of demon is credited with a different gender. The incubus is regarded as masculine and is held responsible for sexually interfering with women, and the succubus is regarded as feminine and responsible for sexually molesting men. Sometimes it is held that there is just one demon which is capable of changing sex to suit the occasion. There are two neat divisions in the process of tracing the origins of these demons: firstly their supposed theological origins, and secondly the documentation of their occurrence throughout history.

Their theological origins are to some degree covered in the

next chapter with the discussion about the Jewish demon Lilith. According to modern Judaic mysticism, Lilith was the first wife of Adam and also the first succubus. She has been credited with being the 'queen of the demons' and the mother of all succubi and incubi. It was said that every time Lilith had sex with Adam a succubus or incubus was born, and that, after separating from Adam, she would steal sperm from sleeping men, or from married couples while they were engaged in nocturnal lovemaking, and make more succubi and incubi from it. Because of this, the succubi and incubi that are loose in the world are deemed to be a result partly of the original sin of Adam and Eve and partly of the carelessness of men in allowing Lilith to steal their sperm.

Those texts that discuss the origins of succubi and incubi almost invariably cite Lilith as their mother, creator and, in some cases, mistress. A typical demonology manual states that 'Lilith was the prince or princess who presided over the demons known as succubi and incubi'.[15] Although Lilith is viewed as being the first succubus, the Jewish *Kabbala* also mentions that the serpent from the Garden of Eden may have been the first incubus. It is often thought that the serpent that tempted Eve was in fact merely a representation of the penis and that the temptation itself refers to the sexual act. The *Kabbala* takes this further and actually has the serpent copulating with Eve and making her pregnant: 'And the Serpent mounted Eve and injected filth into her; she gave birth to Cain. From thence descended all the wicked generations into the world.'[16] This action would make the serpent an incubus and would also drag Eve into the sphere of blame for the unleashing of evil on the world.

The references to Lilith, Adam and Eve are the only widely used theological explanation for the creation and existence of succubi and incubi. They can, however, only be traced back to writings that are, at most, 1,200 years old. Succubi and incubi have a recorded history that goes back several centuries before this, making it likely that the Lilith stories were built on the tradition of the succubi and incubi rather than vice versa. If the Lilith stories are unlikely to be the true historical origins of these demons, then perhaps looking at their recorded occurrence in history could give us a clue to the extent of belief in and antiquity of these demons.

In fact, tracing the written history of the succubi and incubi has proved to be a very difficult task indeed. While many ancient religions have their gods and goddesses which are deemed capable of having sex with humans (see Chapter 5), there does not appear to be any equivalent to the roles afforded to the succubus and incubus.

Their recorded history seems to be synonymous with the advent of Christianity and it is certainly through this religion that their notoriety has grown. In terms of the earliest recorded case of the actions of a succubus or incubus, there is no mention of them at all in the Bible (indeed, there is only one suspect mention of Lilith in the Old Testament) or in any other texts that pre-date the advent of Christianity.

It seems highly likely that the succubi and incubi are yet another historical manifestation of the sleep paralysis and hypnopompic hallucination experiences discussed in Chapter 1. The translation of the Latin verb *incubare*, from which the word incubus is derived, is 'to lie upon', while *succubare* means 'to lie under', which hints at the sensation of weight that many people report feeling on their chests. More importantly, succubi and incubi have been related to a whole group of little-understood demons, all of which are credited with pressing down on people. References to 'pressing' demons can be found from civilizations dating as far back as ancient Rome, Gaul and Germany, where they were variously called Dianus, Alf and Hanon Tramp. Other ancient references include those to the Greek demons known as Ephialtes ('the leaper') and Pnigalion ('the throttler'). All these demons were supposed to sit on people's chests during the night, partly suffocating them, making the link with sleep paralysis very strong indeed. It therefore seems likely that the most notorious demons of the Middle Ages have their cultural origins in the old-hag attacks.

The early church theologian St Augustine of Hippo compared them to the ancient Gaulish demons known as '*dusii*' (also sometimes called *duses* or *dusiones*). *Dusii*, however, differ greatly in their actions from the succubi and incubi, and are in fact Prussian demons that were thought to possess the bodies of men and then take them to far-off regions. Although some writers in the Middle Ages believed the *dusii* to be a third type of sexually molesting demon, their actions are not normally deemed to be sexual in nature.

Therefore, although there are fleeting references to demons or spirits that may or may not be the ancient equivalents of succubi and incubi, we cannot for certain attribute them to the pagan or organized religions that pre-dated Christ. What is certain, however, is that talk of succubi and incubi was already circulating within the earliest church congregations and it is in this context that we find the first brief mentions of these demons by name. It is possible that the earliest Christian reference comes in the apocryphal 'Acts of the Apostle Thomas', where St Thomas relates the story of a woman who was for over five years visited at night by a demon that would sexually abuse her. The first recorded use of the terms succubus and incubus appears in the fifth-century writing of St Augustine, who is widely acknowledged as one of the people largely responsible for steering the philosophical direction of the Catholic church as we know it today. In his famous discussion on the limits of Christianity, *The City of God*, he says of these demons:

> It is commonly reported from both personal experience, and from those of others that are undoubtedly trustworthy and honest, that the sylvans and fawns, commonly known as incubi, have often injured women, both desiring them and acting carnally with them: and that certain devils, which the Gauls call *Duses*, do continue to practise this uncleanness, and tempt others to it, all of which is confirmed by such persons, and with such confidence that it would be impudent to deny it.[17]

St Augustine is insistent about the existence of these demons, and he unquestionably attributes the same sexual actions to them as would crop up in writings again and again through to the modern age.

Between Augustine's writings and the beginning of the twelfth century the subject of succubi and incubi was treated with suspicion and disbelief by many church writers. The few references that are made to them do, however, show that belief in these spirits was still strong among the lower clergy and their congregations. There are a few brief references to them in the eight and ninth centuries, but it is not until after the first millennium that the status of the succubi and incubi moves from what had previously been considered to be mythology by the church into the realm of fact.

The rise in interest in the activities of the succubi and incubi can be directly related to the church's increasing worries about the widespread use of pagan worship and witchcraft. To the minds of the church elders, the moral abuse of sexuality was a major factor in the worship of witches, and the thought that there existed demons that were capable of copulating with men and women fitted well with their notion of widespread perversity in the community. By the time the witch trials had started in the fifteenth century, not only were succubi and incubi a fact of life to many theologians but they had also been given a whole new role to play within society.

## The actions of the demons

Details about the appearance of the succubi and incubi and, more importantly, just how it is that a supernatural being can copulate with a physical one such as a human being, are scant. This is because the issue of what these demons actually looked like, and what they were capable of doing, was not settled until the publication of the witch-hunters' handbook, the notorious *Malleus Maleficarum* (see Chapter 6). Prior to this, succubi and incubi had only been mentioned in the vaguest of terms and any descriptions of their physical appearance or actions were limited to phrases such as 'at night she was oppressed by a demon' or 'she enjoyed the constant society of an incubus'.

Before the turn of the thirteenth century, an attack by a succubus or incubus was seen as something beyond the control of the victim. People are described as the passive recipients of the unwanted attentions of the demons. This perception changed in the early part of the thirteenth century, when it became accepted that a person who had been attacked by one of the demons was not an innocent victim picked at random but a willing participant in the union. At the very lowest level, this meant that the person had been tricked into consenting to have sex with the demon, usually by the succubus or incubus appearing as a beautiful man or woman or as the person's sweetheart.

This initial change of attitude is reflected in what is possibly the first recorded story of an incubus attack, which appears in the 'Acts of the Apostle Thomas'. St Thomas came across a woman who had been receiving the unwanted attentions of an incubus for over five years. To remove the demon, St Thomas first tried to persuade it to leave of its own free will, but the demon merely said that it would return to torment the woman once the saint had left. To prevent this, St Thomas baptized and anointed the woman in the name of Jesus, and she was troubled no more.

This account is typical of the way that many succubus and incubus attacks were described before the start of the witch trials. The succubus or incubus would appear as a handsome male or female youth, and would initially trick its way into the bed of the victim. Once the victim had consented to sex, the demon would return night after night for several months or years, with the victim being unable to stop it. At this point, the person would turn to a priest or other church official who would remove the demon.

The pattern described by St Thomas is adhered to so closely by later tales of succubus and incubus attacks that it is likely that many of them are simply variations of the St Thomas story, with other religious characters substituted in the role of St Thomas. There is, for example, a tale accredited to St Bernard that differs hardly at all from that of St Thomas. In 1135, St Bernard was said to have cured a woman who had been suffering an incubus attack for seven years. He gave his staff to the woman, but the demon said it would come back once the staff had been returned to Bernard. As in the story of St Thomas, Bernard then blessed the woman and cured her of the unwanted attentions of the incubus.

O. Brignoli, writing in 1714, relates a story of how a 22-year-old man in 1650 confessed that he had been lying in bed one night when the door opened and his sweetheart, a girl named Teresa, walked in. She told him that she desired to be with him and, although he suspected something was amiss, he agreed to let her stay the night. After a night of passion, Teresa revealed herself to be, in reality, a succubus and the youth realized he had been tricked. Nonetheless he allowed the succubus to visit for several months until, struck with remorse, he sought the help of the church, which removed the succubus by the actions of prayer.

In these early tales, there are two interesting points. The first is that the victim is, in the eyes of the church, blameworthy for initiating the attack by giving in to the demon's request for sex. The Christian church, from its inception, had serious inhibitions and taboos about sex in all its forms; the moral to be taken from this tale was that, if you have pre-marital sex, then you risk taking a succubus or incubus as a partner and not being able to get rid of it afterwards. In this respect, it would seem that stories in the St Thomas vein are a thinly disguised warning against the moral dangers of pre-marital sex. People should be wary of anybody wanting to take their chastity, even their sweethearts, as they might just be a lustful demon in disguise!

The second point concerns the way in which the demon cannot just jump on the victim and force them to have sex. Instead, the first copulation between the demon and the victim has to be consented to, which is another reason why the demon would want to disguise itself on the first occasion. After the initial union, the demon can come and go as it pleases, and will, from then on, not only reveal its true identify to the person but also rape and torment them for months afterwards. This aspect is reminiscent of the folklore tales of vampires which need initially to be invited into a room or building, but afterwards can come and go as they please.

Many other tales follow the same pattern – a man or woman is tricked by a succubus or incubus into surrendering their chastity and the demon then visits for a period of months or years until the church steps in and removes it through prayer. In these tales, the demon is nearly always said to have troubled the person for a period of seven days, seven weeks, seven months or seven years. The consistency of the figure seven in these cases may suggest that they are variations of the same folk tale. In terms of punishment, the attitude towards people being tricked by demons suggests that they were deemed to have made a mistake, based on lust rather than a desire to do evil. As most of these early stories of succubus and incubus attacks would seem to be more of a moral warning than to have an actual historical basis, written records of people being punished seem to be non-existent.

At some point in the thirteenth century, the perception of a demon attack being an unfortunate case of lax morals gave way to a more sinister and complex view of the actions of succubi and incubi and how they copulated with human beings. As the church's obsession with witchcraft and the actions of the devil grew stronger, so the role of the succubus and incubus within late-medieval society changed. The rise of the witch trials, and the witches' rituals themselves, are described more fully in Chapter 6. All we need to know here is that there was a build-up in awareness of witchcraft by the authorities between the tenth and fifteenth centuries which resulted in an increasing number of people being brought before the courts on a charge of practising witchcraft. Succubi and incubi formed a major part of these trials.

Contrary to the secondhand stories of people being tricked by a succubus and incubus, the role of the demons changed so that they became a common and intricate part of the ritualized nocturnal worship of the witches. The close connection, in the eyes of the church, between open and perverse sexuality and the worship of the devil made the traditional role of succubi and incubi as copulating demons a natural one to include within the sphere of the witch trials. The two demons would now be present at the witches' Sabbat (their nocturnal devil-worshipping ceremony) and welcomed by the witches, who would have sex with them as part of their devotion to the devil and all things evil. The succubi and incubi had suddenly moved from being tricksters in a Christian moral fable to being very real and unpleasant entities invited by a witch to copulate with them.

The most frightening aspect of this was that very few people actually admitted to having had sex with these demons. Fornicating with a succubus or incubus was an accusation levelled at witches, to which many would only agree after periods of imprisonment or torture. Most of the witches tried in the Middle Ages were accused of having consorted with them, normally during the course of the Sabbat, and to agree to this accusation was to sign your own death warrant. For example, in 1645 Elizabeth Clarke (sometimes called Bedinfield), a one-legged old woman from Manningtree, Essex, was brought before the magistrates by Matthew Hopkins, the self-confessed Witchfinder General. At the trial, Clarke admitted that after three nights' restless sleep the devil appeared to her in the form of a country gentleman and said, 'Besse, I must lie with you.'[18] Clarke agreed and, when asked for a full description of the demon that molested her, replied that he was 'like a tall, proper, black-haired gentleman, a properer man than yourself!' This must have dented Hopkins' pride, and when he asked her whom she would rather sleep with, the devil or himself, Clarke shouted out 'the devil!' This may have sealed her fate, as Clarke, together with three others, was executed later in that summer.

## Malleus Maleficarum

During most of their existence, the succubi and incubi had remained a hidden, ill-described phenomenon that seemed to be more of a threat than a reality. There was little discussion as to what these demons were, what they looked like and how they, being spiritual entities, could have physical intercourse with mortal humans. These questions were to be answered, in amazing detail, by the book that was, above all others, to bring the succubi and incubi from the realm of myth and demonology into the everyday reality of the Middle Ages. The book concerned is the *Malleus Maleficarum*, an outstanding and frightening book (written by two Dominican priests, Henry Kramer and James Sprenger, in 1487); its history and relationship with the witch trials are discussed in detail in Chapter 6. Suffice it to say that this book was the witch-hunters' handbook, telling the authorities how witches (and their familiars) worked, how their actions could be identified and how they should be punished.

There are no fewer than five sections within the *Malleus Maleficarum* that deal specifically with succubi and incubi and the way in which they operate. These were designed by the authors to answer every conceivable question that theologians might ask about the capabilities and modi operandi of the succubi and incubi. The *Malleus Maleficarum* is, however, a misogynous text (see Chapter 6), and so, although succubi are mentioned, it is mainly the actions of incubi on women, and how women can leave themselves open to incubus attack, that are dealt with.

According to the *Malleus Maleficarum*, the demons called succubi and incubi were no longer thought of as being the offspring of the demon queen Lilith (see Chapter 3). They were instead deemed to be angels who had fallen from the grace of God and had been, as a punishment, made to copulate with human beings: '... where the sin is greater, there is the punishment greater; and the higher angels sinned more greatly, therefore for their punishment they have the more to follow these filthy practices.'[19] Indeed, so great was the punishment of having to have sex with human beings that the succubi and incubi did not inhabit the normal hell with the other demons but instead some lower, more horrific hell specifically reserved for those who undertook the sin of fornication.

This view of sexual intercourse as a 'filthy practice' and the ultimate sin, whether it is between demons and humans or between unmarried consenting adults, is a theme that runs right through the *Malleus Maleficarum*. Sex, as far as the authors Kramer and Sprenger were concerned, was a curse from God and it was something that, at a pinch, could be tolerated in marriage for the sake of having children, but was under no account to be enjoyed as a recreational pastime. To want sex was to invite feelings of lust and, in an extension of the moral in the story of St Thomas and the incubus, may just invite the devil into bed with you.

In all the stories I have read about the actions of succubi and incubi, there is a frustrating lack of detail about how these demons accomplished the physical act of copulating with humans. Are they solid beings? Do they trick the person into thinking they are having sex with something corporeal, or is it something altogether more esoteric? We are simply never told. Fortunately for curious voyeurs of demon sexuality, such as myself, the *Malleus Maleficarum* answers all these questions and more in its own prejudiced but unique style. The demons, we are told, make themselves an 'aerial body' out of mist or fog and then animate it by 'spiritual' means. Thus the demons are neither totally solid beings nor totally spiritual entities but instead some form of possessed cloud of condensation that looks and feels real but is actually nothing more than mist. In the form of this mist, the succubus or incubus is able to copulate physically with a man or woman. This contrasts with the earlier descriptions of succubi and incubi being in every way like a normal, and often good-looking, human being. Where the authors of the *Malleus* got this notion from is unclear, and they do not back it up with any examples of people seeing or feeling these misty bodies.

Interestingly, and for no apparent reason, Kramer and Sprenger believed that the succubus or incubus, in the form of this mist, was visible to witches but not to anybody else. To illustrate this point, the following anecdote is given:

> ... the witches themselves have often been seen lying on their backs in the fields or the woods, naked up to the very navel, and it has been apparent from the disposition of those limbs and members which pertain to the venereal act and orgasm, as also from the agitation of their legs and thighs, that all invisibly to the by-standers, they have been copulating with Incubus devils.[20]

This vision of half-naked women being spotted in woodlands with their legs waving in the air is far removed from the early tales of a demon that would appear at midnight to trick its way into the beds of unsuspecting people.

In fact, the whole notion of who is or is not liable to be attacked by a succubus or incubus would appear to have changed within the *Malleus Maleficarum*. Gone are the random nocturnal attacks of the past. Now, in order to suffer the attentions of a demon the person must have sinned greatly or, even worse, invited the demon into bed with them. In summarizing who can be attacked by succubi and incubi, the *Malleus* says:

> First, as in the case of witches themselves, when women voluntarily prostitute themselves to Incubus devils.
>
> Secondly, when men have connection with Succubus devils; yet it does not appear that men thus devilishly fornicate with the same full degree of culpability; for men, being intellectually stronger than women, are more apt to abhor such practices.
>
> Thirdly, it may happen that men or women are by witchcraft entangled with incubi or succubi against their will. This chiefly happens in the case of certain virgins ... and it would seem that such are bewitched ... [who] cause devils to molest such virgins in the form of incubi for the purpose of seducing them into joining their vile company.[21]

With regard to when and where a succubus or incubus could be expected to attack a person, the *Malleus Maleficarum* is also quite specific. The witches' gatherings, such as the Sabbat, were particularly favoured, and the demons would turn up to these and have sex with those mortals who were there to worship the devil. They could also appear, at night, to witches on their own or to people who had been cursed by witches. There was also room for innocent victims (i.e. those who were not practising witchcraft) to be attacked by the demons if they had been born as the result of copulation between a demon and one of their parents or if they had been cursed by their midwife:

> ... it can be said in conclusion that these Incubus devils will not only infest those women who have been generated by means of such abominations [i.e. have been born from sex with a demon], or those who have been offered to them by midwives, but that they will try with all their might ... to seduce all the devout and chaste maidens in that whole district ... [22]

In one of many examples of eccentricity in their book, Kramer and Sprenger single out women with beautiful hair as being also very much at risk. Their reasoning for this is unique: '... either because they devote themselves too much to the adornment of their hair, or because they are wont to try to excite men by means of their hair, or because they are boastfully vain about it ...'[23]

Feast days were also a flashpoint in the demons' calendar, since they would try to take advantage of people's drunkenness and revelry to trick them into having sex. The church's dislike of feast days (other than religious ones) in the Middle Ages is well known because of the direct link with the pagan festivals that they once represented, and because dancing was considered by many to be the pastime of the devil.

Considering that they had so much to say on the natural history of these demons and their effect on the morality of the day, Kramer and Sprenger are very reticent about how best to prevent a succubus or incubus attack. The traditional method, as used by St Thomas, St Bernard and others, was to pray heavily and, if that failed, to give the victim a religious icon to take to bed with them which would keep the foul entity at bay during the hours of darkness. None of this is mentioned at all in the *Malleus*. Instead, we are rather weakly told that 'prayer is not always helpful' and that exorcism should be used as a last resort. Many cases are then quoted in which the demon has resisted holy water, prayer, sacrament-taking and other attempts at removing it. For example, the authors describe '... an enclosed nun, a contemplative, whom an incubus would not leave in spite of prayers and confession and other religious exercises. For he insisted in forcing his way into her bed'.[24]

There is no mention of the practice of writing the names of angels on amulets or other objects, as is the case with Lilith. The nun's problems were solved when she repeated the word 'benedictine' which could, at a great stretch, be related to the Lilith practice of name-calling (see Chapter 3). The general consensus seems to be that, while you could not stop the attentions of a persistent demon, you could be punished for it.

It was thus, in the unusual writings of the *Malleus Maleficarum*, that the succubi and incubi truly took their hold in medieval society.

They were no longer a frightening bedtime story told by church elders but a hideous and terrifying demonic manifestation that threatened to take advantage of every moral error, from hairbrushing to dancing on feast days. Worse was the direct association of these demons with the practice of witchcraft. Kramer and Sprenger made especially sure that signs of fornicating with succubi and incubi were high on the witch-hunter's list of evil at work. So successful was this latter point that cases of succubi and incubi attacking people, which had hitherto been largely folk tales, started to flood into the courts as part of the evidence against those suspected of being witches.

The succubi and incubi, whether they were real or imaginary, were to reach their peak of infamy during the fifteenth to seventeenth centuries, when they were mentioned in a great many witch trials. A full account of a incubus attack that came to court can be found in the tale of Anne Jeffries, an illiterate Cornish peasant girl who, in 1645, was found lying paralysed on the floor in a state of semi-consciousness. When recovered, she reported how she had seen six small men enter the room, who began to kiss her and then took her to a fabulous palace. In the palace she was seduced by a full-sized man but was interrupted when a crowd of people burst in and she woke up on the floor. The girl was later arrested on a charge of witchcraft but was only imprisoned for a short time. This case has some notable similarities to the old-hag attacks that were described in Chapter 1, and has even been compared to modern-day alien-abduction cases (see Chapter 12).

Such full accounts of succubus and incubus attacks are, however, very rare in transcripts from the witch trials, and their mention in court is normally just one of several charges laid against each witch.

## Belief beyond the witch trials

The gap between the end of the witch trials and the so-called age of reason was actually quite small, being only a matter of a few decades. By the end of the 1670s, the practice of publicly executing people, and more especially women, on the charge of witchcraft had all but ceased. The last-known edition of *Malleus Maleficarum* was produced in Lyons in 1669 and, because its central purpose, to identify and punish witches, was no longer widely practised, the next published edition would not be until 1900. By then it was definitely only read for its extraordinary historical value or for curiosity. The first English translation was not published until 1946.

With the termination of the senseless violence associated with the witch trials there came a general understanding that many of its central accusations did not perhaps exist after all. This includes the belief in succubi and incubi, which was really only upheld through the forced confessions of women and men accused of the crime of sorcery. This is not to say that these demons did not still have their supporters, nor that there was not still a great fear of them among the general population. In the sporadic witchcraft trials that still occasionally occurred across Europe during the eighteenth century, succubi and incubi were mentioned every now and then. The slow process of scientific examination was, however, beginning to gain a hold, and as society organized and urbanized itself away from its wretched medieval and church-bound past, so the notion of demons, devils and witchcraft began to recede from the public's imagination.

One of the last and most vocal supporters in the belief of succubi and incubi was Father Ludovicus Maria Sinistrari de Ameno, a Franciscan theologian born in Italy in 1622. Aside from being one of the Catholic church's greatest authorities on human psychology and church law, Sinistrari (as he is commonly known) also produced one of the few books ever to be devoted entirely to the subject of demon sexuality and, in particular, succubi and incubi. This work, which is entitled *De Demonialitate, et Incubis, et Succubis*, was probably written in the dying days of the witch trials, around the 1670s. Nonetheless, it is an authority on the sexuality of demons, and Sinistrari does everything in his power to convince the reader of the reality of succubi and incubi and about how great their threat is to mankind. Aside from the usual vague and unreferenced stories about succubi and incubi raping nuns, monks, nobles and peasants, Sinistrari makes many of the same points and addresses many of the same problems regarding these demons as does the *Malleus Maleficarum*.

He asks how intercourse is physically possible, how it differs from the act of bestiality, who is liable to be a victim and what their punishment should be. His conclusions are similar to those of the work of Kramer and Sprenger of two centuries earlier. Sinistrari does not, however, make them as forcefully, nor offer such violent solutions to people who have been 'polluted' by the demons.

There is an altogether more philosophical feel to Sinistrari's writings. He argues passionately that the term 'bestiality', originally defined as 'sex with different species' by St Thomas Aquinas, should not include sex with succubi and incubi, as these are not flesh-and-blood creatures and cannot therefore be considered to be animal species at all. He offers no real answer as to how the physical act of copulation is achieved, but does at least admit that some women only imagine or dream their demon attackers. He also, somewhat wearily, notes that holy relics, exorcism or prayer are all incapable of removing a succubus or incubus, and that this places them in the same category as demons that take possession of the human body or mind. This is interesting, as many historical cases of demonic possession have been equated with modern-day mental illness such as schizophrenia, which, unsurprisingly, cannot be cured by prayer alone. Perhaps some cases of demon rape were similarly based on psychological disorders, or could even have been the result of the sleep disorders discussed in Chapter 1.

Much of Sinistrari's attitude to succubi and incubi can be summed up in his belief that: 'There are quite a few people, over-inflated with their little knowledge, who dare to deny what the wisest authors have written, and what everyday experience demonstrates clearly: namely, that the demon, either Succubus or Incubus, has carnal union not only with men and women but also with animals.'[25] From this we can see that, even by the end of the seventeenth century, Sinistrari was receiving severe opposition from his contemporaries about the existence of succubi and incubi. When he died in 1701, Christendom lost its last vocal supporter of these sexual demons.

## The modern era

Belief in witches and demons had all but ceased by the turn of the nineteenth century. Instead, people had the new-found wonders of chemistry, physics, geology, astronomy and mathematics to amaze and amuse themselves with. Thoughts of demons were far away.

In the latter half of the nineteenth and the first half of the twentieth centuries, there was a revival in interest in witchcraft as a historical topic. In the works of Montague Summers, Charles Olliver and others, there are historical references to succubi and incubi. These authors did not advocate belief in the demons. However, as with many occultist practices and beliefs, succubi and incubi, or at least the belief in them, were later to be resurrected in the dying decades of the twentieth century.

Disillusionment with conventional forms of Christian worship in the western world has led to the creation of a more fundamentalist branch of Christianity whose worshippers are known loosely as 'evangelical' or 'born-again'. In a 'back-to-basics' approach to their religion, many individual churches have reverted to taking the Bible at its word, rather than the liberal interpretation of it that most mainstream Christian branches practise. This has, in many cases, meant reviving Christian beliefs from previous eras, including belief in the devil as a personification of evil, the truth of witchcraft and demonology and, tied in with all these things, the existence of our old friends the succubi and incubi. Evangelical Christian writing about these demons is often extreme and, in some cases, as nonsensical as that of the *Malleus Maleficarum*. In this modern age, much propaganda is distributed via the internet as well as through old-fashioned 'Bible-thumping' sermons. The following is a classic example taken from an evangelical Christian web site:

> Forget medieval times and folklore, these demons [succubi and incubi] are for real! The demons have sex with both men and women as the person sleeps, AND YOU KNOW IT. It's not a dream, and it's not your imagination. If you have encountered this situation, DELIVERANCE and Spiritual Warfare can stop it.
> A woman called us once and told us about these demons, and that she was afraid to go to sleep because of it. She said that the demons would often lift her bed up in the air, and drag her across the floor. She never got back to us, and probably never got DELIVERANCE.
> Another woman wrote to us once and told us that demons were having sex with her as she slept. Her husband, a Pastor, said it was just her 'imagination'. DEMONS ARE FOR REAL! She did DELIVERANCE and Spiritual Warfare, and we got an e-mail from the woman the very next day saying, 'Praise the Lord. What a wonderful night's sleep I had! No demons attacking my body. NONE!'[26]

Other Christian literature claims that nine out of ten women are being attacked by 'sex demons', but do not know it, and should seek immediate spiritual guidance; or that lustful thoughts or pre-marital sex will entice the demons to attack people.

In opposition to these Christian writings, the motives behind which differ little from those of the medieval church, there are actually now occultist books available which tell you how to encourage demons to have sex with you. Most of these involve basic relaxation and self-hypnosis techniques (i.e. trying to induce a hypnagogic state) and then focusing on the arousal of the body's erogenous zones until another entity takes over and brings on an orgasm. But, aside from these strange outpourings, the common belief in succubi and incubi is well and truly dead. In fact, few people nowadays have ever even heard of them. This does not mean that the modern world does not have its equivalent to the medieval copulating demons. As discussed in Chapter 1, there is still a strong belief in the reality of supernatural beings that are able to have sex with humans. In fact, there are probably far more reported cases of supernatural sexual assault today than there ever were during the height of the witch trials and, unlike the tortured confessions of the witches, these stories are given voluntarily.

## Phantom pregnancies

Before we leave the medieval world of witchcraft, superstition and copulating demons once and for all, there is one last topic that needs to be cleared up. It was a problem that much vexed theologians of the day and, again, formed an active role in the courtroom trials of witches. It revolved around a central question – if an incubus can have sex with a woman, is that woman then capable of becoming pregnant from the demon and so spawning a child that is half-demon and half-human?

Perhaps unsurprisingly, this possibility is little discussed today but it was a major worry in the Middle Ages. The *Malleus Maleficarum* has a number of sections devoted to this question and uncharacteristically concludes that 'no procreation is possible'. For once, however, the *Malleus* did not provide the last word on the matter and opinion remained divided.

The medieval church already knew that it was possible for heavenly beings to mate with humans from the passage in Genesis which states that 'the sons of God went into the daughters of men'. It was also known that a divine union could result in the birth of a child, as was demonstrated by the impregnation of the Virgin Mary by the Holy Spirit which resulted in the birth of Jesus Christ. Other examples of Biblical angelic impregnation resulted in children that were giants. According to the Jewish *Kabbala*, Adam and the demon Lilith fathered a demon every time they copulated. Could a demon really produce flesh-and-blood offspring, however, when it was only a spiritual being itself? There were certainly no shortage of claims of demonic children during the witch trials. One old French story relates that:

> ... in the district of Marrée lived a girl who was with child through the wiles of the Devil. It puzzled her parents not a little to account for her state, for she habitually shunned all manner of dancing and would not marry. On pressing her with questions she confessed that the Devil slept with her every night in the shape of a fine young man. The parents, not content with this explanation, made sudden entrance into the chamber where she slept with torches in their hands. They saw in the bed with her a horrible monster quite inhuman in aspect whom, refusing to leave the

bed, they fetched a priest to exorcize. Finally the monster was prevailed upon to leave, which he did with frightful noise and breaking of furniture, removing a portion of roof with rage. Three days later the girl gave birth to a monster, the ugliest that was ever seen, which the midwives strangled.[27]

Many similar stories can be found from the days before the witch trials, including examples where nuns had apparently been impregnated by the devil (or in one case Jesus). Before the witch hysteria, girls were generally not deemed to have been at fault if they had been taken advantage of by a demon or angel and so there can be little doubt that some unplanned pregnancies were blamed on supernatural forces. It may even have been that some malformed babies were assumed to be part 'monster'. Needless to say, during the witch trials themselves, some women under torture would confess to having borne children for the devil and then murdered them as part of their black worship. Updated versions of these reports can still be found in many of the Satanic ritual abuse scares that have occurred since the 1980s (see Chapter 8).

Other than direct impregnation via a demon attack, the church also believed that demons could enter a woman via her ears; this led to the practice of covering the head with cloth. The Cathars, a medieval Christian sect of southwestern France, also believed that:

> ... when the spirits come out of a fleshy tunic, that is a dead body, they run very fast, for they are fearful. They run so fast that if a spirit came out of a dead body in Valencia and had to go into another living body in the Comté de Foix, if it was raining hard, scarcely three drops of rain would touch it! Running like this, the terrified spirit hurls itself into the first hole it finds free! In other words into the womb of some animal which has just conceived an embryo not yet supplied with a soul; whether a bitch, a female rabbit or a mare. Or even in the womb of a woman.[28]

As an example of this, the detailed Cathar records from the village of Montaillou describe a case where, after a horse died:

> ... its spirit entered into the body of a pregnant woman and was incorporated into the embryo of the child she was carrying in her womb. When the child grew up, he achieved the understanding of good. Later he became a parfait. One day, with his companion, he passed the very place where the horse had lost its shoe. The man, whose spirit had been in a horse, said to his companion: 'When I was a horse, one night I lost my shoe between two stones, and went on unshod the whole night.' Then they both began to search between the two stones; and they found the shoe and took it with them.[29]

This Cathar belief perhaps has more in common with the belief of reincarnation rather than actual demon impregnation. Nonetheless the spirit still has the ability to enter a woman's body and infiltrate an embryo.

Other religions regularly cite examples of fruitful intercourse between animal spirits and human beings. Tibetans are said to believe that the human race originated from the union of an ape with a demon; the Iroquois Indians believe that it was a union between wolf spirits; and the Eskimos that it was a union between bears. Even the twins accredited with founding Rome, Romulus and Remus, were said to have been the sons of a god.

Some religions still reflect these legends by the use of bestiality, symbolic or real, within their ceremonies. One report of a ceremony from India records that a horse would be smothered, and that '... a woman, usually the leading lady of the district, was then compelled to lie down alongside the corpse of the animal. Both woman and horse were then carefully and completely covered with a large sheet of opaque material. In that position she performed a very obscene act with the horse symbolizing the transmission to her of its great powers of fertility.'[30] Other records of bestiality in history are somewhat less religious in nature, including the story that Catherine the Great would allegedly strap herself underneath her horse so as to obtain sexual gratification!

In modern western culture, the belief in demons producing children via women has disappeared although, as with much of medieval demonology, there are probably some religious sects who still promote the idea. The idea has nonetheless been kept alive with supernatural films and books such as *Rosemary's Baby*, where an unsuspecting woman is made pregnant by a demon, and the *Omen* series of films, where the Anti-christ is borne on Earth via a jackal.

# 3

# THE QUEEN OF DEMONS

In Chapter 2, the historical origins of the most commonly encountered of the sexual demons, the succubi and incubi, were explored. This chapter looks more closely at the theological origins of such demons. Whereas history merely records the factual aspects regarding sexual demons, theology attempts to find an account of their origin that is compatible with the belief system within which it operates, such as Judaism or Christianity. Succubi and incubi were particularly problematic for the church to explain. It nonetheless managed, with some help from Jewish tradition, to come up with a credible story, involving the personification of evil in the form of Lilith and her demonic offspring.

## The personification of evil

Many gods are credited with the ability to have sex with, or impregnate, humans. There are few traditions, however, of darker beings such as demons being able to do likewise. This is because in many ancient religions there are no strictly evil beings. Instead, a god, in a reflection of the human persona, is capable of being both good and evil, depending on their mood. In monotheist religions, such as Christianity, Judaism and Islam, having a god that is both good and evil has presented a theological and moral problem that survives to this day. How can a supreme being, who created the world and stands for all that is good in it, also allow everyday suffering to afflict its people?

This question is still widely asked today, particularly when religious people suffer disease or mishaps. There are, for example, many cases of churches collapsing on their congregations during earthquakes, or boats or aeroplanes full of pilgrims going down with no survivors. This problem has in most cases been overcome by creating a separate supernatural being that is the moral opposite of the god. This opposing being is normally deemed to be inherently evil and, while it can never be as powerful as the supreme being, it is nonetheless held responsible for all the evil acts in the world. Hence crop failures, earthquakes, disease and famine can all be justified by blaming them on the actions of an evil being. In the case of Christianity and Judaism, that being is the devil, who, in the same way that God has his angels, has a team of demons to whom he delegates certain evil tasks.

It is within this Judaic and Christian tradition of personified evil that we can begin to trace the theological history of demons and other beings that are able to mate with men and women and, according to some sources, are capable of producing offspring as a result of their foul copulations.

## Lilith the demon queen

The most important of the Judaic demons credited with the ability to have sex with humans is Lilith, who is often given the title 'queen of the demons'. According to Judaic tradition, she is the oldest of the world's demons, and it is felt by some scholars that her legend actually pre-dates that of the first Old Testament writings. She was certainly around in Babylonian times and still forms a part of Judaic tradition.

In modern times, Lilith is best known for her association with the story of Adam and Eve and the Garden of Eden. This legend can be traced, in written form, to the satirical work entitled *The Alphabet of Ben Sira,* which was anonymously written sometime between the eighth and tenth centuries AD. Whether this legend dates back further than this, or was simply the creation of the author of *The Alphabet*, is not known.

The argument for Lilith's existence and activities stems from the contradictory nature of two passages in the Old Testament book of Genesis. In the first chapter, we are told: 'So God created man in his own image, in the image of God he created him; male and female created he them.'[31] Only a short distance further on, however, we find that '. . . the Lord God said, it is not good that the man should be alone'.[32] If God had initially created man and woman, then why was Adam alone a short time afterwards and in need of Eve as a companion? The logical answer, according to *The Alphabet*, was that Adam must have had a wife before Eve and that, as Eve was said to be the first woman, that this first female must have been a spiritual being. It is probably best to let *The Alphabet* take up the story from here:

> [God] then created a woman for Adam, from the earth, as He had created Adam himself, and called her Lilith. Adam and Lilith began to fight. She said, 'I will not lie below,' and he said, 'I will not lie beneath you, but only on top. For you are fit only to be in the bottom position, while I am to be in the superior one.'
>
> Lilith responded, 'We are equal to each other inasmuch as we were both created from the Earth.' But they would not listen to one another. When Lilith saw this, she pronounced the Ineffable name and flew away into the air. Adam stood in prayer before his creator: 'Sovereign of the Universe,' he said, 'the woman you gave me has run away.' At once, the Holy One, blessed be he, sent these three angels to bring her back.
>
> Said the Holy One to Adam, 'If she agrees to come back, fine. If not she must permit 100 of her children to die every day.'

To cut a long story short, Lilith refused to return to Adam and, when the angels threatened to drown her in the sea, she said to them:

> 'Leave me! I was created only to cause sickness to infants. If the infant is male, I have dominion over him for eight days after his birth, and if female, for twenty days.'
>
> As a concession, Lilith said that a child could be protected by wearing an amulet with the names of her three pursuing angels on it.
>
> 'Whenever I see you or your names in an amulet, I will have no power over that infant,' said Lilith.
>
> Adam, then being on his own again, was given Eve by God.[33]

This story, which was apparently created out of two conflicting sentences in the Book of Genesis, is how Lilith is best known in the modern world. In an apparent argument over who should be on top during sex (Adam favouring the missionary position), Lilith deserted Adam and, cursed by God to have 100 of her children die every day, became an angry and embittered spirit. This argument over sex and Lilith's loss of face in front of God has been seen by some theologians as a metaphor for a perpetual struggle for domination between the male and female sexes.

Because of her threat to kill newborn children, fear of Lilith was so great among some Germanic Jews that there sprang up a tradition of watching newborn baby boys continuously for the first seven nights of their lives, until their circumcision on the eighth day, lest Lilith the demon queen should come and take them during the night. Children found dead in their cribs were said to have been victims of Lilith's vengeance. Now such deaths are normally associated with Sudden Infant Death Syndrome (SIDS) or, to use its more common name, cot death.

Of more interest to us here is another series of legends associated with Lilith in which she is portrayed as being not only the queen of the demons but also the queen succubus, and, indeed, the mother of those demons known as succubi and incubi.

Beyond the story given in *The Alphabet*, there are a great many other traditions attributed to Lilith, the origins of most of which are obscure but are unlikely to pre-date the story given in *The Alphabet*. In the *Kabbala*, a Jewish mystical text written in twelfth-century Europe, the tradition of Lilith as a succubus is revealed in full detail. In this tradition, which builds upon the story in *The Alphabet*, we find Adam married to Eve but, since the killing of Abel by Cain, Adam has lost the urge to copulate with Eve, saying, 'Why should I beget children for terror!'[34]

After 130 years of abstinence, Adam and Eve separate, making Adam vulnerable to Lilith's charms once more. Disillusioned by the world, Adam begins to sleep with Lilith again, with each successful sexual union resulting in Lilith giving birth to a new demon for the world. In the *Kabbala* these demons are described as being '... the evil spirits of the world who are called the Plagues of Mankind. And they lead the sons of man astray, and dwell in the doorway of the house, and in the cisterns and the latrines ... '[35]

These demons, the offspring of Adam and Lilith, are considered to be the succubi and incubi that are discussed in Chapter 2. Lilith herself has, however, not entirely left the scene yet, for, after the death of Adam, she too is supposed to have turned her attention towards mankind. Because of God's curse, which decreed that 100 of her children must die each day, Lilith has an urgent need to keep producing demonic offspring. She can, however, only become pregnant by using the semen from mortal men. One of her tasks in the world is therefore to collect the fresh semen from mankind.

She does this in two ways. Firstly, she acts as a genuine succubus, actually having physical sex with men while they are sleeping. The man is subconsciously aroused by Lilith and copulates with her without waking – the only evidence of her actions being some spilt semen or sometimes an erotic dream. In other words, any man experiencing the discomfort of a wet dream has, in reality, been tricked by Lilith into having sex with her and thus inadvertently making her pregnant. On this the *Kabbala* says:

> ... and she comes forth, and makes sport with the son of man, and becomes hot from them in the dream, in that desire which man has, and she clings to him, and takes the desire [i.e. semen] and from it she conceives and brings forth other kinds of demons into the world. Those children whom she bears from the sons of man come to women, and they conceive from them and bear spirits ... .[36]

This passage indicates that the demons produced from Lilith's wet-dream encounters are in fact incubi that are only capable of having sex with and impregnating women.

The second means by which Lilith could get hold of male semen was to collect it from wherever it had been deliberately or accidentally spilt by the man. In practice, this meant that she would steal from men who had been masturbating or from couples who had just had sex but had managed to spill some semen. The masturbation element of this is not to be found in the *Kabbala* or other medieval texts, and would seem to be a later legend or perhaps a contemporary one that it was not seen fit to write down. The issue of Lilith being in the marriage bed was, however, of much more concern and receives a number of mentions, including:

> And behold, the dark husk, that is Lilith, is always in the sheet of the bed of a man and a woman who copulate, in order to take the sparks of the drops of seed that go to waste, because it cannot be without this, and she creates from them demons, spirits and Lilin. And there is an incantation to drive away Lilith from the bed and to bring forth holy souls, which is mentioned in the holy Zohar.[37]

The traditional means of keeping Lilith away from the marital bed is the same as that designed to keep her away from the souls of newborn children. If the names of her three pursuing angels are written around the room, she will leave the house alone.

There are a great many other traditions associated with Lilith, most of which do not concern the core thesis of this book. In the *Kabbala* there is sometimes said to be a similar but slightly less powerful female demon, called Naamah, who is also capable of raping men and giving birth to succubi and incubi. Lilith is sometimes credited with clearing up the confusion created by Naamah and on occasion adopts Naamah's unwanted offspring. Adam is sometimes said to have slept with Naamah as well as Lilith, and in the Book of Zohar other Biblical characters, including Noah, Abraham, Isaac and Jacob, are similarly said to have been seduced by Lilith. She would indeed appear to have been a promiscuous and wanton demon, content to use her sexuality to cause trouble and, more importantly, to fill the world with more hideous demons, among whose ranks are the succubi and incubi.

## Searching for Lilith's origins

The written traditions of Lilith's relationship with the Old Testament and the sexuality of mankind are, in comparison with other religious texts, very young indeed, being written only a matter of 1,200 to about 800 years ago. Virtually everything we know about the Jewish tradition of Lilith comes from *The Alphabet* and the books of the *Kabbala*. There is evidence that some of what was written about her in these books, particularly the *Kabbala*, was in fact anti-Christian in its tone. For example, the fact that Adam was tempted by Lilith after being celibate during his separation from Eve has been seen as a swipe against the Christian doctrine on abstinence from sex, the implication being that celibacy makes people more open to temptation from evil.

Despite these recent legends, Lilith is obviously a major sexual demon and her links with the better-known succubi and incubi is an important one. Although the Jewish writings may be recent, it is possible to trace her occurrence back many centuries before this and through a great many religions. Her role appears to have changed little over the centuries.

In spite of her strong links with Judaism, Lilith herself only manages one solitary mention in the Old Testament and even this would not seem to justify her image as a nymphomaniac, baby-killing demon. In the Book of Isaiah the following passage has been seen as referring to her: 'The wild beasts of the desert shall also meet with the wild beasts of the island, and the satyr shall cry to his fellow; Lilith shall rest there, and find for herself a place of rest.'[38] It must be pointed out that not only does this reference shed no light on why Lilith should be thought of as an evil demon, but also that her name is sometimes translated from the Hebrew as 'the screech owl', and this has led some scholars to dismiss this reference as being nothing to do with her.

Although references to her in the Bible may be scant, Lilith does turn up in other ancient religious texts. She is mentioned in the *Epic of Gilgamesh*, which was written between 2500 and 2100 BC, although, again, not in connection with either child murder or supernatural rape. She is merely referred to as 'the demon Lilith' who is frightened away by Gilgamesh. Again, however, doubt has been placed on the validity of this translation and the reference therefore remains ambiguous.

Her unquestionable historical debut comes in the Babylonian *Talmud,* where she receives no fewer than four mentions, none of them complimentary. In fact, taken together, these references portray her as nothing but a long-haired demon with wings and a promiscuous tendency:

> Rabbi Jeremia ben Eleazar said, 'During those years, in which Adam, the first man, was separated from Eve, he became the father of ghouls and demons and Linin.' Rabbi Meir said, 'Adam the first man, being very pious and finding that he had caused death to come into the world, sat fasting for 130 years, and separated himself from his wife for 130 years, and wore fig vines for 130 years. His fathering of evil spirits, referred to here, came as a result of wet dreams.[39]
>
> Lilith grows long hair.[40]
>
> Lilith is a demoness with a human appearance except that she has wings.[41]
>
> Rabbi Hanina said, 'One may not sleep alone in a house, for Lilith takes hold of whoever sleeps alone in a house.'[42]

Lilith appears again in her more familiar role as a child-murdering seductress in a series of incantation bowls found in Persia (now Iran). In these bowls are a series of rhymes designed to keep away Lilith. On one bowl she is described as being: 'The evil Lilith, who causes the hearts of men to go astray and appears in the dream of the night and in the vision of the day. Who burns and casts down with nightmare, attacks and kills children, boys and girls ...'[43]

Using these ancient quotes, it is possible to see that belief in Lilith is very old indeed, possibly dating back as far as 2500 BC, and that her persona as a succubus and killer of children was in place some centuries before the writing of *The Alphabet,* from which her modern image has been obtained.

There is evidence that she was still feared until very recently in some parts of the world. Amulets for newborn babies, under 200 years old and bearing an inscription to keep Lilith away, have been found in Iran. There is also a traditional Jewish folk tale that speaks of Lilith being found in the bedroom mirror of a young girl. Possessed by the spirit of Lilith, the young girl '... ran around with young men who lived in the same neighbourhood'.[44]

In more recent times, her image has been revived by magicians, including the infamous Aleister Crowley, and even by some feminists, who see her independent stance against Adam as being a stand against male dominance. Psychologist Carl Jung used her as a prime example of suppressed femininity within the male sex, and there have been a number of books and plays either written about her or based on her legend.

Lilith is indeed an important religious figure and probably justifies her title as queen of the demons. She is the first known of the supernatural raping spirits that would later be known as succubi. More importantly, she is the designated mother of the many thousands of succubi and incubi that were believed to be abroad in the world during the Middle Ages. There are, however, no recorded accounts, either first – or secondhand, of attacks by Lilith, whereas her succubus and incubus offspring have hundreds of testimonies to their actions.

# Part two

## SEX FOR USE WITH WORSHIP

# 4

# WORSHIPPING THE PHALLUS

At the turn of the twentieth century, when Freudian psychoanalysis was still very popular, historians and theologians began to find sexual relevance in a great many modern and ancient religions. Much of this was dismissed at the time as being a rather tedious sexual obsession that had sprung from the repressed minds of the Victorian middle classes. Since that time, much of what was written about the sexual nature of many religions has been deliberately ignored or forgotten, the topic having become unfashionable for quite a while. Some of what was written came under the heading of 'phallic worship', a great deal of which is concerned with the ancient religions and cults that were operating at around the time of the Old Testament.

Much of the evidence cited in favour of phallic worship helps to explain not only passages in the Bible but also a great deal about modern religious customs, including the genesis of beliefs about supernatural entities being able to have sex with children and, as is discussed in Chapter 8, accusations of modern Satanic ritual abuse. Phallic worship, as the name implies, is the act of revering the penis, or phallus, normally as a symbol of fertility or as a representation of divine power. The trademarks of religions that practice phallic worship are the effigies of erect penises, often exaggerated in length, that are added on to statues of their gods, or which may be freestanding objects. Some such religions are also noted for their sexual promiscuity, fertility rites and orgiastic practices, which, by modern conservative Christian standards, seem to be shocking, degrading or even inhuman.

## Ancient phallic worship

The act of phallic worship is a very ancient practice, and is liable to pre-date all the currently practised religions on Earth. Its origins are unrecorded and unknown, but it is felt likely, by some historians, that the first organized religions would have concerned themselves with phallic worship, or even have used it as their base credence. The penis, because of its size, shape, ability to become erect, and association with sex and reproduction, would have been a natural object for our ancestors to worship. Just as ancient man recognized the importance of the sun to his crops and therefore to his well-being, so too would he have recognized that without sex (which was an enjoyable experience in itself), there would be no children to carry on the lineage, help farm the land and keep him in his old age. In the same way as the sun was worshipped in order to ensure that it helped the crops to grow, so the penis would have been worshipped to ensure fertility for both the man and the woman. Equally, in some parts of the world the female genitalia, normally represented by a raised oval shape or a long thin crack, were worshipped in addition to the male ones, but for precisely the same reason.

Evidence of the past existence of phallic worship can be readily found in the archaeology of many parts of the world. There are the individual carved Roman, Egyptian, Greek and Babylonian phalli that have been found across Europe and the Middle East. There are the hill carvings of England, most notably the one at Cerne Abbas, in Dorset, most of which have, or would have had, phallic representations. There are the murals, wall carvings and hieroglyphics that feature phallic representations or depict gods with erect penises. There are the Irish Shelah-na-Gigs that represent open-legged women displaying their genitalia and are still used as symbols of fertility today. Finally, anybody who has ever visited a Mediterranean country will have surely encountered a statue or a postcard of that most famous of all phallic gods, Priapus, whose monstrous phallus projects at an angle of 90° from his groin.

## Judaism and the ancient world

We know from contemporary commentators that the practice of phallic worship was widespread in the ancient world, and that it was particularly popular with followers of the Canaanite and Phoenician god Baal and the Moabite god Baal-Peor. The names of both gods mean 'the one who opens', something that is thought to be a reference to the breaking of a woman's hymen (see Chapter 5). There are many references to these two gods in the Old Testament and there is much evidence that, while Judaism may not have originated from either of these cults in particular, it was probably a phallus-worshipping religion in its origin.

George Ryley Scott, a researcher of ancient phallic worship, says on the matter:

> Yahweh, the god of the Hebrews, was himself a phallic deity, the rite of circumcision in itself indicating his real nature. In Exodus we read how Zipporah cast at the feet of the angry Yahweh the bloody foreskin of her son as a form of appeasement. Like Baal-Peor, Yahweh was referred to as 'the opener', thus: 'And God remembered Rachel, and God hearkened to her, and opened her womb.' The frequency with which Yahweh was represented in the form of a bull, and commonly referred to as the 'Bull of Israel' is another indication of his phallic origin.[45]

Although the subject is a controversial one, there is much anecdotal evidence within the older books of the Old Testament to back up the claims of Scott and others of a phallic Hebrew god.

It is openly acknowledged that the Jewish forefathers worshipped other more pagan gods before finding their one true god, Yahweh. For example, Abraham openly continued to erect 'pillars' (i.e. phallic representations) after converting from his pagan religion (thought likely to be that of Baal) to Judaism.

Phallic symbolism is rife in the first books of the Old Testament; barely a chapter passes without coded references to people worshipping pillars (sometimes referred to as stones) or columns which, in the context of the descriptions given, clearly represent phallic objects. Joshua worshipped a pillar at Shechem, as did Solomon at Gideon. Even one of the most famous stories of the Old Testament, that of Jacob's ladder, has a phallic reference in it. After his vision of God, Jacob built an altar and said, 'This stone, which I have set up for a pillar, shall be God's house.' Noah prayed to a phallus in the ark, and some have even argued that the oval shape of the ark could represent the female genitalia.

Evidence is also provided of worship of the female genitalia in the Bible. Thomas Inman states that the female reproductive force in the Bible, which is called *asherah*, is synonymous with the Syrian term for the vulva, '*Asherah*'. According to Inman, the term *asherah* has been deliberately mistranslated into the English word 'grove', implying an orchard or row of trees. This translation does not make any sense in many parts of the Bible when people are reprimanded for worshipping 'groves'. For example, we are told that 'the Children of Israel did evil in the sight of the Lord, and forgot the Lord their God, and served Baalim [= Baal, a phallic deity] and the groves'.[46]

There are even, according to Scott, signs of what is known as the 'phallic oath' whereby anybody making a promise or oath would place their hand upon their own penis or even that of a second party. This was a common practice that is still reflected in some superstitions and customs today, and in its time was the equivalent of raising your right hand or swearing on the Bible. Scott and others believe that the word thigh has been substituted for the word penis in the following Old Testament quotes:

> Put, I pray to thee, thy hand under my thigh: and I will make thee swear by the Lord, the God of heaven, and the God of earth.[47]

> ... and he called his son Joseph, and said unto him, if now I have found grace in thy sight, put, I pray thee, thy hand under my thigh, and deal kindly and truly with me.[48]

Even the authoritative *Encyclopedia Biblica* recognizes this fact, saying of the practice:

> With regard to the practice of putting the hand under another's thigh, it seems that it grew out of the special sacredness attached to the generative organ; fruitfulness being of specially divine origin, the organ of it in man could by the primitive Semites be taken as symbolizing the Deity.[49]

Although the books of the Old Testament would appear to be full of hidden, but describable, references to phallic ritual practices, the subject is still a very controversial one. It is by no means theologically accepted that Judaism had either phallic origins or a strong phallic element to it. It is often counter-argued that the size and, to the modern world, unfamiliar terminology of the Bible is such that it is possible to find written evidence to back every type of preconceived idea about biblical times, including phallic worship.

Much of the evidence cited does, after all, rely heavily on believing that words like 'pillar' and 'grove' are ancient code for phallic objects or ritual practice. The references to phallic worship in the ancient Hebrew faith may have become hidden with time, or were perhaps even non-existent. The same cannot be said of a great many other religions where the sexual element to worship is more plainly recorded.

## Other ancient phallic religions

Although the guarded references we have noted to phallicism in the Bible are interesting, the reticence displayed in the Old Testament was unusual for its time, since practically every other religion in the Europe and the Middle East was concerned with notions of worship of phallic objects.

In ancient Egypt, it was written that Typhon murdered his brother Osiris and cut up his body into small pieces that were subsequently hidden about the land. Isis, the wife of Osiris, managed to collect together all the fragments of her dead husband's body, with the exception of his genitalia, which Typhon had cast into the River Nile. In reverence to her husband, Isis erected a number of statues representing the cut-up pieces of Osiris' body, the greatest of which was the one for his unrecovered phallus. Statues of Osiris' phallus were to be found in every Egyptian temple and were worshipped with great reverence. Osiris was later to be represented by an ox; which was apparently selected by the priests because of its strength and virility. Isis was similarly worshipped as the principle female opposing Osiris and was often pictured holding a sistrum, an object that represented a womb. She later came to be represented by a cow, the female equivalent of the bull or ox. Other phallic Egyptian gods include Ammon, Kneph and Min.

The Egyptian practice of worshipping bulls is thought to have spread eastwards into Assyria, Persia and eventually the Indian subcontinent. In these parts, and also in parts of ancient Greece and Rome, the bull was worshipped as a sign of male virility and fertility, and temples dedicated to the bull would often be adorned with phallic objects.

Probably the best known of the ancient phallic gods are those of Greek or Roman origin. Priapus, Bacchus, Dionysus, Mercurius, Hermes and Mutinus were all endowed with great powers of fertility or sexual prowess and were depicted as having monstrous genitalia. The female equivalents included Aphrodite, Ceres, Venus and Flora. The festivals associated with these gods, both male and female, are now notorious for their hedonism and sexual excess, traditions of which have filtered through to our society in the form of scare stories about Satanic ritual abuse (see Chapter 8).

Phallic symbols played an important role in Roman and Greek life, and not only were the temples awash with them but also every household, and people would even wear miniature phalli around their necks or carry them upon their person.

## Modern religions

The phallic religions mentioned so far have all died out or were assimilated into other religions, most notably Christianity and Islam, so that little of them exists today outside of their archaeological artefacts or historical records.

There has, in recent years, been a western revival in the practice of some ancient phallic cults, the most notable of which is the so-called art of Tantra. Tantra is, in origin, an Indian religion the texts of which date back to around the tenth century, but which was stamped out in the last century by both the British and the orthodox Hindus. Tantricism revolves around the worship of two principal deities, Shiva and Shakti, of whom Shiva was the more powerful. Much Tantric philosophy is related to the obtaining of a state of higher consciousness through physical exercise, meditation and sexual practices.

It is the sexual practices undertaken during Tantric rituals that have attracted the most criticism, as they allegedly involve group sex, incest and adultery. Age, beauty and mutual attraction apparently play no part in the proceedings – just the rites of sexual intercourse that will, if done correctly, lift the person closer to the gods. Those who are advanced in the techniques can apparently go on to have sex with the gods themselves.

The truth regarding the stories about Tantric sexual ceremonies is hard to come by, and the few westerners who claim to have been initiated into secret Asian Tantric cults produce stories that have a similarity to those of both the witches' Sabbat and the tales of ritual abuse discussed in Chapter 8.

Although only a small fraction of the Tantric religious doctrine revolved around sex, it is this element that has become of most interest to westerners, and during the last century a number of Tantric cults became active in both Europe and America. Many of the occult temples that were set up at the end of the nineteenth century, including the notorious Ordo Templi Orientis, were based on the direct importation of Tantric sexual practices. These temples caused outrage during their time and spawned many offshoots. One follower was the so-called 'wickedest man in the world', Aleister Crowley, who went on to found his own brand of 'sex magic' that caused at least one death and led to his expulsion from several countries.

There are still a great many sexual occultist groups in action and sex magic is now considered to be a mainstream part of occultism.

Although many occultists claim that, in common with Tantric philosophy, the correct practice of sexual magic can lead to improved health, longevity and heightened psychic powers, and can be used as a form of worship, most people acknowledge that it is in fact mostly theatrical in nature.

Nonetheless, I know from firsthand sources that sexual magic is still widely practised today, and that, rather than involving sordid orgies, most of it is symbolic rather than comprising actual physical sexual acts. A good friend of mine, who has been involved in sex magic for some years, said that many people who join his group with a view to getting free sex often leave it feeling very disappointed!

# 5

# SEX TO HONOUR THE GODS

The belief that it is possible for divine or supernatural beings to have sex with humans is a basic and widespread one. Many branches of mainstream Christianity, most notably Catholicism, accept that the Virgin Mary was impregnated by the Holy Spirit before giving birth to Jesus Christ. Although it is not widely promoted, many other religions also have a similar tradition whereby their prophets are the offspring of a union between divine beings and a mortal human. In these cases too, the birth is frequently said to have been from a virgin woman.

Ancient Egyptian, Middle Eastern, Indian, Greek and Roman traditions all empower their gods with the ability to copulate with, and sometimes impregnate, humans; and there are many tales of maidens being tricked into giving their virginity to the gods, or of being raped for their beauty. The Greek sun-god Hercules, for example, is said to have met and had intercourse with Celtine, the daughter of a Celtic king, and the son that she bore him, Celtus (Galates in some versions), later became the founder of the northern European Celtic tradition.

Neither are men immune from the sexual appetites of the gods. The Roman goddesses in particular were noted for their love of mortal men, and some, such as Flora, were even reported to be prostitutes. Some gods were noted for their sexual appetites and were worshipped on feast days with ceremonies that were essentially orgies (see the Bacchanalia in Chapter 9). Lesser supernatural beings, including angels, demons, ghosts, evil spirits were also deemed to be able to copulate with humans, a tradition that has survived to

# Sex to honour the gods

the modern day with the stories of ghost and demon rape (see Chapter 1).

The belief that gods could have sex with, and even fertilize, human beings was not just an esoteric notion or an abstract belief but in many cases an assumed fact that became part of religious or marriage ceremonies. In particular there was the belief that the gods would smile favourably upon any woman who offered her virginity up to them.

## Sacrifice of virginity

The sexual conservatism of most modern religions makes us unused to or appalled by some of the ceremonies, practices and rites associated with other religions. In Chapter 4, it was shown that the many of the ancient religions mentioned in the Bible concerned themselves with worshipping effigies of the erect penis as a symbol of fertility, vigour and power. Often in association with these so-called phallic cults was the belief that it was possible for the gods (or a named god in particular) to have sex with human beings. This belief in divine copulation would often be acted out ritually by the custom of a woman sacrificing her virginity to the god in question. There is much historical evidence to suggest that in ancient times the bride-to-be would be called upon to physically lose her virginity to the statue of the god.

In phallic cults, many of the statues of the gods were endowed with protruding and oversized penises as a sign of their virility. Most famous of these was the Greek god Priapus, whose monstrous erect penis is often completely out of proportion to the rest of his body. Many other ancient gods, and quite a few modern African and Asian ones, are similarly endowed.

Therefore, in order for the god to be seen to copulate successfully with the virgin, the girl would actually have to have sex with the statue itself. St Augustine, writing in the fifth century, says of the practice of giving a girl's virginity to a statue: 'Priapus is there upon whose huge and beastly member the new bride was commanded to get uppe and sitte.'[50] Others also refer to the practice. Lactantius mentions the god 'Mutinus, in whose shameful lap brides sit, in order that the god may appear to have gathered the first-fruits of their virginity'.[51]

Sometimes the phallus would not be attached to a statue but would merely be a phallic object ritually inserted into the vagina, in order to break the hymen, by a priest or family member. Again this was done to symbolize that the god was taking the girl's virginity. The priestesses serving the ancient god Baal (considered to be an arch enemy of Judaism) would have their hymens broken by a stone phallus, and in historical times in the Philippines a smooth stick would be employed for the purpose.

This ritual sacrifice of virginity was reported to be continuing in India during the nineteenth century, with one commentator recounting that 'every pagoda [temple] contains a male member made of iron or ivory which is forced into the vagina of the bride by her parents or relations, until it causes an effusion of blood indicative of the rupture of the hymen'.[52]

There are possible links between the use of artificial phalli and reports from medieval witches of having had an artificial phallus inserted into them during the Sabbat ritual (see Chapter 6). Even in the Bible we find a hint that artificial phalli were sometimes used for physical sexual purposes. 'Thou has also taken thy fair jewels of my gold and of my silver, which I had given thee, and madest to thyself images of men [i.e. made a phallus], and didst commit whoredom with them.'[53]

In many temples, the crude practice of using a statue of a god or artificial phallus to break the hymen was replaced by a priest who would ensure that the girl's virginity was taken by more natural means. This usually meant the priest physically copulating with the girl, but sometimes the hymen was broken by the priest using his finger or some blunt object. In ancient Egypt, the role of the god Anubis was said often to be played by a man, and in the nineteenth century it was not unknown for infertile girls to seek the company of priests or monks in the hope of curing their barrenness.

The right of a god to take a girl's virginity seems abhorrent to most of us within western society, but in the times when it was happening both husband and bride were, according to contemporary reports, very happy to see the practice through for a number of reasons. The custom of sacrificing a girl's virginity to the gods is a very ancient one, and has been related back to the practice of offering the gods the first fruits of any harvest, or the first catch of any hunt, as an appeasement. Such first-fruit offerings are still made today, and this is the undoubted origin of the Christian harvest festival or thanksgiving services. Similarly, the offering of a woman's virginity to the gods would attract their favour and ensure that she would bear many sons and daughters.

There is also the question of the bleeding that occurs when the hymen is first broken. In many ancient societies, and a few modern ones, a woman's menstrual blood was considered to be unclean, unlucky or even poisonous (see also Chapter 6). For these reasons, women were often banished during their monthly periods, and the thought of having sexual intercourse during this time was out of the question. Indeed, when I was in central Africa some years ago, a tribesman forbade me from washing in a river because I was downstream from where some women were swimming and he felt that the water might have been poisoned by their menstrual blood.

If menstrual blood was considered poisonous, then the bleeding associated with the loss of virginity was thought to be ten times more potent. Men feared that if they got the blood upon themselves then they would be cursed or crippled in some way, and so it was that they were happy to let a priest or statue of a god, who was divinely immune from the effects of the blood, take the girl's virginity.

The right of a priest or god to take a newly-wed girl's virginity might well remind some readers of a medieval practice that occasionally crops up in romantic movies or novels. The practice, called the *jus primae noctis*, is an ancient right given to the lord of the manor to deflower any newly-wed girl on his property.

This practice has, fortunately, been illegal for centuries, but it nonetheless shows a connection between Europe's feudal past and its pagan ancestry. The practice may also find expression in some of the now defunct African and Polynesian customs whereby a father would often take the virginity of his own daughter, claiming that he had the right to the 'first-fruit of the tree he had planted'.

## The temple harlots

In many ancient religions, and just outside living memory in India, there was another unusual means by which women could gain the favours of the gods using their sexuality. In this case it was not through copulating with a person or statue deemed to have the power of the god but by making themselves sexually available through the temple itself in what today might be considered at best an outrageous display of promiscuity or possibly even prostitution.

Anybody at all familiar with the Old Testament will be able to find numerous passages referring to sexually available women being present at temples. The large and famous temple of Solomon was awash with women, phallic symbols and even male prostitutes. In other religions, the attachment of women to the temple was considered to be a natural and contemporary part of the religious set-up.

Girls would be attached to the temple for various reasons. The temple of Mylitta in ancient Babylonia required that every girl must, at some point in her life, go to the temple and remain there until a passing man claimed the right to pay to have sex with her. Once this had been done, the woman was free to go and the money she received would be placed on the altar as an offering to the goddess. The historian Herodotus tells us that beautiful girls would only remain there for a matter of hours while less attractive ones could spend months or even years at the temple waiting to be freed. It is also thought that this practice is what is being referred to in the apocryphal 'Epistle of Jeremy', who says, 'It is said that the Babylonian women with cords about them sit in the ways, burning bran for incense; but if any of them, drawn by some that passeth by, be with him, she reproacheth her fellow, that she was not thought as worthy as herself, nor her cord broken.'[54]

Virtually every ancient temple, including the Judaic ones, is recorded as having prostitutes or sexually available women attached to it. In the modern world, prostitution has a very low standing in society, and it is generally practised by those who cannot raise money by any other means. This was not always the case, and in fact most temple prostitutes were regarded very highly, since it was considered that they were effectively worshipping the god or goddess of the temple with their bodies. In many cases, to be chosen as a temple prostitute was a great honour and ensured that the woman concerned would live a luxurious lifestyle and be highly regarded. In this respect, temple prostitutes fulfil much the same role as ancient gladiators or even modern boxers. They did a job that most people did not want to do themselves but took pleasure in; as a result, they were richly rewarded and were highly regarded within society.

For example, the Greek geographer Strabo informs us that the temple of Aphrodite at Corinth took the most beautiful girls from the noble families of the district and traded them as temple prostitutes. He says that this was considered to be the highest profession for a girl as she was, after all, worshipping the goddess with her body, and that on retirement each girl was married into a high-status family. In some parts of India, where many so-called phallic practices occurred until relatively recently, it was customary for the first-born daughter to a family to be given to the temple to serve as a prostitute. This practice was stamped out under British colonial rule, but actually differs little from the once-common Catholic hope that at least one son in a family would join the priesthood and thus sacrifice any ambitions of marriage and fathering children.

Not all those selling their bodies were female – a good many temples also had male prostitutes. One H. More, travelling through Peru in the sixteenth century, observed that '... there were boys consecrated to serve in the temple, and at the times of their sacrifices and solemn feasts the Lords and principal men abused them to that detestable filthiness'.[55]

Other ancient ceremonies, including the Roman feast of Venus, were noted for their homosexual practices and it is often felt that the fury with which the Old Testament denounces homosexuality has much to do with its widespread practice in rival religions and cults of the era.

## Gnostic sects

Although much of the early Old Testament guardedly refers to the practices of phallic worship and the association of its temples with prostitutes, from the time of Moses onwards bigamy, prostitution, sodomy and sexual promiscuity were not considered to be part of Judaic law. Moses was particularly against the generally accepted idea of temple harlots, and his more famous pronouncements on the topic include the following:

> Do not prostitute thy daughter, to cause her to be a whore; lest the land fall to whoredom, and the land become full of wickedness.[56]

> Thou shalt not bring the hire of a whore, or the price of a dog, into the house of the Lord thy god for any vow.[57]

The ten commandments also place the Judaic tradition firmly on the path of righteousness and monogamy, with no tolerance for prostitution, idolatry, adultery or sexual promiscuity of any kind.

From what we know of the major European and Middle Eastern religions of the time, Judaism was practically alone in its stance against permissiveness, with the Canaanites, Assyrians, Egyptians, Babylonians, Greeks, Romans and others all continuing in phallic worship, sacrifice of virginity, and temple prostitution. These practices continued to occur up to and beyond the advent of Christ and, even after the Roman Empire had been converted to Christianity in the fourth century AD, were still practised in parts of Asia and Africa up until the colonial invasions of the nineteenth century.

The advent of Christianity was a major event in the history of

Europe and Asia Minor and one which had a serious bearing on the place of sexuality within mainstream religion. The exact origins, status and meaning of Jesus Christ's life have long since been lost in time and in the political turmoil that affected Roman-occupied Judea during the first and second centuries AD. There are no contemporaneous records of the life of Christ and much of what we are told about him and his teachings comes from the Romanized gospels, all of which were written several decades after Christ is said to have died. Although it is little known outside of history textbooks, the Roman Catholic version of Christ's teachings and actions, which is the version that is accepted by most Christians today, was but one branch of a whole host of different Christian sects that sprang up during the first century AD. These other branches of Christianity are commonly referred to as gnostic sects, and many were very small and short-lived. They do, however, reveal the degree to which early Christian society was obsessed with sex and, in particular, abstaining from it.

The gnostic Christian sects were commonly based around a single charismatic individual who would promote his own interpretation of Christ's message. One such sect arose in second-century Rome around a man named Marcion, who believed that Christianity had a separate god from that of the Jews and who, even more controversially, believed that the virgin birth and childhood of Christ, as depicted in the gospels, were lies.

Marcion was vehemently anti-sexual and even more anti-Judaic. How could the god of the Jews be the one true god when it was he who had devised the humiliation of sexual intercourse, the discomfort of pregnancy and the pain of childbirth? This Jewish god, according to Marcion, was ignorant, evil and spiteful and inferior to the true God of the Christians, whom he worshipped. In common with his belief, Marcion's followers were compelled to reject marriage and sex, even for reproductive purposes. Marcion was persecuted for his beliefs by the early Roman Catholic church and was eventually excommunicated in AD 144, after which time his sect disappeared from history.

Many of the gnostic sects took the old problem of how to explain the existence of evil in a world created by a good god to a logical extreme, concluding that physical objects must contain evil while spiritual ones must be purely good. In some cases, such as the sect that arose in Corinth a short time after Christ's death, the human body was identified as being purely evil while its soul was purely good. Some members of the sect took this to mean that they had licence to indulge in sexual gluttony, safe in the knowledge that their souls could not be affected by their physical actions on Earth. Others, still within the same sect, thought the reverse and took vows of absolute chastity, with husbands and wives withdrawing sexual rights from each other and newly-weds refusing to consummate their marriage.

The problems within the Corinthian church was one of the first major problems that St Paul had to deal with. His writings on the matter form the New Testament Book of Corinthians, where he has much to say on the matters going on in the city: 'It is reported commonly that there is fornication among you, and such fornication as is not so much as named among the Gentiles, that one should have his father's wife.'

Corinth was not, however, the only place that was apparently adding its own sexual interpretation to the Christian message. Between approximately AD 80 and 150, huge numbers of small gnostic sects came and went. Most of these sects demanded some form of refrain from sexual activity, be it total chastity or simply restraint within marriage. Others, however, interpreted the message of freedom given by Christ as an excuse for orgies and so-called 'love feasts'. The penultimate book of the New Testament, The Epistle of St Jude, has been interpreted by some theologians to be a thinly disguised attack upon sexual excess within a specific, but unnamed, gnostic sect from this time. Jude says:

> Even as Sodom and Gomorrah, and the cities about them in like manner, giving themselves over to fornication, and going after strange flesh, are set forth for an example, suffering the vengeance of eternal fire. Likewise also these filthy dreamers defile the flesh, despise dominion, and speak evil of dignities.[58]

As Christianity became more accepted and widespread in the Roman Empire, so gnosticism declined and, after a series of votes taken at the Council of Nicaea in AD 325, the foundations of modern Roman Catholicism were laid.

During the first millennium AD, when the church was establishing itself in Europe, many of the phallic practices associated with older religions were tolerated and even assimilated into Christian practice. From this we have derived many common practices such as dancing around maypoles, 'green men', and certain festivals and holidays. From the start of the eleventh century, however, such practices were less and less tolerated by the church until they were stamped out almost totally. The church became intolerant of anything pagan and especially of any form of sexual licence, which was viewed as morally corrupting and undermining the power of God. Little of this view of sex has changed in the last 500 years, and there are a great many modern Christian practices that would appear to differ little from those of either the early gnostic sects or, indeed, earlier sex-obsessed religions.

In the modern church, sex is viewed as being, at the very least, sinful, if not downright evil. Catholic priests must remain celibate and both convents and monasteries are full of people who have devoted their virginity (among other things) to the service of God. Contraception is a huge theological issue in the Catholic church and the ordination of women priests and the possibility of allowing divorcees or homosexuals to marry has split the Protestant church in recent years. The periodic attempts by the church to assert its authority on perceived breaches in morality have normally resulted in a great deal of pain and suffering for ordinary people (see Chapter 6). There have even, in a mimicry of the gnostic sects, been modern occultist reinterpretations of the life of Jesus. Some insist that he was married to Mary Magdalene and suggest that the wedding at Cana, when he turned water into wine, was in fact Christ's own wedding. The evidence for this comes from the crowd coming to Jesus to ask for more wine as, under Jewish custom, it is the groom that is responsible for providing the drink at a wedding. Another common theory insists that not only did Christ marry but also that his children escaped to France after the crucifixion and that his lineage has subsequently been protected by a series of historical groups that include the Knights Templar, freemasons and others. There is, however, little documented evidence to support any of these claims and they are just interpretations of the story of Jesus, like those devised by the leaders of the gnostic sects.

If, however, Christ had married and fathered children, much of European and later world history might have been radically different. Much of the church's doctrine on sexuality comes from an attempt to mimic Christ's presumed chastity. Christ himself, according to the gospels, actually had little to say on the matter in comparison with his wider philosophy of tolerance and charity. Indeed, if Christ could have given a clearer direction on sexuality and the Christian way of life, perhaps one of the darkest periods in European history could have been avoided. This period concerned itself directly with issues of religion, sex, sexuality and the supernatural, and it is to this era that we shall turn next.

# 6

# WITCHCRAFT, THE DEVIL AND THE MIDDLE AGES

This book has touched upon the medieval witch trials a couple of times already and with good reason. This period, occurring as it did directly before the urbanization of the western world and its subsequent path to the industrial revolution, represents the last great phase of church intervention in the affairs of state. It also represents the last phase of widespread belief in the interference of supernatural beings in the daily affairs of ordinary human beings, and there are many tales of sexual abuse (on both an individual and an organized scale) and sexual practices that can be learned from this time.

I have already discussed the association of succubi and incubi with the witch trials, but these, and other sexual demons, were only one small part of the witch trials, the duration of which and their ability to affect the lives of ordinary people being quite extraordinary. In this chapter, I wish to look at the whole mentality behind the witch trials, and, in particular, attitudes towards women, the accusations of sexual deviance at the Sabbat, and descriptions of sexual intercourse with the devil himself, of which there are several.

## Origins of the witch trials

The witch trials were a uniquely Christian phenomenon. While there are many religions that have their own witches and evil demons, none have ever acted in the same manner or on the same scale as the Christian church did between the fifteenth and eighteenth centuries.

The origins of the witch trials lie in the Christian belief that good and evil are polarized and opposing forces which are locked in constant battle with one another in their attempts to direct the course of mankind. In the good corner was Jesus, God and their angelic host. In the bad corner was the devil, his demons and evil spirits. Each side was deemed quite capable of recruiting helpers from the human race. God would have saints, capable of performing healing miracles, while the devil would have witches, capable of performing witchcraft.

This elaborate dividing of good and evil into two distinct camps was the only means by which the church could explain the presence of death, sickness and misfortune in the world. Other religions had many gods who could perform acts of both good and evil depending on their mood, and so it was up to the people to appease them. If people wanted a good harvest, then they had to pray to the gods of the sun, rain and crops to make sure all was well. The Christians had one omnipresent God and to suggest that he was capable of performing evil was blasphemous. Instead, evil had to be portrayed as a separate entity which, while not being as powerful as God, was nonetheless capable of bringing harm to the world. It was through the need for such an evil figure that the concept of the devil was born.

The Christians took their belief in an opposing and purely evil spiritual being known as the devil from later Judaic beliefs. The Jews too had been troubled by the problem of evil in the world and had created the devil as a result. To them, and later to the Christians, he was seen as a demonic conspirator constantly lurking in the wings, performing acts of evil and trying to tempt mankind into sin. Just as God had his angels, so the devil had an army of demon helpers at his bidding. It was the works of the fifth-century church theologian St Augustine that fully assimilated the devil into the Christian faith.

It was also largely St Augustine who first forged a sexual role for the devil within society. In his writings, St Augustine would appear to have been greatly troubled by the possibility that demons, or the devil himself, could have sex with a woman and subsequently make her pregnant. His voluminous writings go into much theological detail about this possibility, with Augustine coming out firmly in favour of the idea. This greatly influenced many other Christian writers in the following centuries, and the topic appears to have been a common one for discussion among the first-millennium clergy.

From the eleventh to the end of the fifteenth centuries, the church became increasingly obsessed with the notion of its own power. It set about removing previously tolerated superstitions and practices that it felt to be too pagan or sexual in nature, and started to build around itself paranoid notions that the world was an utterly evil place full of the works of the devil. The church particularly believed that the devil had managed to convert a great many people to his cause, all of whom were now working against God. These people were deemed to be witches and wizards who had been given supernatural powers by the devil so that they might cause mischief and evil. Although it had long been believed that there were such things as witches and demons in the world, a campaign was slowly, but surely, initiated against them. One historian says of this period:

> ... witchcraft was universally held to be a dark and horrible reality; it was an ever-present, fearfully ominous menace, a thing most active, most perilous, most powerful and true. Some may consider these mysteries and cantrips and invocations, these Sabbats and rendezvous, to have been the merest mummery and pantomime, but there is no question that the psychological effect was incalculable, and harmful in the highest degree.[59]

The church's campaign against the devil initially took the form of a persecution against minority sects such as the Jews, Cathars, Waldensians, Knights Templar and other similar marginalized organizations, all of whom were accused of orgiastic practices and murder. The hunt for the devil and his witches, however, soon spread into the villages and towns of everyday European Christian society.

The origins of the witch trials of the fifteenth, sixteenth and seventeenth centuries are still a matter of debate. Many scholars believe that their origins lay in the persecution of the Cathars in the south of France. Others, the most notable of whom is Norman Cohen, believe that it was an extension of the persecution of the Waldensians that began in 1487. In truth, nobody is really sure exactly how they began.

When the context of the witch trials is looked at in comparison with the earlier persecutions, it can be seen that they were probably an extension of these previous inquisitions. Even relatively late works on the history of witchcraft, such as those by the historian Montague Summers, firmly link the practices of witches to those of the Jews, Cathars, Knights Templar, Waldensians and others and, as is discussed in Chapter 9, recount identical stories of sexual perversions and murder at supposedly hidden ceremonies.

Although the period of mass witch trials came later, the first prosecutions and executions for witchcraft do overlap with some of the earlier persecutions. Many of the Knights Templar confessed under torture to worshipping the devil at secret ceremonies. Only a matter of years after the dissolution of the Knights Templar came the first prosecution for sorcery by the church, when Dame Alice Kyteler was found guilty of sacrificing live animals to devils in 1324. Other isolated cases occurred over the next 100 years until, in the 1450s, the first of the mass executions occurred.

In 1459, many men and women were burned at Arras in France after confessing that they had been attending 'hellish dances', and similarly in 1485 people were burned for cavorting with the devil in the Constantine district in Germany. The crime of witchcraft was, therefore, already being widely used in the late fifteenth century, although recorded tortures and executions because of it were isolated and rare. Belief in the works of the devil was gaining strength throughout the church, and it could only be matter of time before a few isolated trials for witchcraft suddenly turned into a full-scale war against the forces of evil.

Many modern moral panics and scares begin with the publication of a commonly available and highly influential book whose contents, however preposterous, are taken at face value (see Chapters 8 and 12). The witch trials were no exception, and it was the publication of one extraordinary book that, above all else, took the witch trials from within a few small German, French and Spanish towns into the whole of Europe and, eventually, to the Americas. The publication of this book was a landmark in western civilization and in attitudes to sexuality and the supernatural.

## Malleus Maleficarum

The pen, we are told, is mightier than the sword, and it is certainly true that, even in our television age, the printed word is still the most powerful means of influencing people. In the Middle Ages, books were highly prized possessions that few people could read, let alone afford, save for the landed gentry and the clergy. Most books were produced by the church for the church and tended to be either Biblical reproductions or collections of prayers and hymns or theological discussions about the nature of God's law.

Such was the case for one initially innocent-looking fifteenth-century work entitled *Malleus Maleficarum*, which translates as 'The Hammer of the Witches'. This book could arguably have been the most influential work of its day and it was to inspire over 200 years of distrust, revenge, hatred, innocent imprisonment, torture and state-sanctioned murder across most of Europe and, later, North America.

It was the *Malleus Maleficarum* that began that period in history now known as the witch trials, much of the central accusation of which was of people having had sex with the devil and other supernatural beings. Of its importance, the historian Montague Summers has said:

> The *Malleus* lay on the bench of every judge, on the desk of every magistrate. It was the ultimate, irrefutable, unarguable authority. It was implicitly accepted not only by Catholic but by Protestant legislature. In fact, it is not too much to say that the *Malleus Maleficarum* is among the most important, wisest, and weightiest books of the world.[60]

The publication of the *Malleus Maleficarum* is sometimes portrayed as being a spontaneous event, caused by nothing more than the enthusiasm of the two priests who wrote it. Nothing could be further from the truth.

In line with the church's worries about continued pagan practices and the evolution of other religions, there had also been an increasing amount of concern about witchcraft and, more specifically, the church's belief that people were fornicating with the devil or his demons in midnight ceremonies. This concern was not a new one. The issue of fornication with evil beings can be traced back at least to discussions held by St Augustine in the fifth century AD, and it had continued sporadically since. Concern gathered in the fifteenth century and, before the publication of *Malleus Maleficarum*, there had been a number of public witch trials in which the central accusation was that people had been fornicating with the devil.

The church was already convinced of the evil in its midst and the beginnings of the *Malleus Maleficarum* can be seen in a now notorious statement (technically called a 'bull') issued by Pope Innocent VIII on 9 December 1484. In this bull the Pope summed up all the church's concern about the increased prevalence of pagan practices and witchcraft in Christian Europe. More especially, it directly concerned itself with the church's belief that its subjects were fornicating with evil. The following extract from the bull is a perfect summary of the medieval church's attitude to this whole area:

> It has indeed lately come to Our ears, not without afflicting Us with bitter sorrow, that in some parts of Northern Germany, as well as in the provinces, townships, territories, districts and dioceses of Mainz, Cologne, Trèves, Salzburg, and Bremen, many persons of both sexes, unmindful of their own salvation and straying from the Catholic Faith, have abandoned themselves to devils, succubi and incubi, and by their incantations, spells, conjurations, and other accursed charms and crafts,

enormities and horrid offences, have slain infants yet in their mother's womb, as also the offspring of cattle, have blasted the produce of the earth, the grapes of the vine, the fruits of the trees, nay, men and women, beasts of burthen, herd-beasts, as well as animals of other kinds, vineyards, orchards, meadows, pastureland, corn, wheat, and all other cereals; these wretches furthermore afflict and torment men and women, beasts of burthen, herd-beasts, as well as animals of other kinds, with terrible and piteous pains and sore diseases, both internal and external; they hinder men from performing the sexual act and women from conceiving, whence husbands cannot know their wives nor wives receive their husbands; over and above this, they blasphemously renounce that faith which is theirs by the Sacrament of Baptism ... [61]

In that lengthy extract we can see that virtually every common problem and malady, from crop failure to impotence, was capable of being blamed on witches. With the arrival of the plague and the prevalence of other diseases such as cholera and smallpox, as well as the poor farming techniques prevalent in Europe, it is no wonder that later on so many witches needed to be found to take the blame for all these disasters. There are also the crucial statements that ordinary people were deemed to have been having sex with 'devils, incubi and succubi', which, while forming a central feature in Innocent VIII's bull, was to assume even more importance in both the *Malleus Maleficarum* and the witch trials that it later provoked.

In that same bull, it was announced by the Pope that two Dominican priests, Henry Kramer and James Sprenger, had been given the task of investigating the claimed incidents of witchcraft in northern Germany and that they were to be afforded every assistance in their task. These two priests, each of whom was noted for his intelligence and outstanding comprehension of theology, undertook their task with glee. Their results were published three years later as the weighty theological work known as the *Malleus Maleficarum*.

The *Malleus Maleficarum* is divided into three sections dealing with:

1. the actions of witchcraft and its relationship to the church;
2. the treatment of those affected by witchcraft;
3. how witches should be made to confess and treated legally.

In line with the theological training of its authors, each of these sections is then subdivided into a series of questions and answers about the workings of witchcraft and how it should be treated. In style and content, the book is really the equivalent of a do-it-yourself guide to witch-hunting.

The *Malleus Maleficarum* does not pull its punches in the methods it outlines for either detecting or treating witches. The book takes the reader through the various physical signs that must be looked for on a witch, and how to make her (witches were always assumed to be female – more about this assumption will be discussed later) confess her crimes of sorcery.

There are sexual elements in all the signs of sorcery that are advocated. A common practice was to look for strange marks or moles on the thigh or breast, which were thought to have been put there by the devil. In the case of moles, or other protruding pieces of skin, it was thought that these were extra teats from which the devil or the witch's animal familiars could drink.

Other sexual signs were confessions of having had sex with the demons known as succubi and incubi (see Chapter 2), but possibly the greatest sign of them all was to have participated in the witches' ceremony of devil-worship called the Sabbat. It was alleged to be at the Sabbat that the greatest acts of sexual depravity took place, including the practice of kissing the devil's buttocks and of having sex with the horned Prince of Darkness himself; these practices are discussed in detail below.

The *Malleus Maleficarum*, while undoubtedly starting and acting as the main focus of the witch trials, was aided by many other people. On the Protestant side was Martin Luther, a German priest who rebelled against the Catholic church. Despite being only a baby at the time of the original publication of the *Malleus*, Luther was to add fuel to the sixteenth-century witch trials.

Luther had an obsession with the devil and his capacity to influence the everyday workings of human life. He claimed that the works of the devil were to be found around every corner, and even to have met him on a number of occasions. Luther's voluminous writings are full of his rantings about the devil and the misfortunes that could be blamed on him.

For example, Luther suffered from constipation and became convinced that the devil had become lodged in his bowels. He thus viewed every toilet movement as a victory over the forces of darkness, and famously wrote: '… if that is not enough for you, you devil, I have also shit and pissed. Wipe your mouth on that and take a hearty bite.'

Luther's many followers were similarly on the lookout for the obvious works of the devil, and as his brand of Protestantism grew in popularity so did the approval for the capture, punishment and torture of witches.

## Sexual practice at the Sabbat

The focus of the witch trials was on the nocturnal ceremonies that all witches were supposed to attend in order to worship their master, the devil. This ceremony was known as the Sabbat; this name, a corruption of the Jewish 'Sabbath', reflected the belief that it was not only witches but also Jews who were in league with Beelzebub. The *Malleus Maleficarum*, the writings of Luther and other works all focus themselves on the goings-on at the Sabbat. It was here that the witches were said to meet with demons and be given supernatural powers with which they could do harm. It was also at the Sabbat that many perverted practices were said to occur, including orgies, homosexuality, murder and fornication with the devil himself. When a suspected witch was arrested, much of the questioning would be focused upon the goings-on at the Sabbat, and it was sometimes on the strength of these descriptions, often extracted under torture, that a witch would be hanged or burnt.

Despite the obsession that the medieval church seems to have had with the thought of various groups practising hidden orgies, as well as with the individual nocturnal attacks by succubi and incubi, the actual detail of what kind of sexual practice occurred is scant in contemporary medieval literature. This may have been because most of the accusations regarding orgiastic practice were at best exaggerated and more likely to be entirely made up. It may also have been that to give explicit details of sexual practice would have titillated the populace too much and may even have encouraged the hidden practices. It could also have been that sexual detail was felt to be unnecessary in the light of other evidence against the witches.

Accounts of orgies at the Sabbat come from a number of sources. In AD 906, nearly 600 years before the start of the witch trials, the Benedictine abbot Regino of Prüm, wrote:

> This too must by no means be passed over that certain utterly abandoned women, turning aside to follow Satan, being seduced by the illusions and phantasmical shows of demons firmly believe and openly profess that in the dead of night they ride upon certain beasts along with the pagan goddess Diana and a countless horde of women, and that in those silent hours they fly over vast tracts of country and obey her as their mistress, while on certain other nights they are summoned to do her homage and pay her service.[62]

When Abbot Regino wrote this, the concept of witchcraft, in the medieval sense, had not yet been formulated and the church was still largely concerned with overcoming pagan practices. Hence he talks of 'abandoned women' instead of 'witches' and, although they cavort with Satan, they are also depicted as being associated with the ancient Roman moon-goddess Diana.

Other references to the Sabbat orgies are equally vague. Martin Delrio wrote of witches at the Sabbat:

> When they are young and tender they will thus be able to bear the hateful embrace of Satan who has assumed the shape of a man. For by this horrid anointing he dulls their senses and persuades these deluded wretches that there is some great virtue in the viscid lubricant. Sometimes too he does this in hateful mockery of God's holy Sacraments, and that by these mysterious ceremonies he may infuse, as it were, something of a ritual and liturgical nature into his beastly orgies.[63]

Some hints as to what kind of sexual perversions were expected to have occurred at these orgies have been given already. In secret ceremonies that were attributed to the Jews, Cathars, Bogomiles and Knights Templar (see Chapter 9) there was talk of kissing an animal, a deity or other participants on the anus. This was not only thought of as being some kind of unnatural sexual perversion, but also implied that homosexuality and bestiality took place at these orgies.

Other hints that homosexual practices were occurring come from Henry Boguet's belief that at a Sabbat 'every kind of obscenity is practised there, yea, even those abominations for which Heaven poured down fire and brimstone on Sodom and Gomorrah are quite common in these assemblies'.[64] Although it does not say so directly in the Bible, from the sixth century onwards it was believed that the sexual perversions talked about in Sodom and Gomorrah were homosexual ones, and from this we have gained the term 'sodomy' for the practice of anal sex.

Actual descriptions of homosexuality at Sabbat rituals all come from the confessions of witches, many of which were extracted using physical or psychological torture and so must be viewed with some suspicion. On 19 January 1611, Madeleine de la Palud confessed that 'the heathens would gather together and on Sunday would be with the succubi and incubi devils, on Thursday commit sodomy, on Saturday commit bestiality and on other days live normally'.[65] In 1614, Gentien le Clerc said that 'then everybody goes to bed, men with men and with women ... the men couple with each other'.[66]

Until very recently, homosexuality was considered to be one of the greatest abominations against mankind and God, and even in our modern society it is not widely tolerated, especially by the church. In fact, homosexuality was still an imprisonable offence until the 1960s in Britain, and was still illegal up until the late 1980s in the Channel Island of Jersey. Many other countries and religions will still not tolerate the practice and it remains illegal in many parts of the world. Accusations of homosexuality are still used as insults in modern society and the exaggerated mannerisms and practices of homosexuals are commonly used as the butt of jokes in films and plays.

Based on the writings of many first-millennium bishops and Popes, most notably St Augustine, accusations of homosexuality were treated very gravely indeed in the Middle Ages, and those found guilty of the practice were punished with severity. It was largely on the accusations of homosexuality that the Knights Templar were destroyed in the fourteenth century and it was common, until the twentieth century, for homosexuals to be imprisoned and tortured for their chosen lifestyle.

Because of its anti-Christian image, accusations of homosexuality were a natural thing to be associated with the practices of witches, for, whereas a populace may not be too outraged at the thought of orgies (they may even have been envious!), they would certainly not tolerate the thought of homosexuality occurring in their midst. The other bonus of associating homosexuality with the Sabbat was that, as with the notion of witchcraft itself, an accusation of homosexuality against somebody is extremely difficult to disprove. A homosexual is physically no different from anybody else and therefore trying to prove that one is not homosexual is very difficult. Thus it was (and still is) the perfect 'crime' to be associated with stories of ritual abuse.

Other than homosexuality, there were three other main sexual practices believed to occur at medieval Sabbats. These were: heterosexual orgies, bestiality, and copulation with the devil.

Despite accusations of homosexuality, it was heterosexual orgies that were most commonly referred to with regard to the Sabbat. Details are, unsurprisingly, rare, and it is normally just mentioned that such practices would occur and they are sometimes merely acknowledged as 'debauchery'. Montague Summers, writing in the 1920s, provides a good example of the sorts of vague statement that would be written about sexual practices at the Sabbat, which more likely reflected the beliefs of the writer than what may have actually occurred. He writes that 'many, unabashed, were giving themselves up to the wildest debauchery and publicly performing the sexual act with every circumstance of indecency'.[67]

In the Middle Ages, orgies were seen as pagan and as giving in to temptations of the flesh. They are also implied to have formed a part of the ritualized worship of the devil. Accusations of heterosexual sex (unlike homosexual sex) at the Sabbat, while frequently mentioned, were rarely used as a direct means of prosecuting people, but merely as a means of reinforcing other accusations of devil-worship.

We also find rare references to the practice of bestiality at the Sabbat which, Madeleine de la Palud confessed, would be committed on a Thursday. Bestiality, in modern terms, conjures up an image of humans copulating with animals, and may even remind us of the accusations of kissing animals' anuses or of the kissing or worshipping of toads, goats and other familiars at the Sabbat. We should be wary, however, of associating the medieval accusations of bestiality with the practice of having sex with animal species other than our own. The meaning of the word bestiality has changed somewhat over the centuries, and in the Middle Ages it had a much broader context than its current narrow definition. In old religious terms, bestiality meant fornication not just with animals but also with certain frowned-upon non-Christian sections of society.

In 1222, a church deacon was burnt alive at Oxford, England, on a charge of bestiality. His crime, however, was not that he had had sex with an animal but that he had married a Jewess. A similar case occurred when Johannes Alardus was burnt to death in Paris, France, for having had several children by a Jewish servant. When commenting on this latter case, Nicolaus Boer wrote that 'coition with a Jewess is precisely the same as if a man should copulate with a dog'.[68]

Others believed that the same was true of all non-Christians and that sex with a heathen could be classed as sodomy as well as bestiality. Professor E.P. Evans comments that: 'It seems rather odd that Christian lawgivers should have adopted the Jewish code against sexual intercourse with beasts, and then enlarged it so as to include the Jews themselves.'[69]

Thus, by the medieval definition of bestiality, it may not have been animals that the witches were being accused of having sexual intercourse with at the Sabbat, but Jews, Saracens (Muslims) or some other non-Christian people. Because of a lack of detail in the claims made about bestiality, it is hard to tell who was being accused of doing what and to whom.

Other than animals or non-Christians, this term might equally well refer to the belief that the devil or other demons would appear at the Sabbat in the form of an animal, usually a goat, and would then proceed to have sex with some or all of the participants at the

Sabbat. Indeed, the appearance of the devil as half-man, half-beast, complete with horns, cloven hooves and a tail, has been related to sexuality. Peter Stanford writes: 'Animals according to the strict Christian sexual code ... have uncontrollable sexual urges which distinguish them from humans. Since he is part animal, the devil attempts to exert his power through his own sexual amorality.'[70] This image of the devil as a sexual deviant was certainly alive and well during the witch trials when, after undefined and general claims of orgies, the next most common sexual practice cited at Sabbats was the act of coition with the devil or other evil beings.

We must here distinguish between the claims regarding sexual encounters with the devil and those with succubi and incubi, as discussed in Chapter 2. Whereas sex with evil beings was often described as taking place with a succubus or incubus, these were often accusations made by courts about happenings at the Sabbat and have nothing in common with the firsthand reports of isolated nocturnal attacks discussed in Chapter 1, the majority of which can be related to known psychological phenomena. In contrast, accusations of sex with the devil were nearly always made by the courts and were often part of the torture-induced confessions of witches about the proceedings of the Sabbat. Such claims abound in the literature.

> To him [the Prince of Evil] is brought the fairest maiden that she may be queen of the Sabbat, and on the altar-stone before his throne she writhes in a voluptuous agony of pain under the all-rending action of his monstrous sex. And now on all sides weird music and discordant chanting arise, the feast has begun, corrupt flesh is greedily devoured, aphrodisiac drugs are absorbed, and madness spreads through the crowd. Faster and more furiously do they dance and stamp, couples sway to the sexual rhythm, hag and youth, maiden and beast, incubi, succubi, devil and human, till the night rings with the frenzied cries of their unbridled passion.
>
> The more monstrous the perversion, the more hybrid the couple, the greater the merit, till the first delicate shades of approaching dawn send the hell-brood scurrying into the darkness whence they came.[71]

This typical description of the proceedings of the Sabbat confirms the widely held belief that not only was the devil being worshipped by the use of fornication but also that he would actually take part in, or in some cases lead, the orgy. Time and again there are references to witches having confessed to being present at a Sabbat where a central figure would lead the ceremony and later copulate with at least one of the assembled congregation. This master of ceremonies was sometimes held to be Satan himself, while at other times he would just be an unnamed figure. Many people, mostly women, went to the stake or were imprisoned for their confessions of having copulated with the devil or one of his demons at the Sabbat.

Although it is by no means certain that many of those who confessed to being present at the Sabbat were ever actually there, it is a commonly held belief that the mysterious devil-like figure that controlled the ceremonies, and later copulated with the witches, was more likely to be a man dressed up as the devil than an actual supernatural being. Even Montague Summers, a firm believer in witchcraft, writes that:

> In many of the cases of debauchery at Sabbats so freely and fully confessed by the witches their partners were undoubtedly the males who were present; the Grand Master, Officer, or President of the Assembly, exercising the right to select first for his own pleasures such women as he chose.[72]

Beyond this, the usually conservative Summers uncharacteristically ventures that many of the women may in fact have been abused with an inanimate object ('artificial phallus') rather than actually having has sex with another human being.

Artificial phalluses do form central roles in other contemporary or ancient religions (see Chapter 4) and there is some evidence for Summer's proposition, based on a very unusual characteristic of the copulating devil or demon at Sabbats that has been reported by a number of women. In their confessions, they clearly state that the being having sex with them had a penis that felt unnaturally cold in comparison with that of a normal man.

In a case in 1645, a widow called Bash attested that the demon that slept with her (a dark and attractive youth) 'was colder than a man'. Similarly, in 1662, Isobel Goudie and Janet Breadheid said that, after having made love to the devil, they 'fand his nature als cold as spring-well water'.[73] Henry More, in his *Antidote Against Atheism*, says that 'witches confessing so frequently as they do that the devil lies with them, and withal complaining of his tedious and offensive coldness'.[74]

Nearly 500 years after these events, it is hard to tell whether these women were describing genuine sexual encounters they had experienced at a Sabbat or whether it was just another commonly perceived feature of witchcraft to which they had been made to confess. It may have been that, when asked in detail about the actions of the devil, it would seem logical to the women that, because he was not human, he would not have felt like a human and so they described him as being cold. Despite allegations of trance-inducing drugs being taken at the Sabbat, it is hard to believe that a woman would not know the difference between genuine sexual intercourse and somebody ritually inserting an artificial phallus into them.

In addition to their sexual content, stories and confessions from the Sabbat also brought forward tales of murder and bizarre ritualistic practices. These stories, while being an important part of the witch trials, have been included in Chapter 9, so that they can be directly compared with similar tales from over the last 2,000 years.

## Misogyny and witchcraft

Aside from its quirky stories of demons, devils and sorcery, the witch trials of the Middle Ages were also responsible for instituting a period of unprecedented violence against women. In all the tales of witchcraft and sorcery that we have discussed over the last few chapters, the central 'witch' is nearly always female. Gender played a very important role within the witch trials and is closely connected with many of the strange sexual undertones and ideas about female sexuality that pervaded the church and society at the time.

The degree to which women were mistrusted and blamed for the ills of witchcraft can once again be seen in the *Malleus Maleficarum*. This book, being a reflection of the mood and superstitions of the time, is wholly anti-female in its tone and extremely sexist in both its assumptions and its content. It is automatically assumed that a witch is a woman and, in the few cases where male witchcraft is mentioned, this too is normally blamed on the actions of women who must have poisoned the man. The attitude of the *Malleus Maleficarum* towards women is adequately summed up in the following quotes:

> As for the first question, why a greater number of witches is found in the fragile feminine sex than among men ... [75]

> All wickedness is but little to the wickedness of women .... What else is a woman but a foe to friendship, an unescapable punishment, a necessary evil, a natural temptation, a desirable calamity, a domestic danger, a delectable detriment, an evil of nature, painted with fair colours ... [76]

> ... they are more credulous; and since the chief aim of the devil is to corrupt faith, therefore he attacks them ... [they] are more impressionable, and more ready to receive the influence of a disembodied spirit ... they have slippery tongues ... women are intellectually like children ... she is more carnal than a man, as is clear from her many carnal abominations.[77]

In fact, the *Malleus Maleficarum* offers us several dozen reasons why women are more likely to be witches or be susceptible to the ways of evil of men, and backs them up with many Bible quotes that, for reasons of equality, have been removed or altered from modern Biblical texts. The hatred (and I do not use that word lightly) that the authors of the *Malleus* clearly had for women is extraordinary and pervades every paragraph of the book. These were not, however, just the isolated ravings of two zealous Dominican priests, but in fact a very accurate reflection of the status of women in male-dominated Middle Ages society. There are many reasons for this mistrust of femininity, all of which have connections with the Bible, sexuality and superstition.

Much of the trouble stems from the Biblical story of the Garden of Eden. Man was created first in the image of God; woman was made from Adam's spare rib as an afterthought (the story of Lilith in Chapter 3 slightly rewrites this Biblical tale). Mankind was therefore the superior of the sexes and attracted more favour from God.

The real problem came with advent of the serpent and the unfortunate incident with the Tree of Knowledge and the apple. It was Eve who was persuaded by the serpent to take the first bite of the apple, against God's advice. This made women weak-willed and more susceptible to the influence of evil, something that is reflected in the accusations of sex with incubi, the devil and others. It was Eve who persuaded Adam also to eat of the apple and got both of them evicted from the Garden of Eden. Women were therefore seen to be responsible for the suffering of men as well. If it had not been for Eve, man would still be living in the Garden of Eden in tranquillity and contentment. Women were therefore responsible for all the ills of the world and the weak-willed susceptibility of Eve, and her propensity to consort with evil spirits and subvert men, was deemed to be represented by females in the Middle Ages.

The attitude towards women in general was appalling and most churchmen, who lived a lifestyle that meant they almost never came into contact with women, and certainly not in a domestic situation, viewed women as nothing more than domesticated baby-machines. Protestant leader Martin Luther said: 'Men have broad shoulders and narrow hips, and accordingly they possess intelligence. Women ought to stay at home; the way they were created indicates this, for they have broad hips and a wide fundament to sit upon, keep house and bear and raise children … Let them bear children to death; they are created for that.'[78]

The statistics of the witch trials show how dangerous it was to be a woman in those times of suspicion and scapegoatism. In 1492, in the German town of Langendorf, the entire female population (apart from two) was rounded up and accused of being witches. In a large survey of the sex of those accused of witchcraft in 1519 to 1700 in Europe and America, it turns out that 72 per cent of all those accused of witchcraft were women, and in many districts the figure was as high as 92 per cent. Only in Russia were marginally more men than women charged with sorcery.[79]

Even in those cases where men were charged with witchcraft, their punishment was invariably less severe than that of their female counterparts. Often the blame in cases of men being involved in witchcraft was shifted onto women; in keeping with the tradition of Eve, the trouble was put down to a woman having tempted the man into the ways of wickedness. Men were more liable to be pilloried or humiliated if they were convicted, whereas women would almost certainly be burnt at the stake.

The *Malleus Maleficarum*'s final section was on the punishments that should be handed out to those found guilty of witchcraft. Its underlying theme was taken from the famous Biblical quote in Exodus 22:18, which clearly states 'Thou shalt not suffer a witch to live.' The *Malleus* took, as it does through most of its text, the term 'witch' to be a purely feminine one, turning it into a gender-biased form that effectively says 'Thou shalt not suffer a woman convicted of witchcraft to live.'

This sex discrimination is reflected in other quotes of the time, especially in the Spanish law which stated: 'A woman who bewitches men or beasts or other things, if it is proved against her, shall be burned. If a man be a magician, and it is proved against him, he shall be shaven in the form of a cross and scourged and banished.'[80]

The prospects were not all that good for women accused of witchcraft in the Middle Ages, and the word of a neighbour was all it needed for a woman to be taken by the state and tortured to make her confess her part in the Sabbat or some other wrongdoing. Although much of this had initially stemmed from the church's attitude towards Eve and the concept of original sin, the whole myth of witchcraft and women was also closely connected with women's sexuality and the sexual act itself.

## Superstitions and women's sexuality

At an early age, most people become aware of the fact that boys and girls have many physical differences, the most obvious being in the genitals. Adolescence exaggerates these differences considerably. In men, the penis grows larger and can become erect, the voice deepens, facial hair develops and the body becomes broader and is more musclebound. In women, breasts develop, menstruation commences and the hips broaden. Most modern societies now understand the biological significance of these changes and their link to sexual maturity and the ability to reproduce, and that they mean little to any perceived spiritual development within humans. In the Middle Ages, the link between sexual maturity and reproduction had yet to be made, and the bodily changes brought about by adolescence only served to heighten the differences between men and women. These differences were not, however, just on a physical level but instead ran deep into the perceived soul of the individual, and were centred, in particular, around the sexuality of the individual and the gender to which they belonged.

In common with their physical stature, men and women in medieval society were viewed as two separate species of human being. Men were spiritually pure, close to God and prone to goodness. Women were impure, tainted by a disposition not only to do wrong but also to influence others to do wrong. The most surprising differences were, however, on a sexual level. In the reverse of what we think today, men were seen as being sexually restrained, capable of controlling their desires and of only needing to indulge in sex as a necessary means of furthering the population. Women, on the other hand, were sexually promiscuous, with an insatiable appetite for men and the ability to drive men (and each other) mad with overt sexual flaunting and vanity.

By the sixteenth century, when the witch trials were in full swing, few women dared to dress in any way that might be seen as sexually attractive and the overtly feminine characteristics of the human body, such as the breasts, legs and hips, were for the most part kept firmly covered. Men, on the other hand, could wear tights, open-necked shirts and, most overtly of all, codpieces to indicate and highlight their masculine qualities. Worse still was the consensus that women were not allowed to display any form of pleasure from sex and that they should under no circumstances go in search of it. This would only serve to heighten the view of women as saucy temptresses whose only objective was to subvert the ways of men.

This view of sex and women has lasted a remarkably long time and there are still remnants of it about in modern society. It is only since the 1960s that women have started to wear clothes that allow the legs and breasts to be revealed in a sexually provocative manner, and that they have been allowed to express an open desire and enjoyment of sex itself. There are many who firmly blame the disintegration of society (if such a thing has occurred) on the sexual revolution of the 1960s, and many problems related to sexuality still exist. For example, the dichotomy of sexuality in the Middle Ages is reflected by the fact that a woman who has had several sexual partners is still often thought of as a 'slut', whereas a promiscuous man is revered as a 'stud'.

At the time of the witch trials, this view of women as being the more sexually active and corrupting of the sexes was reflected in the beliefs of the day. Many superstitions centred around the menstrual cycle and, in particular, the monthly period. Menstruation was seen as the ultimate sign of womanhood and the period was compared with the medical practice of bloodletting, which was used as a cure for a great many diseases. Bloodletting was believed to remove 'bad blood' and evil from the body, and was widely practised, especially in the use of leeches. When women had their monthly period it was viewed as a sign that the female body, that vessel of evil and wrongdoing, was purging itself of its badness. For this reason, menstrual blood was considered to be poisonous and was to be avoided at all costs, a belief that is still reflected in some African societies, where menstruating women are made to leave the village or stay in special huts.

The connection between the reproductive cycle and menstruation had not yet been made, and so while a woman was menstruating she was considered to be purging herself of her evil. After the menopause, however, when her periods had ceased, it was believed that the evil that had previously been bled from the body was in fact now building up within her, gradually turning her towards evil. It was for this reason that many older, post-menopausal women, and especially those who were widowed or spinsters, were viewed as being more likely to be a witch. A modern commentator on the witch trials, Linda Roper, says:

> A post-menopausal woman, the old witch was in a sense a dry woman who, instead of feeding others well, diverted her nourishment to her own selfish ends. Older widows were viewed as having the power to ruin young men sexually, and youths were warned against marrying such women because they were sexually ravenous, and would suck out their seed, weakening them with their insatiable hunger for seminal fluid and contaminating them with their own impurities.[81]

The reference to men's seed within this last quote echoes another interesting and sexually orientated belief associated with female witches. As was seen in the story of Lilith and in the lore of the succubi and incubi, male semen was viewed as the life force within man and, as such, was something to be treasured. Masturbation or reckless sex was seen as a waste of this vital fluid, and it was thought that witches were permanently on the lookout for opportunities to obtain men's seminal fluids. It was viewed as particularly suspicious that men could only ejaculate once or twice during sex, while women could have prolonged sex and sometimes several orgasms in a row. The only logical reason that could be found for this was that women must be trying to remove all the semen from men by making them have sex and ejaculate more than once at a time.

Again, older women were seen as being more voracious in this respect than their younger counterparts, because they could not attract as many young men and so were prepared to 'suck dry' any man that did consent to go with them. The practice of fellatio was seen as particularly dangerous, involving as it did the penis being placed directly in the mouth of the witch – an action that seemed to involve the semen literally being sucked from the man's body. Drunken men were particularly at risk, for not only could they be tempted to go with a witch more easily but drinking was also deemed to increase the body's production of semen (medically, the reverse is actually true), which could then be removed by the witch.

Another major assumption about women was that they possessed an insatiable desire for sex, which meant that they would go to almost any lengths to fulfil their sexual appetites, including sleeping with incubi and even the devil himself. The *Malleus Maleficarum* is quite specific on the matter: 'All witchcraft comes from carnal lust, which is in women insatiable … . Wherefore for the sake of fulfilling their lusts they consort even with Devils.'[82]

Women were thought to be capable of lesbianism, bestiality or using artificial phalluses to indulge themselves in the absence of men. Again, older women were deemed to be the most sexually active among the witches, and the concept of the 'old-maid witch' has filtered down to us in the form of the old hags of fairy tales and in modern cartoons where witches are always depicted as being old crones riding broomsticks. At the Sabbat, older witches do not fare much better, with at least one authority insisting that the devil would have sex with 'the pretty witches from the front, the ugly ones from behind'.[83]

In addition, old women, because their breasts could no longer produce milk, were thought to develop teats elsewhere on their bodies, especially on their thighs, from which the devil or her animal familiars could suckle. These teats were often sought after in the witch trials and any mole, sty or piece of loose skin would be considered to be an extra nipple.

Finally, as if the prejudice of age was not bad enough for women, the everyday occupations of women could lead them into suspicion. It was particularly dangerous to be a midwife or so-called 'lying-in maid' (a nurse who would look after mother or child for the first weeks after birth). Because of their association with children, which were considered to be used as human sacrifices during the Sabbat, these women were liable to be found guilty of any harm that came to mother or child in the months or even years after the birth. Witches were said to be able to offer the newborn female children to the devil without their mother's permission so that, come adolescence, they would become witches themselves or be more susceptible to attacks by incubi. Other beliefs were that the midwife could swap or steal the child from the mother, putting an identical one in its place. These women were also at the mercy of the women they tended and could easily find themselves accused of witchcraft simply for disagreeing with their mistresses.

By the time the witch trials ended, there was scarcely a woman alive who could express or show any sexual desire without fearing for her reputation or even her life. While this attitude fluctuated over the years, with the sexual provocativeness of the late eighteenth century followed by the repressed sexuality of Victorian society, many of the superstitions and attitudes of that day can still be seen in the sexual iconography and attitudes of today. It is still common to refer to disliked women as 'witches', or old women as 'hags' or 'dried-up'. The image of the woman as the temptress or vamp is also still very much alive.

Even after decades of sex-equality legislation, we are still a long way from achieving a society in which the attitude of men towards women is truly balanced.

## End of the witch trials

The bulk of the witch executions were over with by the middle of the seventeenth century, with the phenomenon of the witch trials disappearing almost as quickly as it had started, although there were still successful prosecutions for witchcraft right up until the second world war. The wave of paranoia, superstition and persecution that characterized the witch trials claimed many hundreds of lives across mainland Europe (Britain, perhaps because of its non-Lutheran

Protestantism, proved more reluctant to try its witches) and even spread across the Atlantic into the New World of America. In fact, it was in America, in Salem, Massachusetts, that the most famous of all the witch trials took place.

Belief in witches, in the medieval sense of the word, is still remarkably strong in many parts of Africa. In the townships of South Africa, people are still being killed at the hands of mobs on suspicion of being witches, while, as described in Chapter 10, the penis-snatching scares of west Africa have had many people running for their lives after being accused of sorcery.

Even though the witch trials may have ended, many of the beliefs about witchcraft and devil-worship have not subsided in Europe or America. Because of the paranoid nature of both government and the society over which it governs, there will always be an equivalent to the witch trials for every generation. In 1950s America, it was the McCarthyite anti-communist hunts, and in the 1980s and 1990s it is the wave of Satanic ritual abuse trials that have swept around the world (see Chapter 8). In Britain, the last successful prosecution on the charge of witchcraft occurred in 1944, when the medium Helen Duncan was imprisoned for fear that she might use her psychic powers to reveal military information on the forthcoming D-Day landings.

The witch trials might seem to be part of a different era in human history, but the potential will always exist for them to begin again and, as I know from my own researches, there are many people who would welcome their return.

# 7

# THE POWER OF LUST

Since the times of the witch trials, concepts about the power that sex and sexuality may have on the individual have changed markedly. In place of the church view that sex was spiritually powerful and could corrupt the individual's chances of going to heaven, there came more esoteric notions about whether there may actually be some form of physical and quantifiable power attached to both the emotional and the physical sides of sex.

After the wave of scientific discovery that produced electricity and the industrial revolution, the gentleman scientists of the late nineteenth century began to turn their attentions towards the matter of understanding the human mind. The early psychologists, most notably Sigmund Freud, were convinced that the key to human personality lay in the sexuality and sexual experience of the individual. Sex went from being a corrupting spiritual influence to something that could corrupt (or at least shape) the psychological make-up of the individual. At the same time, it was beginning to be recognized that sex was also a strong factor in the entire workings of society. Many comparisons were made between the way animal societies organize themselves around the need to copulate and produce offspring and the way that human society, albeit more subtly, organizes itself in a similar manner.

As the twentieth century dawned, some of those who had concerned themselves with the controversial area of psychical research believed that they could see a link between the psychic powers that they observed in people and their sexuality. Although there had always been hidden sexual overtones in many of the living-room seances that had taken place during the Victorian spiritualist craze, the new generation of psychical researchers believed that they could see something more tangible attached to human sexuality and, in particular, to the sex act itself.

They believed that sex was so strong an emotional experience that it was capable of generating its own separate psychic force that, like electricity, was hidden but nonetheless real and quantifiable. This force was considered to be so strong that it could on occasion build up inside the body to such a degree that it would leak out and cause localized havoc. It might even become trapped inside the body and damage the health of the individual. Many attempts were made both to study the effects of this sexual energy on the individual and to try to measure and even store it.

## Making the Earth move

The date of 15 December 1977 was not a happy one in the north London Harper household. For nearly three months, the family had been plagued by a poltergeist that had not only ransacked the house but also focused itself on the Harper's oldest daughter, Janet. On that particular day not only did the poltergeist speak in a rough growling voice, something that is very rare in such cases, but it is also claimed that Janet Harper was teleported through a solid wall into the next-door house. As proof that she had been there, she left behind one of her books that had been observed to be in her bedroom only moments beforehand. In addition to this apparently miraculous teleportation, there was the usual round of objects flying through the air on their own, or appearing and disappearing at will. Witnesses outside the house claimed to have seen not only Janet levitating in her bedroom but also cushions materializing on the roof of the house.

According to the chief investigators into the Harper poltergeist case, 15 December 1977 marked the peak of the poltergeist's power, with more strange phenomena being observed in that one brief day than at any other time in the 14 months that the poltergeist was resident with the Harper family. The same date also marked Janet Harper's menarche; in other words, it was the day that she began to menstruate. Tellingly, one of the questions asked by the 'poltergeist' that day was, 'Why do girls have periods?'.[84]

Almost a century earlier, on 28 August 1878, an 18-year-old girl named Esther Cox from Amherst, Nova Scotia, underwent a terrifying ordeal. That evening she had agreed to go for a drive in a horse and cart with a local boy named Bob McNeal. The couple had driven to a remote woodland spot where McNeal made sexual advances towards Esther and asked her to walk into the woods with him. Esther refused and in a fit of anger McNeal pointed a gun at her and ordered her to go into the woods. Esther was convinced that McNeal meant to rape her and was only saved when another vehicle came down the road. Esther was noted to be a sensitive girl and the incident left her in a highly distressed state.

One week later, Esther was lying in bed with her sister Jennie when she again became distressed and, having previously kept the McNeal incident to herself, suddenly blurted the whole story out. After comforting Esther, Jennie blew out the candle, but within a few seconds both girls heard a scratching noise. Convinced that a mouse was in bed with them, the girls screamed and lit the candle once more. No mouse could be found but the scratching noises continued. The same thing occurred the next night, and this time the noises were traced to a box underneath the bed. The girls pulled the box into the middle of the room where it promptly rose into the air of its own accord. Their screams brought in their brother, who told them that they had been dreaming.

Stranger things were to occur in the following weeks. On several occasions, the bedclothes were ripped from the girls' bed during the night, loud rapping noises were heard coming from walls all over the house, messages were scratched into the walls, and objects within the house were observed to move on their own. Most worrying was the poltergeist's habit of setting fire to objects, including, on one occasion, Esther herself. These events were all connected to Esther and, as if to confirm that the attempted rape by McNeal was the cause of the trouble, on one occasion Esther went into a 'trance' and told the whole family about the incident in the woods. Significantly, the poltergeist told Esther that its name was 'Bob'.

These two cases are classic examples of the perplexing psychic phenomenon known as a poltergeist haunting. Until relatively recently, it was generally believed that poltergeists were malevolent spirits that somehow attached themselves to an individual person, feeding off their energy and causing psychic mayhem. In fact, the word poltergeist is itself derived from the German words *polter* (noisy) and *Geist* (spirit). However, with the advent of organized psychical research it was noticed that most poltergeist cases had a great deal in common and that they even conformed to a predictable pattern. At the centre of this observable pattern was the fact that nearly all poltergeist cases are focused around teenage girls. This has led many parapsychologists to wonder whether poltergeists have more to do with puberty than with disembodied spirits feeding off damaged auras.

The psychic power that is said to cause the manifestation of poltergeist hauntings has been given the name 'recurrent spontaneous psychokinesis', or RSPK for short. Almost as soon as the puberty connection had been found, people were suggesting that RSPK could be an energy or psychic power produced by sexual chemistry inside the body. There seemed to be good evidence for this. Janet Harper, for example, was known to be obsessed with the fictional television detectives Starsky and Hutch, while the Esther Cox poltergeist seemed to make endless references to the occasion in the woods when her chastity was threatened by Bob McNeal. Other cases have even closer ties.

Another poltergeist in Somerset, England, centred itself around a family of four, and produced many of the usual phenomena including moving objects, rapping noises and strange smells. When investigators were called in, they automatically assumed that the two teenage children were the focus of the activity, but were surprised to discover that it was in fact their 49-year-old father. Questioning revealed that the man was suffering from impotence brought about by work anxiety. After treatment to restore his sexual prowess, the poltergeist activity ceased. An almost identical case occurred in which a 48-year-old man was the focus of a furniture-moving poltergeist. He too was found to be medically impotent. After treatment, the paranormal activity ceased almost immediately.

Stranger than this are the cases of so-called 'spectral spoilsports', in which a resident house ghost apparently takes exception to any form of sexual activity in its presence. The *Daily Mirror* carried a story about a 21-year-old girl who had rented a London flat which apparently had a resident poltergeist that resented the presence of men. Men who came to read the utility meters were apparently assaulted by an invisible force, and had their reading equipment ripped from them and hurled down the stairs. Even worse occurred when the woman had men to stay overnight with her. These unfortunates would have the bedclothes ripped from on top of them and then be dragged out of bed onto the floor. In an attempt to resolve the situation, a seance was held; in the course of this, the spirit of a former servant girl at the property said that she did not want to see sex performed in front of her baby.

There are many cases where couples making love have almost literally had the 'Earth move' around them, with objects jumping off the walls or moving of their own accord. The husband of medium Frieda Weisl once complained to psychic investigator Harry Price that all the objects on their mantelpiece would be swept to the floor whenever Frieda reached orgasm during intercourse.

Many famous spiritualist mediums apparently underwent some form of sexual arousal during their trances with, as the seance progressed, their moans and groans becoming ever more sexual until, when apparently at the point of orgasm, objects in the room moved on their own or appeared from mid-air. The historian Alex Owen found many links between Victorian sexuality and the actions of women in the seance room. Owen firmly linked these to the mood of society rather than to any psychic force, but others prefer to believe that the link between mediumship and sex was a physical one and that this could explain the similarity between many seance-room techniques and those seen in poltergeist cases.

These cases, assuming they are accurately reported, and the association of adolescents with poltergeist-type phenomena, do seem to suggest that there could be a link between human sexuality and the RSPK psychic force. If, however, this is the case, then what aspect of sexuality could be causing it? Whatever it is, it must be more prevalent around the time of puberty than at any other time in life. The first psychic investigators to study this problem did so in the early part of the twentieth century, and were all followers of Sigmund Freud, the founder and promoter of psychoanalysis. Freud, then as now, was best known for his belief that many everyday anxieties and neuroses can be directly related to sexual problems within the individual. This Freudian view of sexuality was extended to the RSPK theory.

Psychologist and psychic researcher Fodor Nandor was convinced that the activity of poltergeists was caused by sexual energies, and he has been joined in this view by other researchers, including Carl Jung, Colin Wilson and William Roll. Nandor cites sexual frustration as the main cause of RSPK. This would explain why poltergeists are normally focused on teenagers, and also why the aforementioned impotent men were at the statistically unlikely centre of paranormal phenomena. Psychic researcher Benjamin Walker says:

> Psychic researchers have repeatedly established that the centre of the poltergeist activity is often a persistent masturbator, and they believe it possible that the biomagnetic energy drawn by the 'poltergeist' is obtained during the release of sexual tension, when the masturbator reaches his or her climax. Excessive masturbation has also been cited as the reason for other unexplained psychic occurrences ...[85]

In fact, some investigators are so sure that RSPK is generated by sexual frustration that they claim to have found evidence of a sexual cause in all the major poltergeist cases. Esther Cox has been said to have been frustrated because she in fact wanted Bob McNeal to have sex with her but could not let herself go (there is no historical evidence for this at all), while other famous poltergeist subjects have been diagnosed as the victims of incest or rape, or as having a desperate urge to lose their virginity.

The evidence for these accusations is, in each of these cases, very thin, and the need to find a single sexual event as the cause of the poltergeist episode shows a marked similarity to the cases of Satanic ritual abuse 'survivors' discussed in Chapter 8. The plain truth is that, while there does appear to be an undeniable connection between puberty and poltergeists, any connection to specific sexual feelings beyond this cannot be proved. Practically all adolescents, and many adults, are sexually frustrated to one degree or another, but only a fraction become the focus of poltergeist cases. If one accepts the reality of adolescent-associated RSPK, then the cause is something beyond just ordinary sexual frustration.

More modern investigators into the poltergeist phenomenon have shifted their focus slightly away from a specifically sexual cause. One of the favoured theories of the moment is that such activity can be triggered by stressful situations or even by the poor health of an individual. This has been largely based on studies that have shown that a disproportionate number of poltergeist cases occur in families that are in some way dysfunctioning. In England, the greatest number of cases comes from divorced families living in state-provided housing (it has been suggested that some of these cases are faked in an attempt to get rehoused). In America, too, links have been found between alcoholic or absentee parents and/or physical abuse. Although these, and many other patterns, can be discerned from poltergeist cases, nobody is any closer to offering a solution to them, let alone isolating any definite sexual component.

Those sceptical of the reality of poltergeists as a genuine psychic phenomenon have suggested that there may be another reason why so many cases are associated with adolescents. It is a commonly held belief that the teenagers at the centre of poltergeist cases are exhibiting not RSPK but rather that other classic side-effect of puberty known as attention-seeking, and that by faking poltergeist-like tricks these adolescents succeed in becoming the centre of attention.

There is actually a great deal of evidence of children playing tricks on their families and psychic investigators in modern poltergeist cases. Several of the investigators who visited the Harper family became convinced that Janet Harper was faking many of the things observed there, and it is true that much of the most spectacular activity reported by the two chief investigators in the case took place when their backs were turned, or when Janet was out of sight. In many other cases, children have been observed to be hiding or throwing objects themselves, banging on walls with their shoes, or throwing themselves out of bed. When caught cheating, most poltergeist foci insist that, while they may have faked some of the later phenomena, what was observed at the beginning of the haunting episode was real. This excuse was one also commonly used by nineteenth-century spiritualist mediums who were caught cheating.

In conclusion, there unquestionably seems to be a connection between the poltergeist and the onset of sexual maturity in humans. Whether this connection is due to RSPK, disembodied spirits or a need to be the centre of attention is not known, and there is evidence to support all three of the main theories, although none of them has yet been proved. The issue of poltergeists does, however, illustrate the basic human belief that there might be energy associated with sexuality or even the sex act itself. The RSPK theory suggests that this energy is capable of being harnessed into something more tangible than just a few loose hormones running around the body. Others have also put forward the idea that there may be energy associated with the human sex drive, and some even claimed to have harnessed it.

### Harnessing orgasmic power

Poltergeists are considered to be an example of a spontaneous leak of sexual energy from a person; but, it is argued, if everybody is capable of generating these energies then there must be a way of measuring and even collecting it.

The pioneer of harnessing the power associated with sexual energy was undoubtedly Wilhelm Reich, an eccentric Austrian psychoanalyst who devoutly followed the teachings of Freud. He was very active in 1920s Austrian psychological circles and was at one time described as being Freud's 'most brilliant student'. Reich was particularly interested in the driving force behind human sexuality, and came to conclude that 'sexuality is the centre around which revolves the whole of social life as well as the inner life of the individual'.[86]

By the end of the 1920s, Wilhelm Reich had drifted far away from conventional Freudian psychology. He was convinced that sexuality was a force in its own right, comparable to electricity or even gravity. He thought that sexual energy flowed through the body and that it was capable of being stored in the same manner as electricity is stored inside a battery. The method of discharging this pool of sexual energy was through the orgasm. The orgasm, said Reich, was 'the capacity for complete discharge of all dammed-up sexual excitation through involuntary pleasurable contractions of the body'.[87] Those who could not achieve orgasm would end up with excess amounts of sexual energy building up inside their bodies, which would eventually cause severe mental and physical problems, including schizophrenia and depression. Reich believed that many common disorders would be solved if the dammed-up sexual energy were to be discharged.

Initially, Reich set about trying to measure his perceived sexual energy by measuring the difference in electrical energy given off by the genitals when both aroused and unaroused. Using volunteers, Reich discovered that sexual excitation did indeed produce a 'bio-electrical discharge' and that this seemed to reduce levels of stress and anxiety in the individual. Sexual arousal, said Reich, was like a thunderstorm, with the orgasm being like a lightning strike, discharging all the built-up sexual energy from the body.

In the 1930s, Reich's studies were periodically disturbed by having to flee from the persecution of Nazi Germany, whose authoritarian regime did not seem to like Reich's notion of sexual energy. He first fled to Norway but, at the onset of the second world war, emigrated to the USA. By the time he settled there, Reich had already come up with some remarkable new theories based on his orgasmic thundercloud research.

Before leaving Europe, Reich claimed to have discovered a new form of living matter that he called 'bions'. These were claimed to be tiny pulsating vesicles of energy that were halfway between dead and living tissue. Bions could develop spontaneously and were, said Reich, capable of turning themselves into single-celled life forms. In his experiments with bions, Reich determined that there were two main types, which he named blues and reds, and that the two kinds, when brought together under the microscope, would fight with each other. Furthermore, Reich claimed to have found the source of his mysterious sexual energy and even to have observed it. He named this sexual force 'orgone' (from 'orgasm' and 'hormone') energy, and compared it with the 'life force' of alchemists. He claimed that orgone energy was observable as a blue force around copulating frogs, and that it was capable of being measured with an 'orgone energy field meter', an invention of Reich's own making.

Although Reich had a considerable band of followers, members of the scientific world were not among them, and the eccentric Austrian received a great deal of ridicule and scepticism about his ideas of sexual energy. Reich, however, was convinced that orgone was the answer to his previously observed problem of dammed-up sexual energy. The human body, he famously wrote, can be seen as 'a sac of fluids and energy' to which the application of orgone energy could help cure cancers, illness and mental disorders. After noticing that metal containers were capable of storing orgone energy, Reich set about designing an 'orgone-energy accumulator' into which patients could be placed, in a sitting position, so that they might absorb some of the orgone energy. The orgone-energy accumulators were large boxes made from alternate layers of organic material, normally wood, and inorganic material, normally metal. The patient sat inside the box, where they often described tingling feelings and relief from aches and pains.

The notion of orgone and healing through sexual energy was, however, attracting the attention of the authorities, whose enthusiasm for the idea was somewhat less than Reich's. The start of his downfall came in 1947 with the publication of an article in *The New Republic* magazine which implied that Reich was running a sex cult from his Maine laboratory. The magazine drew the attention of the US Food and Drug Administration (FDA) which immediately began a covert investigation into Reich's activities.

By this time, Reich was showing signs of having overdosed on his own sexual energy and was writing books claiming that orgone energy was the fundamental building block of life (the 'cosmic orgasm') and that all the great leaders in history, including Christ, suffered from a lack of orgone management. Reich started engaging in more and more bizarre and dangerous experiments, many of which involved the use of radioactivity, which he considered to be the polar opposite of orgone energy (a sort of anti-orgone). One such experiment (the 'Oranur experiment') resulted in the serious radiation poisoning of several people who, despite Reich's attempt to cure them with orgone, became very ill indeed.

This was the final straw for the FDA, which took out a court order effectively banning Reich from carrying out any further orgone experiments and forcing him to destroy much of his equipment. Reich was livid and accused the government of wanting to cover up his work, something that reflected his increasing paranoia in later years. Determined to carry on with his research, in 1955 Reich was caught moving an orgone-energy accumulator across a county line and was taken back to court. Reich chose to defend himself and gave a series of long and paranoid speeches from the dock. These had little effect and he was found guilty of selling fraudulent machines (the orgone-energy accumulators) and sentenced to two years in prison.

Unfortunately, prison was obviously not a good accumulator of orgone energy for, on 3 November 1957, Reich died after serving only nine months of his sentence. His ideas, however, caught on with New Agers and the newly born UFO community, some of whom still promote his beliefs today. His Orgonomic Laboratory in Maine has been preserved as a museum and there are regular Orgone Conventions where the latest advances in sexual energy research are discussed.

Although Reich's notion of sexual energy and orgone may seem to have been eccentric and, towards the end of his life, extreme, he was not alone in his beliefs. A great many modern occultists use 'sex magic' to try to achieve higher spiritual planes, in the belief that the sex act is 'full of magical endowment'. The sixteenth-century occultist Aratus says: 'As the physical union of man and woman leads to the fruit from the composition of each, in the same way the interior and secret association of man and woman is the copulation of the male and female soul, and is appointed for the production of fitting fruit of the divine life.'[88]

The medieval alchemists also believed in life or animal forces that are related to human sexuality, and that sexual energy may play a part in their search for the recipe for the magically potent 'philosopher's stone'. Many modern cults also claimed to have found spiritual or actual energy in the sexual act, and most of these sects require a strict sexual code, be it free love or celibacy, from their followers.

## Shunamitism

One of the most unusual beliefs in the power of human sexuality is related to the value of chastity rather than the act of copulation. The reverence of virgins is not a new phenomenon. The Catholic church worships the Virgin Mary and ancient societies of all kinds have had their temple virgins, their eunuchs and, of course, the legendary vestal virgins, all of whom were deemed to embody a form of divine power through their abstinence from sex. Even in modern society, the virgin is still seen as a symbol of purity and majesty, and anything that needs to be described as pure is given the prefix virgin – virgin snow, virgin olive oil, etc.

Shunamitism is an occultist practice that takes the belief in sexual energy one step further, and holds that it is possible to transfer energy from one person to another simply by being in close contact. Specifically, shunamitism refers to the transferring of youthful energy from a young virgin to an older person through the act of lying next to each other. Although both the virgin and the other person must lie naked next to each other, intercourse is not permitted as this will 'earth' the sexual energy stored in the virgin and thus not achieve the desired transfer of life force.

The unusual name of this practice comes from the reference made to it in the Old Testament when King David was old and frail:

> Now King David was old and stricken in years; and they covered him with clothes, but he gat no heat. Wherefore his servants said unto him, Let there be sought for my lord the king a young virgin: and let her stand before the king, and let her cherish him, and let her lie in thy bosom, that my lord may get heat ... . So they sought for a fair damsel throughout all the coasts of Israel, and found Abishag a Shunammite, and brought her to the king .... And the damsel was very fair, and cherished the king, and ministered to him: but the king knew her not.[89]

There are examples of shunamitism from relatively recent times back to ancient Rome. It is recorded that the Roman Claudius Hermippus lived to be 115 by sleeping, but not having sex with, virgins. Pope Innocent VIII, the initiator of the witch trials (see Chapter 6), was also reported to use young boys to stroke him during his later years.

In more recent times, a Madame Janus of Paris, France, ran an eighteenth-century shunamitism house which employed over 40 virgins. Clients, who were invariably male, would be washed, massaged and then sandwiched in bed between two virgin girls. Anybody caught deflowering the girls would have to pay a huge financial forfeit.

Shunamitism has also had its dark side. The child-murderers Gilles de Rais and Elizabeth Bathory were reputed to drink or bathe in the blood of virgins in the belief that it would keep them from ageing and give them supernatural powers. There are also the horrific experiments carried out in the Nazi concentration camps that seem to have more than a passing resemblance to shunamitic practice. The following is an extract from a letter to Heinrich Himmler about experiments that were being carried out on prisoners at Dachau camp:

> The test persons were chilled ... Removal took place at a rectal temperature of 86 degrees ... In eight cases the test persons were placed between two naked women on a wide bed. The women were then instructed to snuggle up to the chilled person as closely as possible. Once the test person regained consciousness, they never lost it again, quickly grasping their situation and nestling close to the naked bodies of the women ... An exception was formed by four test persons who practised sexual intercourse between 86 and 89.5 degrees. In these persons, after coitus, a very swift temperature rise ensued, comparable to that achieved by means of a hot-water bath.[90]

The conclusion was that the subjects did not revive any more quickly with the naked girls than with blankets or warm baths. It should be added that these horrific experiments were done in an attempt to find the best method of reviving airmen who had fallen into the sea but, for our terms, seem to prove that shunamitism may not have any scientific basis.

# Part three

## ORGIES, SCARES AND PANICS

# 8

# SATANISM IN THE SUBURBS

In November 1989, a six-year old boy was found cowering inside a cupboard at his school in the English town of Rochdale. The boy had obviously been disturbed by something and, when questioned by the headmaster, began to tell some very strange and unpleasant stories. Worried by what he had heard, the headmaster contacted the local social services, and in February 1990 two women social workers were assigned to the case.

The boy told the social workers that he had been forced to take part in unusual rituals whereby a number of supernatural entities, including ghosts named Jim and Bob, had taken him from his room and forced him to stab babies to death. He also said that his family had kept him locked in a cage, forced him to bury and then later exhume the corpses of the babies he had murdered, and fed him drugs, including a magic solution described as 'fizzy tea'. It was also claimed that number of supernatural events had occurred, including the case of a man who could grow to 3m (9 ft) tall at will.

The social workers acted immediately, and took the boy, and three of his brothers and sisters, into the care of the authorities. All the other children were closely interviewed and, in one form or another, confirmed the six-year-old boy's stories, and even added new elements to them. As a result of these interviews, another 16 local children were taken from their parents in a number of dawn raids in June, July and September and held in council care.

When, in September 1990, the national press got hold of the story, Rochdale social services told them that the children were being held because they were the victims of suspected ritual sexual child abuse. Such stories make sensational reading and, after years of being ignored, the issue of sexual abuse had been particularly strong in the late 1980s. The Rochdale case was, with its stories of ghosts and drugs, different from the hitherto reported cases of paedophilia and incest. Some reporters felt that the case was not quite right and warranted closer examination. It was particularly closely investigated by reporters from the *Mail on Sunday*, a middle-class tabloid whose readers, ironically, were statistically more likely to believe tales of Satanism and black magic. After six months, the newspaper concluded that the whole story had been based on a myth and that all 12 parents and all 21 children from five families had been wrongly accused of ritual sexual abuse. Despite this, and several similar investigations, it was to be another six years before the Rochdale social services admitted their error and returned the children to their parents.

The Rochdale case is an example of a phenomenon that has become known as Satanic ritual abuse. It is just one of hundreds of similar cases that have been reported from all around the civilized world since the early 1980s.

Satanic ritual abuse, as exemplified by Rochdale, occurs when a local population, often in conjunction with the local social services, believe that there are groups of Satanists or occultists in the community who are conducting secret ceremonies. Across the world, these ceremonies seem to have common themes, including child murder, sexual abuse, bestiality, cannibalism, the appearance of ghosts, devils and demons, and a variety of weird locations, including castles, dungeons, underground caverns and even a swimming pool full of sharks. All these ceremonies involve the use of children, the abusers of whom are usually family members, teachers or playgroup organizers. The Satanists invariably only get found out when one of the children they are accused of abusing talks to the authorities; sometimes their victims only remember their abuse decades later, when it is too late to prosecute.

The phenomenon of Satanic ritual abuse has now spread to every part of the Christian world, particularly English-speaking countries, and there are few westernized countries that have not had at least one court case involving Satanists. Some countries have had tens or even hundreds of such cases, leading many churches to set up special vigilante groups to help defeat the threat from urban Satanism. The subject itself is, however, a controversial one and there have been wide-ranging investigations into the phenomenon by several government agencies, the findings of which have all been negative.

The issue is certainly contentious, but could Satan and his helpers really be at work in the town and village communities underneath our very noses?

## The devil rides into Nottingham!

In October 1987, on the Broxtowe housing estate in the city of Nottingham, England, the police and social workers descended on the house of an extended family and took seven of their children into care on suspicion that they had been sexually abused by their parents and relatives. Eighteen months later, the investigation had widened so that by the time the case reached the courts ten adults from the Broxtowe estate were found guilty of 53 offences against up to 27 children, all aged under eight. All were sentenced to lengthy prison terms.

The facts of the case, as revealed in court, were horrendous and received a great deal of media publicity at the time. This case, like the Rochdale one, had an air of unreality about it, and after a while it appeared that the allegations being made against the adults were not only bizarre but also in many cases physically improbable, if not impossible.

Much of the evidence against the accused adults had been gained by a strange degree of co-operation between the foster families that had taken care of the Broxtowe estate children and the social services. It turned out that the foster parents had been asked to keep detailed diaries of everything that the children had said as part of the investigation into the case. At the time, the police questioned the legitimacy of this tactic and whether any of this evidence would be usable in a court of law. The social services believed that the police were trying to obstruct their investigation and, after much bitterness, the police refused to investigate any of the claims made in the diaries. The social services, however, were convinced of the reality of the diaries and were sure that not only had the children been sexually abused but also that there was an extended ring of Satanists at work in the Nottingham region.

The diaries kept by the foster parents contained information, given by the abused children, that appeared to provide clear evidence of secret and hideous orgies held to honour the Prince of Darkness and his forces of evil. At these ceremonies all manner of sexual abuse, cruelty and even murder occurred. The ceremonies always took place at night and were variously said, by the children, to have occurred in tunnels or underground rooms at a church, in a big castle full of sharks and boats, at a pub, in a cemetery, at a house with a swimming pool full of crocodiles, sharks and a dragon, and also on a boat. Those figures that the children recognized at the ceremonies apparently included Superman, clowns, witches, a magic lion and characters known as Mr Brown and Mr Pooh Pants.

The diaries said that the children had witnessed many impossible events at secret orgies. It was continually mentioned that babies were shot, jumped on, stabbed, burnt, hung around people's necks, cooked alive in microwave ovens, eaten, chopped up, killed by policemen, buried and ripped from pregnant women's stomachs. One child said he saw Jesus being murdered and his body was cooked and later eaten off a silver platter. Most of the children said that they saw people taken off the street, killed and eaten. The children themselves claimed to have been cut open, killed and mutilated, but then magically made better. They had also been made to drink blood, eat spiders, stab sheep, and had been turned into frogs by witches. There were also descriptions of sexual abuse and of videotapes being made of the whole ceremony.

Given the nature of these Satanic ceremonies, it is perhaps not surprising that the police had such reservations about investigating the claims, most of which had been taken from the diaries the foster parents had kept on the children. It was their belief that the information in the diaries was nothing more than a mixture of common childhood fantasies about witches made to look more sinister by the unorthodox questioning methods of the foster parents and social workers. It was also felt that the children were too young to give reliable evidence. The youngest was 21 months at the time the abuse supposedly took place, with the oldest only being seven years old.

The police initiated their own separate enquiry into the affair, entitled the 'Gollom Report', which concluded that there was no evidence of Satanism, witchcraft or other ritual abuse on the Broxtowe estate. It said that there was a lack of evidence to support the original allegations of abuse and the evidence of the corroborating adults was unreliable. They also believed much of the information in the diaries to have resulted from an unhealthy co-operation between the social services and the foster parents at bi-weekly meetings that occurred between the two groups.

The sceptical 'Gollom Report', not surprisingly, resulted in a complete breakdown in communication between the police and social services. This did not stop the case, as more and more accusations continued to emerge from the social services, who even believed they had found the sites of the secret ceremonies in various private and public places, including a church, a public hall and two houses with swimming pools. The situation was rapidly getting out of control and drawing much unwanted publicity onto the Nottingham social services; so, in July 1989, a so-called Joint Enquiry Team (JET) was formed, consisting of four police officers and four social workers, none of whom had had any previous involvement with the case. Their results were published at the end of the year in the 600-page 'JET Report'.

The findings of the 'JET Report' were damning: 'We had not found any corroborative evidence in the Broxtowe case and no longer believed the children's diaries substantiated the claim of Satanic abuse. In our view they represented other influences and were open to alternative explanations ... We have come to the hypothesis ... that evidence can actually be "created" by social workers as a result of their own therapeutic methods.'

The report was an embarrassment to many people, including the then British Prime Minister, Margaret Thatcher, who had publicly praised the Nottingham team in 1988 for having stopped such a foul practice in its tracks. Despite the British Department of Health recommending that the 'JET Report' be published to prevent similar miscarriages of justice elsewhere in the country, the report was withheld from the public. This has led to many accusations of a cover-up between the then British government and the social services, or even of a collusion with the Christian right wing, who have strongly supported the idea of Satanic ritual abuse. There had also, in the aftermath of the Nottingham scandal, been a number of high-profile newspapers and television programmes claiming to have evidence of Satanism at work on the Broxtowe estate. All their evidence was later to be proved false, including a videotape that apparently showed a Satanic ritual in action. This actually turned out to be a home movie of a rock star who practised bondage in his spare time.

A copy of the 'JET Report' was, some years later, leaked onto the Internet; this finally allowed critics of the case to see how badly it had been handled. Nottingham Council has spent a considerable amount of time and money trying to get copies of the report removed from the world wide web, but at the time of writing there are at least a dozen websites which have copies of it available.

Despite some people still claiming that Satanism is alive and well in Nottingham, there is still no physical evidence that any ritual abuse took place in the Broxtowe estate.

## The dawning of a new phenomenon

The Nottingham case was the first British example of the Satanic ritual abuse scare phenomenon, and is typical of it. Although Satanic ritual abuse scares did not reach Europe until 1987, they had been very common in the USA since the early 1980s and, as with the Nottingham case, were the cause of much local and national trouble.

The American cases also involve examples of adults being accused by the authorities of sexually or physically abusing children in obscene and hidden ritualistic ceremonies that normally have Satanist overtones to them. The history of these scares is relatively simple and readily identifiable. As to what it is that causes the scares to erupt in the first place, and what it is that has driven them from America to practically every other civilization on Earth, these are more complex questions to answer.

Most authorities on Satanic ritual abuse agree that the start of the scares can be directly attributed to the publication, in 1980, of the book *Michelle Remembers*. This book, written by Canadian psychiatrist Lawrence Pazder in conjunction with his patient Michelle Smith, was a sensational account of the horrendous encounters that Smith underwent at the age of five at the hands of a group of Satanists. Pazder had recovered the memories of Smith's abuse using hypnosis, and the book was heralded as *prima facie* evidence that Satanists were active within the USA. Much of the material in the books of Pazder and Smith now makes up the basis of many Satanic ritual abuse cases; this material includes descriptions of underground ceremonies, murder and torture of babies and innocent people, people trapped in cages, and the so-called 'brood mares' whose job it was to provide fresh babies or foetuses for the coven.

*Michelle Remembers* was an instant bestseller and triggered the publication of a whole series of similar 'survivor' stories, including the highly influential *Satan's Underground* by Lauren Stratford which was later proved to be a work of fiction, the author admitting to making up all the details of Satanic ritual abuse. The sheer number of books, articles and television programmes, particularly talk shows, that gave details of the accounts of 'survivors' of ritual abuse at the hands of devil-worshippers raised the profile of Satanic ritual abuse within the public consciousness. Based on the evidence of these survivors, it appeared that there was a network of underground Satanists at work in mainland USA and that they were kidnapping, abusing and killing adults and children, and that they may even have been breeding children specifically for the purpose of sacrificing them. People of all kinds, and especially some sectors of the church and authorities, were now on their guard, looking for evidence of Satan's helpers at work. Needless to say, it was not long before such evidence was forthcoming.

In September 1983, a part-time worker at the McMartin pre-school nursery in Manhattan Beach, California, was arrested after a parent complained that he had sexually molested her son while he was at the nursery. The man was later released through lack of evidence, but a local police chief circulated a letter to over 200 parents detailing the unproven allegations of sexual abuse at the McMartin nursery. The letter also requested that parents question their children to see if they could confirm that sexual abuse had occurred at the nursery. With the rumour-mill in action, it was not long before local television and newspapers were mentioning the nursery in connection with child-pornography rings. Hundreds of parents came forward with stories of sexual interference, and within six months there were over 360 children on record as having been abused by the staff at the McMartin nursery. After medical examinations, 120 of these children were later considered by social workers to have some physical evidence of sexual abuse on their bodies.

In March 1984, seven adults were arrested and charged with 208 accounts of sexual abuse against 40 children. Telephone polls at the time showed that 90–96 per cent of adults in the area believed them to be guilty. By the time the McMartin case came to court, however, the testimonies of the children went far beyond allegations of routine sexual abuse. They claimed to have been taken into secret tunnels and abused in ceremonies dedicated to the worship of the devil. It was the descriptions of these Satanic orgies that were to form the backbone of the evidence against the accused adults.

In court it was claimed that during these ceremonies animals were sacrificed, babies were killed and their blood drunk, and that the bodies were later buried or burnt. Some of the children told fantastic tales of being taken to Los Angeles in a hot-air balloon or said that they had been flushed down toilets, or travelled through sewers to places where they were sexually abused by adults, cleaned up and then returned to the nursery to be picked up by their parents. Others claimed that film stars, pop stars and politicians were present at these ceremonies.

The physical evidence for any of this was thin (to say the least) and in 1986 the charges were dropped against five of the defendants, with 52 charges of abuse remaining against the last two adults. After a series of trials in which the juries remained split, with the majority in favour of acquittal, the remaining two adults went free in 1990, much to the horror of townsfolk and the local police.

The case had stirred up such a fervour in Manhattan Beach that some people took matters into their own hands and decided to try to find the necessary physical evidence themselves. There were two obvious factors in the case that they felt could be corroborated – the talk of tunnels and rooms underneath the nursery school, and the burial of babies' and animals' bodies in the land around the school building itself.

At various times during the trials, the children had precisely described the location of 13 trapdoors within certain classrooms. They had also talked of two huge underground caverns beneath the school, where some of the worst ritual abuse was said to have occurred. In an effort to find the trapdoors, tunnels and caverns, parents from the town ripped up the school's flooring and dug random holes and trenches in the yard, several of which were more than 5m (16ft) deep and 20m (65ft) long. Nothing was found, apart from a 1940s rubbish dump. Ground-penetrating radar was later used in the hope that, as with recent police cases, the location of buried bodies would be revealed. This also produced negative results.

This lack of evidence only seemed to confirm what the county authorities already knew – that there was no physical evidence of Satanic ritual abuse having occurred at the McMartin nursery school. The floor of the school proved to be concrete, which, as was later noted, is impossible to infill or alter without leaving marks – one only has to look at where pavements have been dug up and re-surfaced to know this.

One of the allegations made in court was that a named adult had killed a turtle by stabbing it through the shell – an almost impossible thing to do given the thickness of a turtle's shell. Some time after the main trials finished, rumours began to circulate that the remains of a stabbed turtle shell and some human remains had been dug up from a classroom. An investigation into these claims showed them to be false, with neither the turtle nor the human remains coming to light, or indeed a place from which they could have been dug up. Despite this, these rumours are still heavily promoted as fact by some pro-abuse campaigners on the case. Even after their court acquittal, the seven accused adults were still believed by over 90 per cent of the town to be guilty of Satanic abuse on their children.

The McMartin case was only the first of a number of high-profile cases within the USA, the majority of which were centred around schools or day-care centres. In most cases, the accused adults were arrested and later released back into a hostile community for lack of evidence.

There are cases where the accused have been found guilty and sentenced to lengthy jail terms. The most notable example is that of Bob Kelly, who was found guilty of 99 charges of ritual sexual abuse and given 12 consecutive life sentences, all of which were later overturned by the appeal court.

In addition to these high-profile cases, there have been hundreds of minor examples of hysteria in small towns right across the USA. The panics generally follow the same pattern as the McMartin (and Rochdale and Nottingham) one and ultimately have no physical evidence to back them up. The Satanic ritual abuse phenomenon became a major talking point within the USA, with high-profile cases being followed by the media and many self-claimed survivors coming forward to participate in campaigns and talk shows on the subject.

Indeed, the talk-show culture of the 1980s and 1990s has been cited as one the greatest means by which the phenomenon of Satanic ritual abuse has been able to spread so far and wide. Although it took a while to leave the shores of the USA, by the late 1980s Satanic ritual abuse had crossed both the Atlantic and Pacific oceans to turn up in Europe and Australasia.

It is said that whatever happens in the USA later makes its way across the Atlantic to Europe and eventually to other parts of the world as well. This was certainly true in the case of the Satanic ritual abuse scares and the Nottingham case of 1987 proved to be the first of 84 similar cases to be reported in the UK between then and 1992. Identical examples also started to be reported from the rest of Europe, Australia, New Zealand, South Africa and Canada.

The number of Satanic ritual abuse cases worldwide now runs into thousands, and it would appear that what was once an isolated American phenomenon has spread across the globe. How, though, can we be sure that all these cases are examples of hysteria and misunderstanding on the part of the public and the prosecuting authorities? After all, just because some of the more famous cases have been proved false, it is still possible that there really do exist organized rings of Satan-worshippers.

## Of fairies and false memories

Satanic ritual abuse is a difficult topic to deal with objectively. To say that it does not exist runs the risk of being interpreted as saying that the sexual abuse of children by adults does not take place, and this is most definitely not the case. Paedophilia is a real and serious threat within our society and there are undoubtedly those who do abuse children sexually and physically; some of these people may well operate in small groups, although evidence of sizeable national or international paedophilia rings is actually very thin on the ground. Like most sexual deviations, paedophilia is something that is more often practised in secret isolation. Just because child abuse exists, however, it does not mean that Satanic ritual abuse also exists, and there are a good many reasons for doubting its reality.

One major problem with the Satanic abuse cases of the last few decades has been the degree to which it has apparently been driven by the media and certain sections of the church. The accusations made in each case are remarkably similar to each other, with the most common themes being stories of children taken to underground locations, taking part in quasi-religious ceremonies and then being forced to watch as babies, animals or people are sacrificed and their bodies disposed of, sometimes by being eaten.

The first case of Satanic ritual abuse to gain publicity was in America in 1983 and came a short time after a wave of hysteria that followed the publishing of the aforementioned 'survivor' book, *Michelle Remembers*. The reportedly true account of Satanic ritual abuse in *Michelle Remembers* is very close indeed to every case of Satanic ritual abuse reported in America, Europe and further afield and most analysts believe that, even though there had been two similar books published in the early 1970s, it was the success of this book that was solely responsible for the origination of the Satanic ritual abuse scares. The two earlier books, *The Satan Seller* and *From Witchcraft to Christ*, which also told firsthand tales of people who had allegedly survived Satanic ritual abuse, had accounts that were different from and much tamer than those told by Michelle Smith and her psychiatrist. The details given in *Michelle Remembers*, which outsold both previous books by the thousand, are undoubtedly the blueprint upon which all modern Satanic ritual abuse cases are based. It also heavily promoted the notion that, like Michelle Smith, people could have been unwittingly abused by Satanists without consciously remembering it. Only the help of a friendly psychiatrist and the use of hypnosis could recover the 'lost' memories.

*Michelle Remembers* caused many other people to believe that they had been abused by Satanists and a large number sought psychiatric help. These people, more commonly known as 'survivors', would generally recall details of their experiences while under hypnosis. These tales were almost always identical to that spelt out in *Michelle Remembers* and before too long television and radio chat shows and the tabloid papers were full of the tales of survivors. There can have been few people in America who were not aware of the issue of Satanic ritual abuse and of the common tales of sexual abuse and butchery that were supposedly occurring under the noses of suburban citizens everywhere. Many Americans believed that the Satanist threat was real and, once they were aware of it, went out searching for evidence of the Satanists at work in their own urban backyards.

The public disquiet about Satanism also turned out to be music to the ears of evangelical branches of the Christian church who had for years been warning of the threat that the devil posed to society at large. In the years after *Michelle Remembers* was published, a number of church alliances were formed specifically to raise public awareness of Satanist ritual abuse. Among these groups were the very active Evangelical Alliance, the Christian Response to the Occult and the even more extreme Reachout Trust. All of these groups actively sought out survivors of Satanic ritual abuse and actively promoted its reality. Practically all of their literature was (and still is) based on the written accounts within *Michelle Remembers, Satan's Underground, Dance with the Devil* and other bestselling survivor books, some of which have since been proved to be faked.

It is perhaps not surprising that, given the large number of survivor stories and the general atmosphere of fear about the reality of Satanic ritual abuse, cases started to be commonly reported by the public. Nevertheless, the fact that the general public believed that this abuse was occurring does not explain how so many cases came to be investigated by the police and the social services and, in many cases, resulted in court cases. The fact this occurred suggests that there was also a desire to believe in the possibility of Satanic ritual abuse among the authorities.

This is a controversial point and one that has generated more bitterness than any other in the analysis of the Satanic ritual abuse scares. The point on which this hinges is whether or not the social workers and police involved in the initial stages of an investigation forced their own beliefs about Satanic ritual abuse onto the children during interviews. The social workers and police say they definitely did not, while their critics say that they unquestionably did. Who is right? And is it genuinely possible to make people, even young children, believe in events that never really happened to them?

A very common criticism in court cases involving accusations of Satanic ritual abuse is that the interview techniques used on children were too suggestive and that the social workers had, in effect, put words into the mouths of the children. The chief means of doing this was to ask leading questions, or put the question in such a way that the answer can only be positive. This technique, when used over time, is capable of making anybody, especially children, believe in events that never actually occurred. Psychologists have, in recent years, recognized that it is possible for one person to implant non-existent memories into another, and have labelled this 'false memory syndrome'.

Although we think of the human memory as being an infallible record of our past thoughts and actions, it is actually a very fragile thing indeed. Contrary to common belief, it is thought that the brain does not store its memories as physical solid images but instead merely carries a summary of our past deeds. When we need to recall a specific event, our brain takes the summary of that event from our memory and then adds its own details to it. In this way, it is possible for us to recall the same event in different ways, and it also explains why memories tend to become more exaggerated over time.

We have all experienced false memories to one degree or another. In a recent reunion with two of my old schoolfriends, we talked about some of the adventures we had had together. Although certain events in these stories were very vivid, including a near-disastrous car crash, we all gave different accounts of the same thing. By prompting each other, we created a hybrid version that, while not false, was certainly not the whole truth either. We went away from the reunion with our memories of those events permanently altered. Equally, every person reading this book will have at some point exaggerated or created stories from their past, and have repeated them so often that they eventually seem utterly real. They are, nonetheless, entirely false memories.

These are examples of self-induced false memories, but it is also possible for a third party to implant memories into people, especially children. Many psychologists have studied this phenomenon and have even taken it upon themselves to implant memories into test subjects. The ease with which they can do so is extraordinary. In one experiment, a four-year-old boy was made to believe that he had been to hospital because he had caught his finger in a mousetrap. The memory was implanted during a series of question-and-answer interviews with the boy over an 11-week period. During his interviews, his replies were recorded, and they changed over the weeks as follows:

*Week 1:* 'No, I've never been to hospital.'
*Week 2:* 'Yes. I cried.'
*Week 4:* 'Yes, I remember. It felt like a cut.'
*Week 11:* 'I was looking down and I didn't see what I was doing and it got caught in there somehow ... I went downstairs and said to Dad, "I want lunch", and then it got stuck in the mousetrap ... My brother pushed me into the mousetrap. It happened yesterday. I went to hospital yesterday.'[91]

The memory of the non-existent hospital visit was simply implanted by the interviewer asking the boy repeatedly about his hospital visit. The interviewer ignored the boy's initial view that he had not been to hospital and simply kept asking him about the experience until, convinced that he must have been to hospital, the boy not only agreed with the questioner but actually elaborated on the experience as well. This technique also works well on adults.

An almost identical means of questioning has been found to be used by the social workers in almost all Satanic ritual abuse cases, and this strongly implies that false memories may have been implanted into the children. The following is a transcript from an interview with a child questioned by social workers in the Nottingham Broxtowe estate case:

*Questioner (Q):* 'We know that your father delivered a foetus and aborted it – he drank the baby's blood.'
*Respondee (R):* 'I didn't know anything about that.'
*Q:* 'You tell us about things that happened when you were there.'
*R:* 'I ate the stomach, my Dad ate the head.'
*Q:* 'You had to eat babies more than once.'
*R:* 'I can't remember.'
*Q:* 'We think you did.'
*Q:* 'Who brought it? A name? Difficult to remember who killed the baby?'
*R:* 'I didn't kill it.'
*Q:* 'Who told you to? Did she give you the knife?'
*R:* 'No.'
*Q:* 'I think she did. You were asked to kill the baby. You had to do it. How was it killed?'[92]

It is clear from this transcript that the interviewer is merely asking (or instructing) the child to agree with their preconceived notion that a baby had been killed and eaten at the 'party'. The rest of the interview carries on in a similar vein, with the child eventually agreeing that the devil was being worshipped, that her friends were also present and that she had witnessed forced abortions, murder and sacrifice at the ceremonies. She was also 'told' which members of her family and community were responsible for the abuse.

This form of interviewing technique differs not at all from that used in clinical false-memory syndrome experiments. It also differs little from that used on witches in the Middle Ages where any answer that does not satisfy the interviewer is considered to be erroneous. In cases of Satanic ritual abuse where more than one victim is involved (which is most of them) this hoisting of pre-existing beliefs onto children explains many of their most unusual features. It explains how every case manages so closely to resemble the traditional model of Satanic ritual abuse as laid out in *Michelle Remembers* and other examples of now commonly available literature. Social workers who have read such books and believe their contents simply ask questions in such a way as to make the children give accounts that closely match them.

It also explains the uncanny similarity between the details given in different children's accounts. The same social worker may question several different children and, again, simply ask questions that get the children to agree with each other and with the social worker's beliefs on Satanic ritual abuse. This was found to have operated in the Nottingham case and was one of the greatest concerns of the JET enquiry team. It also explains how many of the children's stories come to be a strange mixture of descriptions of occult murder and childlike features that are more commonly seen in fairy tales. For example, in the Nottingham case the children gave highly detailed accounts of baby murders and sexual abuse, and yet also described seeing witches on broomsticks, fairy castles, crocodiles, sharks, lions and people flying through the air. Thanks to the biased questioning, we can deduce that the details of murders came from the imagination of the social workers while the fairy-story elements were added by the children. If this was not the case, then we must believe that there are such things as fairies and that they have assisted in Satanic ceremonies across the world.

The leading questioning of social workers and the police may well have produced false memories within children, but could the same explanation really be used on the adult 'survivors' who came forward in their hundreds claiming to remember abuse that occurred to them decades before? The answer is, perhaps unsurprisingly, yes. False memories are capable of being implanted into adults as easily as children, but in slightly different circumstances. Although the leading questioning is still capable of implanting false memories, it requires that the adult be hypnotized before it works really well.

Nobody is really sure what hypnosis is or quite what it does to either the human personality or the brain. Some believe that it does nothing more than relax people; others that it is a form of light sleep; others still that it is a window into the inner reaches of the mind. Since its discovery in the late eighteenth century, hypnosis has been used as tool for diagnosing both the physical and the mental well-being of an individual. Since the turn of the twentieth century, many psychiatrists have used hypnosis as a means of recovering lost or hidden memories from disturbed people. This practice is based on the Freudian belief that the mind is capable of burying unpleasant memories, so if the psychiatrist can uncover such memories then the neuroses and mental problems of the patient can be understood and ultimately cured. Thus, when some psychiatrists are confronted with a disturbed patient, the first thing they will do is hypnotize them to try to recover the hidden memories that they believe are the cause of the problem. In recent years, the role of hypnosis as a psychiatric tool, and indeed the whole concept of hidden memories, have come into some doubt.

Although the hypnotic trance state is still not fully understood, it is now very clear that its use in recovering lost memories is minimal, if it exists at all. Laboratory experiments have shown that hypnotized subjects cannot recall additional details about events which they do remember, let alone ones that they cannot. Instead, the hypnotic subjects become very open to suggestions put to them by the person asking the questions. Like the children being interviewed by the social workers, it becomes very easy to convince a hypnotized person that they have had an experience that has never actually occurred. In other words, it is very easy to implant false memories into a hypnotized subject.

There is very strong evidence to suggest that this has occurred in many of the best cited examples of Satanic ritual abuse survivors. As with the strong link between teams of social workers who believe in Satanic ritual abuse and the geographical spread of such cases, there is a strong connection between those psychiatrists who believe in Satanic ritual abuse and the number of patients they find that they believe are victims of it. Almost all the American cases of

Satanic ritual abuse survivors have been diagnosed by a very small circle of psychiatrists who believe in the phenomenon and use hypnosis to recover memories. The majority of psychiatrists in America have never encountered a survivor, and yet there are a few select ones who manage to find tens of people who have been abused by Satanists. This imbalance suggests that it may well be the psychiatrists themselves who are creating the problem, something that has been suggested in more than one study of the survivor scenario. The problem of the reliability of hypnosis as a psychiatric tool is further discussed in Chapters 10 and 12.

It should also be borne in mind that there are many people who seek attention, fame or money, and will say or do anything to get what they want. The author of one famous survivor book, *Satan's Underground*, Lauren Stratford, has admitted that it is a hoax, and the facts listed in others are either vague or wrong. No survivor of Satanic ritual abuse has ever managed to provide any physical or medical evidence of their ordeals, the details of which would have left some of them with serious internal or external scarring (for example, Michelle Smith claimed to have had body parts grafted onto her, and others claim to have had forced abortions).

## Strange statistics

Returning to the cases involving children, the final proof of the degree to which these cases are reliant on social workers or other adults implanting false memories into children comes from some unusual statistics associated with Satanic ritual abuse cases as a whole. For example, in the UK, over three-quarters of the 84 cases reported between 1987 and 1992 were centred in just three areas of the country. In fact, 14 of the cases were diagnosed by just one team of social workers in Nottingham, including the previously discussed Broxtowe estate case. The same pattern can be seen in the USA, with most cases being tightly clustered in a few small regions. This unusual pattern of distribution would appear to suggest that geography is an important factor in the diagnosis of Satanic ritual abuse. This weakens the case for its being a widespread and independent phenomenon.

Following on from this, it would also appear that such cases are only ever diagnosed and pursued by members of the authorities who believe in Satanic rituals. There is clear evidence that these people are not objective in their investigations of such cases, and start their enquiries by assuming that not only is Satanic ritual abuse a reality but also that the case they are dealing with is an example of such abuse. It is this preconceived belief that leads to the unorthodox questioning techniques and, ultimately, the implantation of false memories into the children.

We have already seen how, in the McMartin case, a police chief directly asked parents to find examples of Satanic ritual abuse in their children and how the Nottingham interviews were led by the social workers themselves. There are also many other instances of non-objectivity by the people in charge of investigating cases, including the so-called 'Little Rascals Abuse Case' in North Carolina, where a San Diego grand jury observed:

> Of particular interest is the information the Jury received about the Little Rascals pre-school case in North Carolina. Eighty-five per cent of the children received therapy with three therapists in the town; *all* of these children eventually reported Satanic abuse. Fifteen per cent of the children were treated by different therapists in a neighbouring city; *none* of the children reported abuse of any kind after the same period of time in therapy. [my italics][93]

In what was an apparently perfect laboratory experiment, only those children interviewed by one set of therapists reported tales of Satanic abuse, which included the usual reports of infanticide and sacrifice. This suggests a conclusive link between individual therapists and the likelihood of Satanic ritual abuse being reported, and lessens the chances that it is a genuine phenomenon.

The final oddity about these cases is their occurrence in time. In the USA, there had not been a single Satanic ritual abuse case before 1983, and in Europe not before 1987. After these respective dates, however, there suddenly came a flood of cases in both continents, later followed by cases in Australia, New Zealand and South Africa. It is as though the Satanic ritual abuse scares were travelling the globe from west to east in a kind of giant 'Mexican wave'. What could be causing this? The probable link between *Michelle Remembers* and the start of the American cases has already been discussed, but what about the spread of the phenomenon outside the USA?

The 1994 official report into the British Satanic ritual abuse scares found a positive link between the activities of evangelical Christians in Britain and the wave of cases that began in 1987. Of particular interest were the undoubted links between some of the evangelical Christian groups and the social-worker community in the UK. Indeed, within the UK, the Christians had organized a number of conferences on the issue of Satanic ritual abuse. These conferences not only promoted the reality of this phenomenon, but also instructed people how to find signs of Satanists at work in the community. Social workers from Nottingham are known to have spoken at one of these conferences in 1989.

It would also appear that similar links exist between Christian groups and police and social workers within the USA, mainland Europe, Australia and New Zealand where other scares have occurred. The influence of this sector of the Christian church has been seen as crucial in the promotion of Satanic ritual abuse scares, and is thought to underlie much of the occurrence of the phenomenon. Such was the conclusion of the British government's report, and the prominence of certain evangelical groups has been noted in most official reports.[94]

## The final damnation

Indeed, the final nail in the coffin of the Satanic ritual abuse scares comes from the many official investigations into organized Satanic ritual abuse that have been undertaken in practically every western country that has suffered from these panics. The British, American, German and Australian governments and the FBI have commissioned investigations into their national occurrences of Satanic ritual abuse, while individual councils and courts have investigated particular cases. All these investigations have concentrated on trying to find the physical evidence which would show that Satanists had been at work and of any sign that they are organized on a local, national or even international scale. Every single one of these investigations has concluded that there is no evidence of any kind of Satanism at work in society at any level. The claims with which these reports have had to deal are extraordinary.

According to those who believe in the reality of the phenomenon, the cases that have been exposed so far are just the tip of the iceberg. It has been estimated (mostly by Christian groups) that up to 50,000 children a year are murdered by Satanists in the USA alone, and 2,000 in the UK. The investigators have naturally asked what has happened to the bodies of these victims and, more to the point, where the victims have all come from. Such large numbers of children would definitely be missed, particularly in places like Britain, where even the disappearance of one child makes headline news.

Some people have invoked the notion of 'brood mares', who are women who are specifically kept alive to breed babies and foetuses for the rituals. This idea was first mentioned in connection with Satanic ritual abuse in *Michelle Remembers* although the idea itself dates back centuries (see Chapter 9). The concept of brood mares is also hard to believe, as over 50,000 women would need to be kept somewhere for this purpose and nowhere, at any time, has a cave, tunnel, hidden room or cellar ever been found that has evidence of being used for Satanic ritual purposes as defined in this chapter (there are, of course, examples of genuine non-ritualized sexual abuse taking place in cellars and caves).

The reports have also noted something else that links in directly with the subject matter of the next chapter. It would seem that many of the accusations levelled against people in Satanic ritual abuse cases differ little from those that were levelled against the Bacchanalia, Sabbat, early Christians and others. All of them have tales of secret nocturnal gatherings, quasi-religious ceremonies and tales of sexual abuse and or murder. In particular there are stories of babies and animals being killed and then eaten, burnt or buried. The questioning techniques used on the children also differs little from those used on suspected witches, further strengthening this link.

There is, in particular, a close relationship between modern Satanic ritual abuse cases and stories of ritual abuse reported during the witchcraft trials. Many people have viewed Satanic ritual abuse as an updated version of the witch-hunts, and many articles on Satanic ritual abuse scares refer to them as modern witch trials. In reality, the link between the Satanic ritual abuse scares and historical stories of ritual abuse goes much deeper than just the witch trials. In fact, according to the history books, every generation since at least Roman times has had its own version of the scares. This is the topic of the next chapter.

# 9

# A HISTORY OF SUPERNATURAL ORGIES

The science-fiction writer Richard Shaver became famous in the 1950s and 1960s because of his short stories about two warring tribes that lived in a secret world beneath the Earth's crust. These two tribes represented good and evil, with one tribe, the Teros, being organized and civilized, while the other, the Deros, was sadistic, perverted and animalistic. Shaver wrote numerous stories about the underground happenings of the Teros and Deros, all of which were popular.

Shaver was not a balanced individual, however, and, after a series of mental breakdowns, came to firmly believe in the reality of the underground world and very publicly promoted the danger that the Deros presented to the human race. Shaver said that the Deros would kidnap women from the Earth and take them into underground caverns to abuse them physically and sexually. They would, he said, be kept in cages and periodically raped and tortured until they had outlived their usefulness, at which point the Deros would kill, cook and eat them. Their remains would never be found.

Few people believed Shaver's stories, but there was a woman from Paris who wrote to him about how she had got into a lift in a building which went down so far as to enter the realm of the Deros. She claimed to have been captured, caged with other women, and raped, until she was rescued by the Teros and returned to the Earth. While Shaver believed her story, the doctors the woman consulted did not.

Shaver's description of the activities of the Deros have a great deal in common with the descriptions given by Satanic ritual abuse victims, and yet he managed to come up with his ideas decades before the current wave of cases.

Similarly, in 1969, a series of rumours spread across the French city of Orléans that clothes shops in the city were part of an organized kidnapping ring that would seize girls and transport them to Arabia for a life of sexual slavery. The situation came to a head when, on 31 May, several shops were surrounded by angry crowds who became convinced that all the shops were linked by tunnels to the River Loire and that there was a submarine there, ready to carry the girls to the Mediterranean. The police managed to control the situation and explained that not one girl had been reported missing from the Orléans area. They, and the French government, were later accused of being involved in a conspiracy to cover up the truth. A later analysis of the situation blamed fears of sexual liberation, which were connected with the clothes stores, for the panic.

Both the Shaver and Orléans stories have remarkable similarities to the Satanic ritual abuse claims discussed in the previous chapter. Shaver's underground ceremonies have a similarity to the Satanist orgies, and the Orléans kidnappings represent the willingness of people to believe in the activities of a subversive group in the midst of an organized society. Yet both of these incidents occurred some years before the current outbreak of Satanic ritual abuse panics. This suggests that there could be an inbuilt willingness within the human personality both to create and to believe stories which centre on a subversive element within society that goes around kidnapping and abusing innocent people.

Proof that this is so can be found in a near-continuous succession of tales of supernatural abuse that stretch back over 2,000 years. The study of the history of accusations of ritual abuse shows that cases like the Nottingham and McMartin ones are in fact just the latest in a tradition that stretches back for millennia. In fact, the modern tales of Satanism pale into insignificance compared with the sexual excesses, torture and murder that have been linked to other cults and religious groups down the ages. Even one of the promoters of the belief in modern Satanic ritual abuse, the Christian church, was itself at one time accused of indulging in orgies of wild sex and murder.

## A history of abusive behaviour

The oldest-known reports of ritualized sexual abuse and murder come from the Roman Empire in the two centuries preceding the birth of Christ. There had, in this time, developed a cult that worshipped the Roman god of wine, Bacchus, and on certain nights of the year members of the cult would meet to worship the god in a festival called the Bacchanalia. The Bacchanalia always occurred in secret and there was, from contemporary accounts, evidently an orgiastic element fuelled by the drunkenness for which the god was known. It is therefore perhaps unsurprising that the Bacchanalia soon gathered a great deal of myth about it.

The Bacchanalia had been around for some time before attracting a bad press. The Greek Euripides wrote of it as early as 429 BC in his play *Hippolytus*: 'Go revel in thy Bacchic rites, with Orpheus for thy Lord and King.' It was in Rome during the second century BC that rumours started circulating which described the proceedings of the Bacchanalia in almost identical terms to today's modern Satanic ritual abuse scares. In an identical manner to modern 'survivor' stories, most of the horrors attributed to the Bacchanalia came from people who had allegedly been part of the cult but had managed to escape from it. The most famous description of the Bacchanalia was given to the Roman senator Postumis by a prostitute named Hispala Fecenia who claimed to have been part of the Bacchanalia but to have later escaped:

> ... when the rites were thus made common, and men were intermixed with women, the night encouraging licentious freedom, there was nothing wicked, nothing flagitious, that had not been practised among them. There were more frequent pollutions of men with each other, than with women. If any showed an uncommon degree of reluctance in submitting to dishonour, or of disinclination to the commission of vice, they were held as victims and sacrificed. To think nothing unlawful was the grand maxim of religion. The men, as if bereft of reason, uttered predictions, with frantic contortions of their bodies; the women, in the habit of Bacchantes with their hair dishevelled, and carrying blazing torches, ran down to the Tiber, where, dipping their torches in the water, they drew them up again with the flame extinguished, being composed of native sulphur and charcoal. They said that the men were carried off by the gods, when, after being fettered, they were dragged into secret caves. These were such as refused to take the oath of the society, or to associate in their crimes, or to submit to defilement. Their number was exceeding great, enough almost to compose a state in themselves, and among them were many men and women of noble families.[95]

Other stories that circulated around Rome told of child sacrifices, incest, urine-drinking, and a host of other things that were supposed to be a standard part of the Bacchanalia. As we shall see, these stories form the core of cult abuse stories throughout history right through to the modern day.

As a result of the prostitute Hispala's survivor story, the Roman senate passed a law banning the Bacchanalia in 186 BC and offered rewards for information leading to the arrest of those involved in the ceremony. Large numbers of people were subsequently imprisoned and the Bacchanalia was considered to have been stamped out, although, in fact, the ceremonies simply became more open and took place during the day rather than at night. Bacchus' name was changed to Liber (still a god of wine) and the drunken orgies simply became known as the Liberalia (or, if the goddess Venus or Flora was being worshipped, the Floralia) instead.

Later, these ceremonies became so accepted by society at large that they involved street parades where an enormous phallus on a chariot was dragged through the town centre. There was, as far as is known, never any formal evidence that human sacrifices, rape or incest actually occurred at the original Bacchanalia ceremonies, and most historians believe that, while some orgiastic practices might have taken place, the consumption of wine was more important than the sex.

The Bacchanalia is the oldest definite confirmation we have of ritual abuse stories, although there are passages in the Old Testament that hint that similar rumours may well have been circulating about other religions, particularly the phallic god Baal-Peor whose worship was exceedingly widespread in the Middle East during biblical times.

In the mid-eighth century BC, the Jewish prophet Hosea said that worshippers '... went to Baal-Peor, and separated themselves unto that shame; and their abominations were according as they loved' and that one specific woman worshipper '... burned incense to them [the gods], and decked herself with her earrings and her jewels, and she went after her lovers ... .'[96]

Other themes of perversity, incest and sacrifice are rife throughout the Old Testament. Some of the stories, like that of Sodom and Gomorrah (from which, thanks to St Augustine, we have derived the term sodomy), are famous, while others are only fleeting references to some of the acts that other idol-worshippers were perpetrating (see Chapter 4). After the assimilation of the Bacchanalia into mainstream Roman society in the century before Christ, we have an almost continuous history of alleged ritualized abuse through to the current day. After the Bacchanalia, the next major phase of ritualistic abuse scares has an ironic touch to it.

## Ritual abuse rumours and the early church

Right from the founding of their religion, the first Christians did not endear themselves to the Roman Empire or, indeed, to the Judaic tradition from which the religion had originally split. During the first three centuries of their religion's existence, Christians were heavily persecuted by the Roman Empire, and stories about Christians being fed to the lions are commonplace today. The current church likes to portray this persecution as being a last-ditch attempt by the Romans to hold back the growing threat to their empire from the divine power and sanctity of Christianity. In reality, the cause of the persecutions has more in common with the Bacchanalia of a couple of centuries earlier and the modern Satanic ritual abuse than any perceived religious threat to Rome.

Very soon after the Christian movement began to grow and define itself, rumours started to occur which suggested that they partook in debauched and unholy rituals and ceremonies. At the end of the first century AD, the Latin religious commentator Minucius Felix said of Christianity:

> As for the initiation of new members, the details are as disgusting as they are well known. A child, covered in dough to deceive the unwary, is set before the would-be novice [who] stabs the child to death. Then – it's horrible! They hungrily drink the child's blood, and compete with one another as they divide his limbs. And the fact they share knowledge of the crimes pledges them all to silence. On the feast-day they foregather with all their children, sisters, mothers, people of either sex and all ages. Now, in the dark, so favourable to shameless behaviour, they twine the bonds of unnameable passion as chance decides. Precisely the secrecy of this evil religion proves that all these things, or practically all, are true.[97]

By AD 60, rumours of incest and cannibalism in Christian rituals were rife throughout the Roman Empire. These rumours are thought likely to have been derived from misunderstandings to do with the Eucharist and the symbolic eating of Christ's flesh and drinking of his blood. There was also, in those times, a Christian festival called the Agape whose literal translation means 'the love feast' and this could have been misinterpreted as some being some kind of orgy. Also, as Minicius Felix states at the end of his description, the Christian secular tradition and their habit of meeting in secret after dark were bound to have created rumours.

On 19 July AD 64, a terrible fire swept through Rome, destroying much of the city and leaving the population extremely angry. The Emperor Nero was unpopular at the time and it was widely suspected that he had started the fire to make space for a new palace he had been planning. To shift suspicion, Nero blamed the fire on the Christians and thus began the first of several waves of state persecution of the Christians.

This persecution was at times severe and Tacitus tells us that suspected Christians were '... covered with the skins of beasts, they were torn by dogs and perished, or were nailed to crosses, or were doomed to the flames'.[98] According to the church historian Eusebius: '... those standing around were struck with amazement, at seeing them lacerated with scourages, to their very blood and arteries, so that now the flesh congealed in the very inmost parts of the body, and the bowels themselves were exposed to view. Then they were laid upon conch shells from the sea, and on sharp heads and points of spears on the ground, [and] after passing through every kind of punishment and torture were at last thrown to wild beasts.'[99]

Because of the ritual abuse rumours associated with them, the Christians were clearly a useful scapegoat for the problems of the Roman Empire, leading one Roman historian to comment: 'If the Tiber reaches the walls, if the Nile does not rise into the fields, if the sky does not move or the earth does, if there is famine, if there is plague, the cry is at once "Christians to the lions!" What, all of them to one lion?'[100]

The Roman persecution of the Christians occurred sporadically until AD 305, shortly after which the Emperor Constantine adopted Christianity as the official religion of the Roman Empire.

The persecution and suppression of the Christians were part of an unpleasant, drawn-out and vindictive process that is still widely referred to by the modern church, and many of the martyrs from that time are still worshipped as saints. The whole episode appears to have originated from nothing more than a bunch of unsubstantiated rumours about the nature of Christian worship. It is therefore surprising, and not a little ironic, that from the fourth century onwards it was largely the Christian church that created similar rumours and, on the strength of these, persecuted any number of religious and other groups that it saw as potential rivals.

## The Christian persecutions

The conversion of the Roman Empire to St Paul's version of Christianity took place in the fourth century, and in the subsequent centuries missionaries set about travelling through Europe and Asia.

By the eighth century, most of western Europe, apart from the Scandinavian countries, had been converted to the doctrine of Jesus Christ, turning the religion into a force to be reckoned with.

The historical re-emergence of the ritual abuse stories does not occur until early into the second millennium AD. The reason for the revival is unclear but one consensus is that as the year 1000 drew closer the church had built up an air of expectation that Jesus would choose this time to make his reappearance on the Earth. When this did not occur, there was a general sense of disappointment and disillusion with the church, and the Pope and bishops of Rome looked around for something or someone to blame. It was from this moment onwards that the accusations of devil-worship and unholy ritualistic murder and sexual practices began to emerge from the church. The devil, and his followers, were held responsible not only for Christ's failure to show at the end of the first millennium AD but also for every possible woe and misfortune over the next 700 years. As in the days of the Roman Empire, accusations of ritual abuse were also used as an excuse to persecute many inconvenient political and religious groups. As with the Bacchanalia and the early Christian 'love feasts', stories of sexual abuse and child murder were the mainstay of these persecutions.

The first recorded mass execution of people accused of ritually eating children occurred in 1022 in the French town of Orléans when a group of heretics were burnt to death for the crime. They had apparently confessed to eating 'heavenly food' – a phrase that was twisted by their inquisitors to mean kidnapped and cooked babies! The rumours emerge in a more familiar and developed form in 1050 when a Byzantium statesman, Michael Constantine Psellos, wrote of the Bogomiles of Thrace:

> They bring together, in a house appointed for the purpose, young girls whom they have initiated into their rites ... and throw themselves lasciviously on the girls ... no matter she be his sister, his daughter or his mother, and after waiting nine months, until the time has come for the unnatural children of such unnatural seed to be born, they come together again ... they tear the miserable babies from their mothers' arms. They cut their tender flesh with knives and catch the stream of blood in basins. They throw the babies still breathing and gasping, onto the fire ... they mix the ashes with the blood in the basins and so make an abominable drink, with which they secretly pollute their food and drink.[101]

The isolated incident at Orléans and the writings of Psellos were to be followed by a much more prolonged period of persecution against a familiar enemy of the church, the Jews. The Jews had always been disliked by the Christian church because they were held responsible for crucifying Christ and because of their dominance within the legal, medical and financial professions, something that had been created by the church refusing to let non-Christians join craftsmen's guilds. The Jews were particularly noted for their money-lending, and there were always nobles and churchmen who owed money to various Jewish financiers or merchants. These people were constantly looking for ways in which they could renege on their debts to the Jews, and the advent of the eleventh-century crusades seemed to offer the perfect opportunity.

When, in 1096, the Jewish financiers of the German town of Mainz refused to underwrite a crusade to the Holy Land, over 1,000 of them were massacred. Similar scenes were repeated across mainland Europe as noblemen encouraged their townsfolk to murder or exile the Jewish populations to whom they owed money. Rumours that the Jews were in league with the devil and that it was their sin that had prevented Christ from returning were circulating as early as the 1020s, and grew steadily throughout the century as excuses were sought to persecute the Jews for their wealth and property. By the twelfth century, the same familiar accusations that had been levelled at the Bacchanalia and the early Christian church were now being directed at the Jews.

Tales that they had tails and horns, and that they were thought to smell of sulphur (known as the *foetor judaicus*), were part of everyday life, and King Philip III of France even required all Jews to wear a badge depicting a horned beast to underline their link with the devil. The synagogue had, as long ago as the fourth century, been described as 'a brothel, a den of vice, the devil's refuge, Satan's fortress, a place to deprave the soul, an abyss of every conceivable disaster or whatever else you will, you are saying less than it deserves!'[102] Stories about sexual depravity, child murder and orgiastic practice were also common.

At Easter in 1144, in the English town of Norwich, a young boy called William disappeared; his body was found some days later in nearby woods. His head was shaved and he had been stabbed many times. It was rumoured that he had last been seen going into the house of a Jewish merchant and, encouraged by the dead boy's mother, rumours soon developed that the boy had been sacrificed in some form of Jewish devil-worshipping ritual. The hysteria became so bad that, after a series of murders, the town's Jews were locked inside Norwich castle for their safety. After being credited with performing a number of miracles, William later ended up being canonized by the church. A similar murder in the German town of Sappenfeld in 1540 resulted in a number of prominent Jews being executed on a charge of ritual child murder.

The murder of William served to reinforce the belief that, at around the time of their Passover, the Jews would kidnap a Christian child and drain him of blood so that it could be used to make their Passover bread. This rumour is reflected in Chaucer's *Canterbury Tales* when a young and devout Christian boy living in the Jewish quarter of town is murdered by Jews whose inspiration is 'Oure first foo, the serpent Sathanas, that hath in Jues herte his waspes nest'.[103]

This tradition of anti-Semitism has continued in modern times with much of the iconography and stories used about the Jews in Nazi Germany. Hitler believed the Jews to be responsible for prostitution, white-slave trafficking and sexual deviancy, and wrote of the '... nightmare vision of the seduction of hundreds and thousands of girls by repulsive, crooked-legged Jew bastards'.[104] Hitler's obsession with the sexuality of Jews has been blamed on his own teenage inability to form relationships with women, but much of what he levels against the Jews is merely a reflection of earlier rumours, including the assertion that they smelt horrible.

Although the Jews were the first and most continual of the groups to be accused of abhorrent sexual and ritualistic practices, they were soon followed by many other similar persecutions involving groups that had, for one reason or another, attracted the displeasure of the church. Next in line were the Cathars, who, prior to the thirteenth century, were a Christian branch who lived in the southwestern region of France in what is now the province of Languedoc. The Cathars' Christianity differed remarkably from that of conventional Catholicism in their dualist belief that God and the devil were deities of equal power. Their lifestyle was a simple one, involving abstinence from material wealth, political power, violence and, apart from for procreational purposes, sex. The Cathars did not bother the established church until, in the twelfth century, they started to gain significant numbers of converts, many of whom were disillusioned with the increasing opulence and power of Rome. At the start of the thirteenth century the familiar rumours began to emerge about Cathar practices. In the 1230s, the Bishop of Paris said of the Cathars: 'Lucifer is permitted to appear to his worshippers and adorers in the form of a black cat or a toad and to demand kisses from them; whether as a cat, abominably, under the tail; or as a toad, horribly, on the mouth.'[105]

After a number of attempts to bring the Cathars to heel, the church lost patience and in 1209 an army of 30,000 men was sent by Rome into Languedoc with instructions to murder anybody not willing to renounce their devil-worshipping beliefs. In the following war, tens of thousands of men, women and children were slaughtered. In the town of Béziers alone, over 15,000 were slaughtered; in a siege of the mountain castle of Montségur, both Cathars and Christians were killed, with one officer, on being asked how they could tell the Christians from the Cathars, credited as saying, 'Kill them all, God will know his own.' (Although widely quoted, the origin of this statement is dubious.)

Although their religion was wiped out, the supposed supernatural abilities of the Cathars remain with us today in the widespread belief that they guarded some kind of great secret (believed by some to relate to the blood line of Christ) or had hidden a great treasure somewhere within the Languedoc region. Others have linked the Cathars to another persecuted medieval sect, the Knights Templar. There is an irony in this since the Knights Templar, an international society of crusader knights formed along much the same lines as those of freemasonry, were themselves accused of satanic ritual abuse. Modern historians say that the Templar '... supposedly worshipped a devil called Baphomet. At their secret ceremonies they supposedly prostrated themselves before a bearded male head, which spoke to them and initiated occult powers. Unauthorized witnesses of these were never seen again. And there were other charges ... of infanticide, of teaching women how to abort; of obscene kisses at the induction of postulants; of homosexuality ... They were accused of ritually denying Christ, of repudiating, trampling and spitting on the cross.'[106]

The Knights Templar, being an organization of honourable knights, might seem to be an odd group to persecute, but many nobles, especially King Philippe of France, owed them large sums of money. This, as with the Jews, was enough to make their eradication necessary; it was Philippe who, in 1312, persuaded the Pope to dissolve the Knights Templar, which led to the torture and execution of many of its members. The organization ceased to exist after this time although, as with the Cathars, many occult rumours still surround it.

Hot on the heels of the Jews, Cathars and Knights Templar came the Spanish Inquisition, and the persecution, based on similar devil-worshipping rumours, of two Cathar-like sects known as the Waldensians and the Sredingins. Such persecution had so far applied to individual groups or occurred in isolated instances;

the greatest-known and widest-spread persecution was yet to come, however, and across Europe over 100,000 people were to be executed for the crime of witchcraft.

## The Sabbat

In the Middle Ages, the church and judiciary (which were much the same thing) became obsessed with the thought that there were large underground organizations within society working to subvert the good works of Jesus Christ. Each of these organizations was thought to express itself through perverted and demonic ceremonies, and the witches were thought to be no different. Whereas the Romans had their Bacchanalia ceremonies, the early Christians their 'love-feasts' and the Jews their Passover festival, the witches were said to have Sabbat meetings. It is this aspect of witchcraft that is most applicable to the current chapter, since almost all the accusations made against the witches' Sabbat can be found in stories attributed to cults that have gone before and since. Much of the *Malleus Maleficarum* concerns itself with the activities of the Sabbat and practically all the witch trials dealt with matters that related to the goings-on at the Sabbat and the people who attended them.

The Sabbat was considered to be the witches' black equivalent of the Christian mass, where they would gather together on specific nights of the year and worship the devil using all the foul means at their disposal. Significantly, these dates were almost always ones that had been significant to pagan religions, such as Hallowe'en. The whole subject of the witch trials, including their causes, details, extent and effects on society, is fascinating and indeed has filled several books. Here we will limit ourselves to looking at those aspects of the Sabbat that are relevant to the cult patterns we are following through history (many of the other aspects of witchcraft are more fully covered in Chapter 6). An excellent summary of what was felt to occur at the Sabbat can be found in Chapter 12 of Henri Boguet's 1590 book *Discours des Sorciers*, where he summarizes the proceedings of the Sabbat as follows:

1. The Sorcerers worship the Devil who appears under the form of a tall black man or as a goat. They offer him candles and kiss his posterior.
2. They dance.
3. They give themselves up to every kind of filthy abomination. The Devil transforms himself into an Incubus and into a Succubus.

4. The hideous orgies and foul copulation practised by the Euchites, and Gnostics.
5. The Sorcerers feast at the Sabbat. Their meat and their drink.
6. However, this food never satisfies their appetites, and they always arise from table as hungry as before.
7. When they have finished their meal, they give the Devil a full account of all of their actions.
8. They again renounce God, their baptism. Satan incites them to do evil.
9. They raise dark storms.
10. They celebrate their mass. Of their vestments, and holy water.
11. Sometimes to conclude the Sabbat Satan seems to be consumed in a flame of fire, and to be completely reduced to ashes. All present take a small part of these ashes, which the Sorcerers use for their charms.
12. Satan is always the Ape of God in everything.

Already, and particularly from this brief summary of the Sabbat, we can see similarities to other accusations that went before the witches. The Knights Templar were accused of kissing each other's buttocks and it was written of the Waldensians that 'the Devil appears to them as a cat, and they kiss him *sub cauda*'.[107] Kissing a human's or an animal's posterior was seen as an anti-Christian and diabolic practice, and is these days still a major insult, which is reflected in the phrase 'kiss my arse!' In the case of the Knights Templar, it was used to imply that the sect was a homosexual one, whereas in the witch trials it was thought to be a means of paying homage to the devil. The proceedings of the witch trials make many references to it. In 1453, Guillaume Edeline was executed after confessing that he '... had done homage to the aforesaid Satan, who appeared in the shape of a ram, by kissing his buttocks in token of reverence and homage'.[108] Agnis Sampson is also on record as confessing that Satan bade people to '... kisse his buttockes, in sign of duety to him, which being put over the pulpit bare, every one did as he had enjoyned them'.[109]

Other charges made against the activities of the Sabbat were more sinister. One of the gravest of these, and again one we have come across previously and will do again, was that children were sacrificed to the devil. In 1610, in the French town of Aix-en-Provence, the following description of the Sabbat was given at the trial of one Louis Gaufridi: 'Sometimes they ate the tender flesh of little children, who had been slain and roasted at some Synagogue [note the Jewish reference here], and sometimes babes were brought there, yet alive, whom the witches had kidnapped from their homes if opportunity offered.' Other descriptions of the Sabbat confirm this belief:

> ... sometimes a pie is baked from babies they have slain or disinterred corpses.[110]

> Moreover the wine which is usually poured out for the revellers is like black and clotted blood ... Isabella further added that human flesh was served.[111]

In 1610 Juan de Echalar confessed that

> ... [toads were] cooked in a stew pot with human bones and pieces of corpses rifled from new-made graves.[112]

These stories of child sacrifice differ little from those of Rome or, indeed, from those of the modern-day Satanic ritual abuse scares, and it was commonly believed that children were either stolen from their mothers at birth or bred especially for the purpose. In this respect, the notorious *Malleus Maleficarum* says, 'There are no persons who can do more cunning harm to the Catholic faith than midwives.'[113] Although details of the actual sacrifices were scant in the trials themselves, many books offered their versions of what they believed occurred to these infants. Montague Summers, writing some centuries after the end of the trials, states:

> There is ample and continuous evidence that children, usually tender babes who were as yet unbaptized, were sacrificed at the Sabbat. These were often the witches' own offspring, and since a witch not unseldom was the midwife or wise woman of a village she had exceptional opportunities of stifling a child at birth as a non-Sabbatical victim to Satan ... . The most general use was to cut the throat of the child, whose blood was drained into the chalice and allowed to fall upon the naked flesh of the inquirer, who lay stretched along the altar.[114]

The numbers of victims attributed to this form of sacrifice are extraordinary, and quite impossible. Over 1,500 child murders were attributed to Madame de Montespan and 140 to Gilles de Rais.

It was widely believed that the fat, blood and bones of the children gave the witches supernatural powers, and that birthmarks, toothache and herpes could be removed or cured by using them. This may be a reflection of more traditional superstitions that the touch of a cold corpse could cure skin ailments. Beyond the accusations of child murder and cannibalism, there were also the stories of orgiastic practices and sexual perversions. These have already been discussed in Chapter 6 and are, like most of the witchcraft accusations, little different from those levelled against modern Satanists.

The end of the main phase of the witch trials in the seventeenth century also brought to an end the extended period of religious persecution that had lasted for over 700 years. From this time onwards, political power in much of Europe and America began to shift away from the church towards the newly formed governments, and science began to explain many factors that had previously been thought to be due to witchcraft. So, at the end of this phase of persecution, what conclusions can we come to?

Firstly, it must be acknowledged that almost all the general accusations levelled against the witches can be seen to have been derived from earlier persecutions, including those of the early Christians, Jews, Cathars and Knights Templar. Stories of child murder, nocturnal orgies, cannibalism, bestiality, homosexuality, sex with gods/demons/the devil and buttock-kissing can all be seen in accusations made against other sections of society over the years.

The difference between the persecution of the witches and that of, say, the Knights Templar was that the Templars were a readily identifiable group of individuals whereas witches were perceived to be hiding within the fabric of society. Thus, rather than being a remote political persecution, such as in the case of the Cathars of southwest France, the witch persecution occurred at all levels of society throughout Europe and North America. Also, because of the need of the court for detailed confessions, we find much more detail about the supposed practices of witches than was given for the other persecutions, although most of this was extracted under pressure.

In reality, there is little evidence to reinforce the accusations of organized practices of witchcraft, particularly that of the Sabbat. There were probably people playing with herbalism, healing, love potions and other superstitious practices (what might be termed 'white magic'), and there may well have even been organized devil-worshippers or paganists, but there were certainly not the large numbers of witches that the trials appeared to uncover.

Even more than this, the descriptions of the Sabbat are plainly based upon those of the earlier persecutions and thus, by definition, must have been false. As is painfully detailed in the Salem witch trials, the majority of witches were simply the distrusted or feared members of society, such as petty criminals, wise women, spinsters, crotchety old men, practical jokers and so on. In many of the cases recorded in the Channel Islands, the witches were people suspected of having stolen or damaged property and, in this respect, the accusation of witchcraft was simply a means of bringing them to justice.

Secondly, there is the degree to which sexuality pervades the whole area of witchcraft. The detail and perversity of sexual practice seem to have been a rising factor throughout the recorded history of Satanic ritual abuse stories. With early Christians, the stories of sexuality merely extended to secret orgies; by the twelfth century we have details of buttock-kissing and homosexuality; with the witch trials, we have all of the previous accusations plus more detailed descriptions of ritualized sex with supernatural beings, bestiality and, of course, the actions of the succubi and incubi. This trend, as we shall see, continues to the present day, when the details given regarding contemporary Satanic cults are very specific, and have often been used to titillate readers. The association of immoral sexual practice with the devil and evil beings was also possibly a means by which the church was trying again to gain dominance over the lives of ordinary people and to stamp out some of the sexual licence left over from more pagan times.

The effect of the witch trials on society was enormous, and the fact that they are still widely talked about today shows their notoriety at the time. Although the trials may have finished in the seventeenth century, the stories of ritualized abuse that fed them were not to disappear so easily.

## Modern witch-hunts

The disappearance of the witch trials in the late seventeenth century put an end to a long period of sustained persecution by the church that began in the early eleventh century (the Inquisition, which concerned itself with Jews and Saracens more than witches, did not fully end until 1826). The stories of organized ritual abuse did not, however, end with the witch trials, but were merely transferred from witches and the Sabbat to other, more clearly defined, groups.

In the late eighteenth century, in the region of Limburg, there was reputedly a secret society called the 'Goats'. With this society re-emerged the same old tales of ritualized sexual abuse and violence. The Goats, whose name alone conjures up a picture of the devil, were said to 'meet at night in a secret chapel, and after the most hideous orgies, which included paying homage to Satan ... they sallied forth in bands to plunder and destroy'.[115] The Goats were disbanded by a series of trials and executions between 1772 and 1780.

A century later it was reported that the Chinese had formulated similar rumours about the goings-on in missionary Catholic hospitals in China. During a period of civil unrest in 1870, one Chinese party used the following slogan against the Catholics: 'Down with the missionaries! Kill the foreigners! They steal or buy our children and slaughter them, in order to prepare magic remedies and medicines out of their eyes, hearts, and from other portions of their dead bodies.'[116] Other records from 1888 have the Haitians holding midnight ceremonies at which 'human beings, especially kidnapped children, were killed and eaten at the mysterious and evil banquets'.[117]

## Conclusions and comparisons

From the details given in this chapter, it must by now be apparent that identical stories of child murder, rape, homosexuality, bestiality and hidden orgies have a pedigree of nearly 2,500 years, and that the Satanic ritual abuse scares of the 1980s and 1990s were just the latest manifestation of this ancient means of persecution.

In fact, it is felt by many folklorists that the inspiration for books like *Satan's Underground* and others may well have been the medieval reports of evil-doing at the witches' Sabbat. Thus the stories of the witch-hunts could have come full circle, having started a similar, if slightly updated, version of the witch trials 300 years after they died out.

This chapter has demonstrated that stories of sexual perversions and murder at quasi-religious ceremonies can be traced back for at least two millennia, that there is little difference between modern Satanic ritual abuse cases and those of ancient Rome, and that at practically every stage of western history there have been identical accusations levelled against distrusted groups of people. It would thus appear that a belief in a hidden but organized sector of society is now a part of our cultural heritage that normally continues under the surface in the form of scare stories, but periodically manifests itself as a full-blown panic or witch-hunt.

In its dormant phase, it is continued in fictional descriptions of occult practices and Satanic orgies, most of which are loosely based on the historical tales from the witch trials. Prior to *Michelle Remembers* the concepts of brood mares, baby-killing and Satanic underground networks were kept alive in the likes of *Rosemary's Baby, Dracula, The Wicker Man* and countless other occult novels and films. None of these purported to be factual and it was only when the survivor tales started to be published that a new and growing evangelical Christian church community decided to take it upon itself to root out the perceived works of Satan.

I have no doubt that we have not seen the last of the Satanic ritual abuse cases and, despite the damning language used in the official reports of the phenomenon, the media will still keeping reporting such examples as fact. Quite apart from the hundreds of innocent people who have had their lives ruined by false accusations of sexual abuse and murder, and the thousands of children who have grown up with implanted memories of having witnessed horrific crimes, a real danger here is that the bad reputation that examples of Satanic ritual abuse now attract probably means that people who are genuinely guilty of sexual abuse have escaped punishment because other fictional charges of Satanism and ritual murder against them have caused the case to be thrown out of court. The overzealousness of individuals to prove their personal beliefs could thus cause the system to work against itself.

As a final point on the subject, once one has recognized the basic characteristics of a Satanic ritual abuse scare, one can find an extraordinary number of parallels within many modern stories that have been used by one section of society to demonize another. Particularly close comparisons can be seen in the anti-Catholic movement that swept through America in the nineteenth century. Fuelling this movement were tales from several nuns who had apparently escaped from nunneries in which ritual abuse was rife.

In a book called *The Awful Disclosures of Maria Monk*, the author claimed to be nun who had escaped from a Montreal convent where she had witnessed scenes of sex between nuns and monks, baby murders and abuse in underground caverns. Several books by other escaped nuns appeared during the century, with titles like *Six Months in a Convent*, *Secrets of the Convent* and *Confessional and Convent Life Unveiled*. All of them describe scenes of sexual abuse, murder and even cannibalism, which helped to stoke the anti-Catholic panics of the time.

The texts of these books are very similar indeed to that of *Michelle Remembers*, *Dance with the Devil*, *Satan's Underground* and other recent Satanic ritual abuse survivor stories. Both the theme of the author being a 'survivor' of ritualized abuse and the details of the abuse itself are almost indistinguishable, despite the fact that over 100 years separates the publication of the last nun survivor book from the first Satanic ritual abuse one. Also, like the modern survivor books, on investigation the nun books were found to be based largely on fiction.

Another good parallel to the Satanic ritual abuse stories lies in the widely believed stories that circulate about so-called 'snuff movies', which apparently feature footage of genuine human sacrifices and sexual murders. The term 'snuff' was invented in 1970 by author Ed Saunders, who had been investigating the story of the Charles Manson personality cult in California. He had heard rumours that a group of devil-worshippers called 'The Sons of Satan' had made home movies of their human sacrifices, and these were known on the street as 'snuff films'. A few years later, director Allan Shakleton was wondering what to do with his flopped low-budget horror movie *Slaughter,* which had, for union-busting reasons, been filmed in Argentina. In the end, he had a flash of genius and, taking the idea straight from Saunders, renamed the film *Snuff*, re-edited and reissued it. This time, Shakleton marketed the film by hinting that it contained footage of a genuine murder. The posters, which showed a picture of a naked woman cut up with a pair of scissors, had the slogan: 'The film that could only be made in South America ... where Life is so CHEAP.'[118] This was certainly true, but the cheapness in question actually referred to the non-union cost of film crews and extras, not the value of human existence. *Snuff* became an instant cult hit and caused outrage across the world; it was directly responsible for the beginning of the myth that film footage of human murders and sacrifice is genuinely available. Such films, still called snuff movies, have been sought after many times but without success, and are thought to be nothing but an urban myth. However, as with the subject of Satanic ritual abuse, this does not stop people from believing in them.

War is a particularly good time to find stories of ritualized abuse and panic as opposing forces make up horrific stories about each other's actions to help rally their troops. During the first world war, there were many stories, on both the Allied and the German sides, that grossly exaggerated the actions of the enemy. The English nurse Phyllis Campbell wrote in *Back to the Front* that the Germans were carrying out the vilest atrocities on women and children. She describes: '... sitting on the floor was a naked girl of about 23. One of her suffering sisters, more fortunate than the rest in possessing an undergarment, had torn it in half and covered the front of her poor body. It was saturated with blood from her cut-off breasts. On her knees lay a little baby, dead.'[119]

Nurse Campbell also claimed to have heard stories of Germans raping, burning and crucifying nuns, of severing the hands and feet of children and of burning people alive. Her stories were widely circulated by the English forces, keen to whip up anger against the opposition. Nurse Campbell's stories have never been proved, however, and there is unquestionable proof that other claims she made, concerning the sightings of angels and phantom armies at the retreat of Mons, were lies.

On 16 September 1916, one nurse, Grace Hume, was reported in the English newspaper *The Star* to have been caught by Germans and had her breasts cut off. Before dying, she had scrawled a note to her sister and passed it on to a nurse. Several other newspapers picked up on the story, which made headline news for a few days. Nevertheless, Nurse Hume was later found alive and well and living in Huddersfield, having never even been called to the front. The letter turned out to be a forgery created by her sister, Kate, who, even after being convicted for the crime, later went on to tell tales identical to those of Phyllis Campbell. A more reliable nurse, Vera Brittain, wrote of the other nurses in her hospital that '... the ladies seemed to try to outdo one another in telling of war horrors'.[120]

In 1990, a Kuwaiti nurse who had escaped the Iraqi invasion of her country that year told of how the invading troops had stormed her hospital and ripped living babies from the incubators, leaving them to die on the floor. This story made headline news across the world and helped whip up fury against the Iraqis. It was only after the liberation of Kuwait the following year that people discovered that none of the incubators in Kuwait had been in use at the time of the invasion and that the incubators were intact.

The last incarnation of the ritual abuse story was one that I came across during the final stages of writing this book. The magazine *Private Eye* carried an article in its 'true stories' section about a Hong Kong journalist who had allegedly travelled to Shenzhen in China only to find that the people there, including doctors, regularly ate medically aborted foetuses. A Mr Cheng said of his foetal cooking: 'I washed the foetuses clean, and added ginger, orange peel, and dried mushrooms to make soup. After taking it for a while, I felt a lot better and my asthma disappeared. I used to take placenta, but it was not so tasty as foetuses.'[121] Do they really eat foetuses in Shenzhen or is this simply a manifestation of Hong Kong's distrust of the Chinese in the aftermath of the colony's return from Britain?

# 10

# THE INVASION OF THE PENIS-SNATCHERS

In the spring of 1983, rumours started to circulate around the city of Houston, Texas, that gangs of 'smurfs' were invading the local junior-high schools, killing the headmaster and then threatening the pupils. The smurfs – small blue cartoon characters with white hats and small tails – were reportedly seen carrying guns and knives, and other rumours alleged that anybody wearing blue clothing would be singled out for attack. The panic reached such a proportion that attendance at schools began to drop and those children who did arrive would refuse to go into the toilets or classrooms for fear that killer smurfs might be lurking there.

The cause of the panic is thought to have come from a Houston television report about a teenage gang called 'The Smurfs', which had been held responsible for a series of crimes in the district. Somebody, somehow, took this story and applied it to the city's schools with the cartoon characters becoming the villains. Word of mouth and the playful imaginations of children did the rest. Nobody ever reported a smurf attack or death to the police and there was not a single eyewitness account of a smurf entering a school. Some of the headmasters rumoured to have been killed by smurfs had to go to extraordinary lengths to prove to their worried pupils that they were alive. One announced to his pupils that Garfield the Cat was on his way to help with the problem.

This panic is amusing to us because we know that small blue cartoon characters could not be responsible for terrorizing or killing people. We know that they simply do not exist and so the panic, which was centred on the over-active imaginations of children, makes us laugh. Nobody was hurt and the tale is simply another one to add to the strange-but-true pages of the newspapers. There are, however, similarities between the Houston smurfs and many of the other stories we have come across in this book, including the Satanic ritual abuse scares, the Popobawa demon of Zanzibar and even the medieval witch trials. The similarities have little to do with the causes of these examples, all of which were different, but relate more to the phenomenon that they represent – technically called a 'culture-bound psychiatric syndrome', but more simply known as a 'social panic'.

## Panic!

Social panics are a remarkably common and yet little-understood curiosity that occur within the complex fabric of human society. They may start at any time in any part of the world. They may only be confined to one small village or town or may, as in the case of the Satanic ritual abuse scares, spread gradually across the globe. Their recorded history would appear to be as long as that of civilization, and it would also seem that such panics are capable of resurfacing independently in different parts of history or in different parts of the world.

The causes of panics are many and varied, and there is no common factor. Some, like the Satanists, start from rumours that build upon commonly held cultural beliefs. Others begin because a genuine experience had by individuals becomes misinterpreted or exaggerated. In this category comes the smurfs, whose origin was in a street gang, and the Popobawa of Zanzibar, where the phenomenon of sleep paralysis was misinterpreted as being a supernatural sexual attack by a demon. Whatever their cause, once the panic has entered a community, it gathers speed and can spread like wildfire.

Although few studies have been made about individual social panics (one of the few that has is discussed later), it is certain that most of them are spread initially by word of mouth, with the media only assisting in a few rare cases. Because a panic is a word-of-mouth phenomenon, its distribution is normally limited to a small region. The smurfs were not reported as having murdered any headmasters in neighbouring towns, and most Satanic ritual abuse cases centre on small towns where it is the local community, often including the law, that ends up pointing the finger and keeping the momentum of the story going.

There are hundreds of examples of social panics each year, and their content is varied. In February 1993, the Chinese town of Chongqing suffered a panic where it was believed that a 'robot zombie' was loose in the town and eating children at random. In a reflection of western horror movies, the robot was said to be repelled by garlic, consequently causing a shortage in the local markets. Other panics are more mundane, and involve people evacuating villages because they are convinced that it will be hit by an asteroid or that certain types of food are poisoned. Keeping to the theme of this book, there can be no finer example of a widespread and deep-rooted panic than that concerning the 'disappearing genitals', which regularly sweeps through parts of the globe.

## The African penis-snatchers

In modern times, the most quoted and famous examples of penis-snatching panics are to be found in the west African coastal countries that stretch between Cameroon and the Ivory Coast. In this part of the world, there have been a number of similar panics that, because of their sexual content and bizarre nature, have attracted the attention of the world's press.

One of the first and greatest of the penis-snatching panics began in Nigeria in 1990. The panic started with rumours that there were strangers from distant tribes roaming the town stealing male members for use as part of their ritual magic. It was believed that the members could be stolen by the magicians simply touching an exposed part of the victim's body, after which the penis would shrink and disappear, leaving the genital region smooth and round like that of a mannequin. Absolute panic ensued and great suspicion and fear was shown towards strangers or those wishing to shake hands or who inadvertently brushed up against others. Soon rumours also began in which it was said that the nipples and labia of women could be stolen in the same supernatural manner.

These rumours were very widely believed and, inevitably, had some serious consequences. In the southern city of Enugu, a riot broke out after a man getting off a bus screamed out that he had had his manhood magically stolen. The person in front of him was dragged off the bus by a mob and beaten. In the ensuing chaos, the police accidentally shot the bus driver dead and injured a woman passenger.

The Nigerian penis-snatching panic calmed down after a couple of months, but belief in the reality of the genital-stealing magicians has never died down in the region as a whole, and has in fact spread more widely since then, often with tragic consequences. In 1996, another wave of panics started again in Nigeria and also in other countries along the west African coast. In a twist to the original story, in those countries outside Nigeria it was often said that Nigerian magicians were the ones going out and collecting penises; this made life very difficult for Nigerian ex-patriots living in the countries concerned.

In August 1996, a mob in Cameroon hanged three men for the crime of magically stealing penises. Several other men were very badly beaten, and instances of penis-snatching were reported from towns up and down the Cameroon coast. One 18-year-old victim is reported as saying that when he shook hands with a Nigerian friend of his '... he felt an electric-like current run through him, and ... that his manhood had retreated into his stomach'.[122] Doctors from the panic-affected regions have said that all the missing genitals were in fact 'unharmed and normal'.

Yet again, in March 1997, the rumours resurfaced in the coastal region of the Ivory Coast and Ghana, where members of a widespread ethnic tribe, the Hausa, were said to be magically removing penises and breasts and then demanding ransom money for them. The consequences of this panic were the most serious yet. In the Ghanaian town of Aboisso, a 3,000-strong mob besieged the council office demanding the blood of any Hausas living locally. In the Ivory Coast capital, Abidjan, a Hausa man from Niger was burnt to death by a mob; this sparked a riot in which thousands of people swept through the city centre, looting shops and ransacking the houses of ex-patriots. Extra police were called in and at least one rioter was shot dead. Many Hausa tribes people left the country fearing for their lives. In an attempt to calm the situation, the Ivory Coast government issued a statement denying the penis-snatching rumours and asking people to remain calm. 'There are legitimate means of punishing evil-doers,' the Interior Minister said.

Although west Africa is the unquestioned centre of these rumours, other more minor penis-snatching panics have been reported from Uganda, Kenya and South Africa. None of these have, however, inspired the mob mentality seen in Nigeria, Cameroon, Ghana and the Ivory Coast.

The penis-snatching panics of west Africa have been of special interest to me as I know that part of the world extremely well and have, at one time or another, visited all the regions and towns named in the various reports of panics. One thing that initially struck me as being unusual about the panics was their geographical distribution. If one plots out their occurrence on a map, almost all of the penis-snatching panics are restricted to the coastal regions despite the fact that each of the countries named stretches inland for several hundred kilometres. The next unusual aspect was why only a handful of countries should be affected and not whole swathes of west and central Africa, where there are over 20 different countries to choose from. Nigeria alone borders seven countries, so why should some populations be affected and others not?

The apparent ability of social panics to restrict themselves to certain regions or districts is one of the key mysteries associated with them. After considering the evidence, it looks as if the answer has to do with a mixture of population geography, economics and the location of a tarmac road. All the African countries affected by the panics have most of their urbanized populations living in cities and towns along the coast. Because of their aridity and the poor infrastructure, the inland regions are more sparsely populated, with a rural agricultural economy. It would therefore make sense that the panics would occur in the larger coastal towns, as this is where the densest populations are. Furthermore, the chief towns affected by the panics all lie along the same international road, which runs continuously from Abidjan in the Ivory Coast to Yaoundé in Cameroon. This road seems to have played an important role in the panics; all the panic-stricken towns are located on this road, and as soon as the road becomes impassable, to the west of Cameroon and the east of Ivory Coast, the panics are no longer reported.

This coastal road is the economic lifeline of the west African region, allowing easy contact and trade between the countries that it runs through. It therefore carries a large number of trucks, vans and lorries, and it is here that the solution to the nature and spread of the penis-snatching panics could lie. Nigeria, because of its large size and oil reserves, is the economic giant of west Africa and exports many of its goods (and workforce) along the coastal road to neighbouring states. The panics started in Nigeria and were widely believed there. It seems probable to me that the panics were then exported by Nigerians travelling along the coastal road from town to town. Although the stories were probably widely believed in these other countries, it would need an incident, like the man on the bus in Enugu, to spark off a riot and draw the issue to the attention of the world at large. Further evidence of the Nigerian connection comes from the belief that it was Nigerian magicians who were doing the snatching and not simply 'strangers' as in the original Nigerian panic.

If the west African penis-snatching panics were indeed spread in this manner, it gives us some evidence that they were perpetuated chiefly by word of mouth. It also suggests that a specific incident is needed to turn what is simply a commonly held belief into a fully fledged panic. There must be hundreds of towns in the west African coastal region where belief in the penis-snatching magicians is strong, but, without an individual or an incident to rally against, that belief would simply remain a local topic of discussion.

The same has been true in the American Satanic ritual abuse scares, where it takes a single accusation against an individual to ignite local beliefs in Satanism and to cause townsfolk to organize themselves into the modern equivalent of a lynch mob.

### Koro – the Asian penis-snatching panics

Although the African penis-snatching episodes may give us an idea of how the phenomenon of panics occurs, they do little to explain what is actually happening to make people believe that their penises, or in some cases breasts, nipples, clitorises or labia, have been stolen. These recent African cases have not been studied in depth, and information on them is hard to come by. There is, however, an equivalent to the penis-snatching panics in another part of the world, and this has not only been studied in some detail but also entered the textbooks as a bona fide psychiatric condition.

In October 1967, on the small southeast Asian island of Singapore, there was a sudden and massive outbreak of the penis-snatching panic. Within a few days, 446 men and 23 women had been admitted to hospital, 97 in one day alone, believing that their penises or, in the case of women, their breasts or labia, had retracted into their bodies and that they were consequently going to die. It took several days of government propaganda to calm the public and to cause a cessation in hospital admissions. Because the panic had been so serious and so unusual, there was a full investigation into it.

The panic, it was found, had its origins in local concerns about the use of female hormones (specifically oestrogen) in commercially farmed chickens. It was believed that some men were growing breasts as a result of eating excessive amounts of chicken meat, particularly the neck, where the oestrogen injections are given. Shortly after this a newspaper reported that a number of men had had their penises retract into their body after eating pork from pigs that had been vaccinated against swine fever. It was said that a number of pigs had themselves died of penis retraction. It was then that the panic erupted. In the days that followed, there were stories of mothers tugging furiously at their daughter's labia to stop their vulvas from retracting, and of men clamping their genitals to trees, tying weights to them or turning up at hospital with friends or relatives pulling at their penises.

In the analysis that followed, it was discovered that 97.5 per cent of those who had been reported as suffering from genital retraction had in fact been Chinese, and not Singaporean, in origin. This statistic suggested to the report's authors that belief in penis-retraction was not native to that area but may have been imported from China. This did indeed turn out to be the case.

In China, this condition is known as *shook yang* (or *suk yeong* or *sou yang*), but in western medical science both the belief in penis retraction and the panics that it sometimes causes are known under the Malaysian name of 'koro'. We will use this latter term here to fit in with convention. The term koro, incidentally, is believed to have derived from the Malaysian word for a tortoise, the implication being that there is a similarity between the way a tortoise retracts the head into its shell and the way the penis disappears into the abdomen.

In China in particular, the belief in koro would seem to be a very ancient one, and it is mentioned in a number of old texts. For example, in his collection of medical remedies of 1834, the Chinese doctor Pao Sian-Ow wrote: '... during intercourse, the man may be seized suddenly with acute abdominal pain. The limbs become cold and the complexion dusky, the penis retracts into the abdomen. If treatment is not instituted at once and effective, the case will die. The disease is due to the invasion of cold vapours and the treatment is to employ the "heaty" drugs.'[123]

A remedy offered by Sian-Ow is to burn some women's underwear to ashes and to rub them over the affected region. In modern cases of koro, the victim, rather than rubbing burnt underwear on himself, will simply try to attach objects to his penis to prevent its retraction. During the 1967 Singapore panic, a commonly used device was a *lie teng hok*, a small clamp used in jewellery making, but chopsticks, string or more conventional clamps were also used. As was indicated in the writings of Sian-Ow, the Chinese belief is that koro is caused by the body temperature being critically lowered by exposure to wind or rain or by the eating of 'raw or cold food'.

The author Anthony Burgess described seeing a koro victim in his autobiography *Little Wilson and Big God*: 'It could end in hysteria and death. I actually saw a Chinese so afflicted in Kuala Lumpur. He stole a superfine jeweller's knife and rammed it in [his penis], screaming on the sunlit street.'

Although koro normally occurs in single cases within China, there have been epidemics reported, at least one of which, in Guangdong, rivalled the events in Singapore. Aside from China, which is the undoubted Asian centre of koro, other epidemics have been reported from Hong Kong, Malaysia, Thailand and, most surprisingly, India. Other individual cases have been reported from a huge range of countries, including Europe and America. Almost all cases seem to involve Chinese subjects; a number of isolated cases in 'westerners' have been diagnosed, but these have all been linked with depression, schizophrenia or even brain tumours.

The Asian outbreaks of koro have been examined in some detail by various psychiatrists. The result of this has been to make koro an officially recognized psychiatric condition within the so-called 'culture-bound psychiatric syndromes', which essentially means that the condition is only to be found in those areas of the world where there is a cultural belief in it. The officially recognized symptoms of a koro attack are defined as the victim having great fear, a delusion that their genitals are shrinking or retracting into their body, palpitations, breathlessness, blurred vision and, occasionally, collapse and body pain. In the 1967 Singapore study it was found that the majority of people who had experienced a koro attack were suffering from paranoid psychosis, depression or feelings of sexual anxiety or inadequacy. This, and the fact that a penis has never once been observed to have disappeared into the body, suggest that koro is a mental delusion and not a physical reality.

In the Singapore panic, 74 per cent of koro cases were cured by using placebo methods (such as attaching clamps or rubbing the body), again showing the mental nature of the problem. In other Asian epidemics, similar placebo methods have been used, including, in a 1993 koro outbreak in Hong Kong, the advice of Dr Cheng Sheung-tak, who at a medical conference said: 'I am a man of science and I tell you that koro is caused by the impish fox spirit stealing the patient's vital energy, and can only be cured by Dr Cheng's ointment, made from stag antlers, deer tail, and deer and seal penis ... it is your solemn duty to recommend it to every family in China.'[124]

The diagnosis of sexual anxiety and inadequacy would certainly fit in well with the Chinese cultural tradition relating to sexual energy, which, it is believed, has to be preserved whenever possible. In particular, the body's manufacture of sperm is thought to require great amounts of physical and spiritual energy and wasting it through reckless sex, masturbation or wet dreams is considered a serious threat to the health of the individual (this parallels some of the traditions attached to the sexual demons described in Chapters 2 and 3). It has therefore been proposed, at least in the case of Chinese koro, that:

> ... in a susceptible individual, hearsay information about koro, along with pre-existing sexual fears and subjective sensations in the genitalia associated with such phenomena as sexual intercourse, urination, defecation, or trauma, leads to the vicious circle of the delusion of genital shrinkage, attendant panic, and enhanced fears of a delusory nature, with even greater panic and crude attempts to prevent the disappearance of the penis.[125]

Thus, for the condition of koro to occur, it requires an underlying cultural belief in the possibility that the penis can, magically or physically, disappear from the body, combined with feelings of sexual inadequacy in an individual. A proper panic, on the scale of the penis-snatching episodes in Nigeria or Singapore, requires the added ingredient of a widely spread and believed rumour as a trigger. In Singapore it was the infected pork, in Nigeria the presence of magicians, and in Hong Kong the belief in an 'impish fox spirit'.

The Asian koro panics also help to reinforce some of the conclusions from the west African panics, and in particular the notion that such panics can be exported. Koro is a Chinese cultural belief and yet it seems to have been exported by Chinese expatriots to places as far afield as India, Malaysia, Thailand and Singapore. In fact, most of the Asian countries that have sizeable Chinese expatriot communities have had koro epidemics. This ability for panics of all sorts, and not just penis-snatching ones, to spread and in many cases remain dormant for years in between outbreaks, is one of the most remarkable qualities of the phenomenon.

It may help to explain the appearance of penis-snatching panics in west Africa. Between 1983 and 1993, the penis-snatching or koro panics underwent a very active phase in which they began spreading further afield from their traditional Chinese epicentre. In 1983, there was a panic in west Bengal, India; in 1989 and 1990, there were panics in Malaysia, Thailand, Hong Kong and Singapore, as well as in China itself. The Nigerian panics began in 1990, right in the middle of this active phase of Asian koro panics. Nigeria was the first African country to suffer from the panics and, although the country is not noted for its resident Chinese immigrant population, it is nonetheless the west African country with the greatest number of ties to the outside world and also has cultural beliefs in magic that would adapt very well to stories of disappearing penises.

Tales of penis-snatching from other parts of the world would have landed on fertile ground in Nigeria, and the fact that they initially arose in Lagos, the largest west African city with the best international connections, might suggest a foreign origin for the story. The fact that the panics spread so easily across coastal west Africa seems to indicate that the region is indeed culturally receptive to the idea of penis-snatching.

Making specific comparisons between the Asian and African penis-snatching panics is very difficult, owing to the lack of any published research on the African epidemics. Clues that it might be the same psychiatric condition of koro come from a rare witness statement in which a Cameroon victim described his penis-snatching experience as a feeling that his manhood was retreating into his stomach. This is one of the recognized symptoms of psychiatric diagnosed koro but, without fuller details, a definite connection is difficult to make; the timing and details, however, make it possible that the African panics are extensions of the Asian ones.

We have so far not discussed penis-snatching panics from Europe, America or any of the other western countries. There have been some slightly smug comments about this, the suggestion being that westerners are not as superstitious as either Asians or Africans and that such tales could never get a hold in a civilized society. Nevertheless, the reason that the penis-snatching panics have never erupted in western countries is because the society there is not culturally disposed to this kind of basic sexual magical belief. We prefer our sexual rumours to be in the form of ritualized Satanic ceremonies, which much better fits our Christian culture and the recent general awareness of child abuse. Just because there are no modern penis-snatching panics, however, does not mean that they have never occurred at all in the west.

There were times when western culture was more predisposed towards believing penis-snatching rumours, when superstition pervaded everyday life and belief in the supernatural was the norm. This was during the Middle Ages, when the witch trials which have been discussed in Chapter 6 took place. Given many of the other claims made at the witch trials, such as those regarding succubi, incubi and the goings-on at the Sabbat, it would perhaps not be surprising if we did find evidence of penis-snatching.

Tales of penis-snatching are, however, actually few and far between in the witch trials, and there are certainly no events that could be described as a panic. Belief in the reality of the phenomenon was certainly strong, and it warrants two sections in the witch-hunters' bible, the notorious *Malleus Maleficarum,* under the heading 'How, as it were, they [witches] Deprive Man of his Virile Member'. The *Malleus* says on the matter: 'There is no doubt that certain witches can do marvellous things with regard to male organs, for this agrees with what has been seen and heard by many, and with the general account of what has been known concerning that member through the senses of sight and sound.'[126]

The writers of the *Malleus* preferred to think that witches did not actually steal the penis but hypnotized the victim into thinking that his penis had disappeared, something that accords well with the psychiatric view of koro. Despite the length of time devoted to the matter in the witch-hunters' bible, there are actually very few examples of penis-snatching being mentioned in the transcripts of the witch trials, and the phenomenon appears to be practically non-existent in the literature. Thus, like the African cases, it is difficult to know whether penis-snatching in the Middle Ages was a reflection of the psychiatric diagnosis of koro or just a myth based on the common fear of infertility.

One of the cases that we do have, however, bears a passing resemblance to a modern and rare example from Uganda, perhaps suggesting that the same psychological thinking was at work. In the fifteenth-century story, a boy from the German town of Ratison had an affair with a girl who turned out to be a witch. When he tried to end the affair he found that he had '... lost his member ... so that he could see or touch nothing but his smooth body'.[127] On the advice of another woman, he trapped the witch and strangled her until she '... touched him between his thighs [and] his member had been restored'.[128] In the Uganda story, on 29 April 1994, a Mr Dembere of Iki-Iki, Uganda, upset a magician at a local market and suddenly found himself without any genitals. On the advice of friends he tracked the magician down to a nearby town and, after shaking his hand, found his penis and testicles restored.

The strangest penis-snatching story from the Middle Ages has to be that in the sceptical commentary of Reginald Scot's *The Discoverie of Witchcraft.* He tells the tale of a man who, after having had an extramarital affair, magically lost his penis. Distressed, he visited the local witch, who freely admitted that she kept, in a tree, a large basket full of male members that her imps had taken from sinners. She '... bade him climb up and take it [his member] back. And being in the top of the tree, he took out [of the basket] a mighty big one, asking her if he might not have the same. Nay, quoth she, that is our parish priest's tool, but take any other which thou wilt.'[129] Reginald Scott was not noted for his belief in either the supernatural or the witch trials and one suspects that his tongue was firmly in his cheek when he wrote down that tale!

At the end of our examination of penis-snatching panics, we have learned much about the manner and means by which such panics can be caused and spread, a lot of which is also applicable to other famous panics. The penis-snatching scares are particularly fascinating because of their history and wide geography and, of course, because of their sexual and supernatural content.

## Mass hysteria

This chapter has so far dealt with the anatomy of the social panic, a curious phenomenon that can continue in many forms for years or even decades. Social panics are often described in the press as being episodes of 'mass hysteria' on a national or even international level. In fact, many modern phenomena, such as the wave of grief following the death of Diana, Princess of Wales, in 1997, are described as being the product of mass hysteria. However, neither the social panic nor the majority of other cases to which the term mass hysteria is applied are in fact examples of this rather unusual psychological phenomenon.

Like the modern distortion of the word nightmare (see Chapter 1), mass hysteria has become a catch-all term used to describe any episode where people apparently act collectively. Hysteria, and particularly mass hysteria, do have specific meanings – they also have a connection with both the paranormal and sexuality. The term hysteria has itself a sexual origin, deriving from the Greek for the uterus (*hystera*), which reflects the ancient belief that the condition is caused by the uterus becoming dislodged from its normal position in the abdomen and stuck in the throat. As men do not have a uterus, it was for centuries believed that only women could become hysterical. When, at a meeting in 1886, Freud suggested that men could also be hysterical, one of the audience cried out: 'But my dear sir, how can you talk such nonsense? Hysteria means the uterus. So how can men be hysterical?'[130]

Hysteria does not, of course, have anything to do with the uterus and is experienced by both sexes. It can take several forms, but the ones that chiefly interest us here are hysteria as a personality disorder and as a dissociation phenomenon.

## Personality hysteria

The sort of hysteria that becomes a personality disorder is the most commonly encountered form of the condition, and is a kind of sensory overload. The screaming hordes of women who followed the Beatles around the world in the 1960s are an example of this. Their screaming, crying and involuntary arm movements are all a form of personality hysteria in which the person is no longer in command of their senses and momentarily loses control. Such a sensory overload normally occurs during times of heightened emotion, and hence hysteria is associated with moments of extreme happiness (such as seeing the Beatles), sadness, fear, stress and so on. In extreme cases, the victim can fall to the ground, twitching involuntarily, or can appear to be possessed, shouting out random words in apparently different voices.

These symptoms are commonly seen at evangelical Christian meetings where the church leader may whip up the crowd to such a degree that people fall to the floor twitching and apparently speaking in tongues (which is known by psychologists as glossolalia). A modern form of hysterical panic, known as the Toronto Blessing, swept through the world's churches in the early 1990s when people would fall to the ground twitching during the height of a service. Most of us have at one time or another seen people who have become hysterical. Few of us will, however, have witnessed the much rarer example of mass hysteria.

Mass hysteria is a little-understood psychological process which, in its most basic form, is where an entire crowd of people suddenly and simultaneously suffer from hysterical symptoms. Mass hysteria will generally only affect a limited and very local group of people for a short period of time. The crowds of girls who were screaming at the Beatles are an explicable example of mass hysteria. Such hysteria was caused by the girls' desire to see the Beatles and, once one person starts screaming, the rest follow. As soon as the Beatles disappeared from view, the hysteria stopped.

More difficult to explain is the case of the English village show at Kirkby-in-Ashfield in 1980, where, shortly after lunch, children began to fall to the ground, apparently completely unable to use their legs. Their symptoms included twitching arms and legs, headaches, difficulty with breathing and miscellaneous pains. By the end of the day, nearly 300 children had collapsed and been admitted to hospital. Perplexingly, nothing could be found medically wrong with them and, after a few hours, all were sent home. Other similar examples have been reported from around the world, including, most recently, an example from Cairo in 1993 where over 1,300 schoolgirls suffered identical symptoms to those of the Kirkby-in-Ashfield village show. In the absence of any medical evidence of illness or intoxication, and because the symptoms exactly match those of a hysterical reaction, such episodes are said to be examples of mass hysteria, although the causes remain shrouded in mystery. It is easy to see how such episodes of mass hysteria could in the past be viewed as, at the very least, evidence of supernatural forces at work. In fact, before the advent of psychology in the late nineteenth century, they were more commonly seen as examples of demonic or angelic possession, and still are in some churches. There has been a sexual element to a number of episodes of mass hysteria, and to two in particular.

The following example is known as affectionately as the 'Devils of Loudon' after the book of the same name by Aldous Huxley; the case was immortalized in Ken Russell's controversial film *The Devils*. The events surround Father Urbain Grandier, who, in the 1630s, was a Catholic canon in the French town of Loudon. Descriptions of Grandier have him as a handsome and intelligent man who was popular within the district but who, alas, may also have deflowered a few of the local girls. He was also notably impudent towards the church authorities, something that had made him a great number of enemies in the higher ranks of French Catholicism. His card was marked and there were a great number of people waiting for the right moment to bring him down. That moment arrived in 1633. During that year at the Convent of the Ursulines, which was located within the walls of Loudon, there was an outbreak of mass hysteria.

Without warning, five of the nuns began to show what, to the church, was an example of demonic possession. They twitched and writhed on the ground, shouting blasphemies, inflicting injuries on themselves, removing their clothes and sexually arousing themselves. Before long every nun in the convent was doing the same, with attempts at exorcism only making matters worse. The Mother Superior at the Convent, Jeanne de Belfiel, was an ill-educated dwarf who seems to have led the other nuns in their hysteria. She is portrayed as having been fixated or obsessed with Grandier, and began to accuse him of being the devil and of placing demons in the nuns.

She, and 12 other nuns, also directly accused Grandier of sexually molesting them in the form of a man and in several other more supernatural guises. This was the opportunity that the church had been looking for, and Grandier was arrested on suspicion of witchcraft and sorcery, and of sexually abusing the nuns.

The Mother Superior described several places on Grandier's body where so-called 'witch marks' could be found. These were traditionally said to be places were no pain could be felt, but as the inquisitors stuck a long needle through various parts of his body, including his testicles, they discovered that Grandier could most certainly feel pain in all parts of his body. His refusal to confess his diabolic crimes led to much greater punishments than this, including the rack, and having his legs gradually and systematically crushed. Still he would not confess and, in August 1634, he was tied to a chair and burnt to death. Rumour at the time had it that at the moment he died a massive drone fly was seen buzzing around his head. As the literal translation of the word Beelzebub is 'Lord of the Flies', this was used to confirm that Grandier was indeed the devil incarnate.

After Grandier's death, the screaming and twitching nuns became far worse, writhing naked in the nunnery and shouting blasphemies at the now considerable crowds of people gathered outside. Father Jean-Joseph Surin was charged with exorcizing the nuns, something that took many months to achieve.

Another witness to the Devils of Loudon was John Maitland who, until his arrival in the town, was a firm believer in witchcraft and possession. When he saw the nuns at work he changed his views instantly and later wrote: 'When I had seen exorcizing enough of three or four of [the nuns] in the chapel, and could hear nothing but wenches singing bawdy songs in French, I began to suspect a *fourbé* [i.e. deceit].'[131] The nuns of Loudon had all the classic symptoms of having been affected by mass hysteria, with the twitching, screaming and obscenities comparable to modern studied cases. The next case is just as striking.

In 1727, rumours spread through Paris about strange and miraculous goings-on in the churchyard of St Médard. It was said that there were writhing women, known as *les convulsionnaires*, in residence who could perform healing miracles and were immune from pain and punishment. Much of what we know of the case comes from an investigation into the affair undertaken by Magistrate Louis-Basile Carré de Montgeron, who, although initially sceptical, was later exiled for promoting his belief in *les convulsionnaires*. His collected testimonies describe St Médard churchyard as being full of writhing women who were apparently arching and twisting themselves into impossible shapes – as with the writhing Loudon nuns, this is a classic sign of hysteria. The real attraction, though, was the apparent inability of *les convulsionnaires* to react to physical and sexual abuse on their bodies. De Montgeron testified that these women could have their breasts trapped between two opposing shovels without harm, that they could eat faeces and drink urine without effect, and that they could also be skewered through the abdomen with poles and beaten on the breasts, stomach and genitals with lump-hammers, again without any apparent harm. Faced with growing crowds and escalating claims of supernatural feats, the French king was forced to shut St Médard in 1732.

The truth of *les convulsionnaires* is hard to fathom and will never be fully understood. It is undoubtedly a case of mass hysteria – the writhing and screams of the women testify to that – but it is hard to believe that the feats described were real. The sexual element in many of the tales makes the affair sound more like a sadistic sexual fantasy and it is often promoted as such in historical texts.

The Loudon nuns and *les convulsionnaires* illustrate many of the facts that we know about mass hysteria. Statistically, examples of mass hysteria are much more likely to occur to groups of women than to groups of men or even mixed groups. Younger women are also more likely to be affected than older ones. Mass hysteria is more likely to occur in a group of people who are connected by a common belief or interest. This is why modern mass hysteria is so commonly seen in concerts and churches, where people have gathered for a purpose. In the case of Loudon the convent was the focus and it was later revealed that *les convulsionnaires* mostly belonged to a minor (and persecuted) Christian sect known as the Jansenists. Inevitably, when groups of women start writhing on the floor and removing items of clothing, a sexual element will result in the story.

## Dissociation hysteria

The second form of hysteria of interest is the controversial topic of multiple personality disorder (some times called dissociative identity disorder), one of the so-called dissociative hysterias. Dissociation is where there apparently appear to be separate mental processes working within the same human brain. The unconscious mind is a dissociative personality that, if Freud is to be believed, works at the same time as our conscious mind but at a hidden level. Other examples of dissociation have profound implications for many areas of the paranormal, especially spiritualism, where many different personalities can seem to inhabit the body of a single medium.

Patients with multiple personality disorder have, as the name suggests, two or more personalities sharing the same body. Some people claim to have hundreds of personalities, which can be male or female, and are often completely unaware of the other personalities in the body. It is theorized that the presence of so many personalities within one body is caused by the patient undergoing a traumatic experience that is severe enough to cause the original personality to fragment into pieces so that the distress of the event remains hidden. Many modern cases are diagnosed, and cured, using hypnosis to recover the original hidden memory, which often relates to childhood sexual abuse.

The disorder itself has a somewhat mixed reputation for, although it has been accepted by the American psychiatric community as genuine, most European psychologists do not believe in its existence. The evidence against it includes the fact that, when the condition was first popularized in 1898, patients only had two or three personalities, but nowadays it is common for them to have tens of personalities. Also, cases only tend to be diagnosed by those psychiatrists who believe in it, and the majority of cases are still to be found in America. The battle between the pro- and anti-multiple personality disorder camps still rages in the pages of various psychiatric journals. There are marked similarities between this disorder and the diagnosis of Satanic ritual abuse survivors discussed in Chapter 8.

One of the major problems with multiple personality disorder is the commonly held belief that its cause within an individual must be due to some form of traumatic experience in the past, usually in childhood. This has led to a problem in both its diagnosis and in the people doing the diagnosing.

Multiple personality disorder is one of those conditions where, as with the Satanic ritual abuse 'survivors', patients often decide for themselves that they are suffering from it. Having made this self-diagnosis, they then seek the assistance of a sympathetic psychiatrist to help confirm their belief. Consequently, those psychiatrists who believe in the disorder do not often have to look for patients to treat or study since, frequently, the patients will find them.

Because of the belief by both the patient and the psychiatrist that a hidden childhood trauma is usually the underlying cause of the disorder, the first thing that a professional will do when confronted with a case of multiple personality disorder is to try to make the patient remember the details of this trauma. The common way of doing this is via hypnosis, which is the accepted tool of diagnosis in cases of multiple personality disorder.

The most commonly diagnosed cause of multiple personality disorder is sexual abuse during childhood, something that would most certainly be traumatic and liable to affect an individual for life. As with the Satanic survivors, however, the majority of childhood memories recovered by psychiatrists conform to a similar pattern and rarely have any physical evidence to back them up. In fact, many recently diagnosed multiple personality disorder victims are claiming to have been abused by Satanists, providing a strong link between the discredited Satanic ritual abuse scares and the largely more accepted multiple personality disorder. Because of this, in recent years the use of hypnosis in cases of multiple personality disorder has fallen under suspicion, and it is suspected that many cases may now in fact be examples of false memory syndrome.

In Chapter 8, we saw how the use of hypnosis could cause a psychiatrist to create false memories within their patient. Cases of multiple personality disorder actually differ very little from those of Satanic ritual abuse. Often, both the patient and the psychologist believe that hidden memories of abuse are the cause of the problem and so indiscreet questioning under hypnosis can easily produce stories of sexual abuse that did not actually occur. The same problem exists with cases of alien abduction and past-life regression, where the majority of diagnoses are still made through hypnosis by psychiatrists who firmly believe in the existence of the disorders they are trying to find. (see Chapter 12).

The uncovering of such examples of sexual abuse in multiple personality disorder cases has caused a huge amount of trauma, because those who have been accused of being the abusers have often suffered social exclusion, violence and even legal proceedings. As with the cases of Satanic ritual abuse, the number of successful prosecutions for sexual abuse as diagnosed under hypnosis runs to only a handful. In fact, in a strange twist of fate, examples of multiple personality disorder have increasingly been linked with Satanic ritual abuse, with some psychiatrists and social workers now believing that a person exhibiting multiple personality disorder is liable to have been a ritual abuse survivor.

The use of hypnosis to recover 'lost' memories has been increasingly criticized in the USA, and there is now a general awareness that many of these memories are nothing more than examples of false memory syndrome. In fact, the conclusions from a number of major studies into people who were unquestionably sexually abused during their childhood are that '... victims neither repressed the traumatic events, forgot about them, nor developed multiple personality disorder'.[132]

One wide-ranging investigation into hundreds of multiple personality disorder cases spread over its 110-year history similarly concluded: 'No case has been found here in which multiple personality disorder, as now conceived, is proven to emerge through unconscious processes without any shaping or preparation by external factors ... it is likely that multiple personality disorder never occurs as a spontaneous persistent natural event in adults.'[133] In other words, the disorder is one of the psychiatric fraternity's own making.

Whether this is true or not is a complex issue. The recovered memories may well be false, but there are unquestionably people out there who exhibit all the signs of having two or more personalities inside them and so, to some degree, whether their condition is of their own or their psychiatrist's making, it nonetheless exists. In this respect, it can be said that multiple personality disorder is a reality. It has certainly been accepted by the courts as a genuine disorder, as the following strange case illustrates.

In 1990, Mark Peterson, a 29-year-old Wisconsin man, was found guilty of raping a waitress known as Sarah. In court, it emerged that Sarah was a multiple personality disorder sufferer who had 18 separate personalities living in her body. Peterson had met Sarah for a date and had got on well with her. On their next date, the couple had gone to a restaurant and afterwards had sex in Peterson's car. A problem had later arisen when Sarah claimed that the personality that had been in charge of her body that night was a 'fun-loving 20-year-old' called Jennifer and that, when her 17 other personalities had found out that Jennifer had agreed to have sex with Peterson, they were outraged. Sarah believed that Peterson had taken advantage of her multiple personality disorder and accused him of rape. The court case descended into farce, as each of Sarah's different personalities had to be sworn in separately as a witness. Nonetheless, Peterson was found guilty and sentenced to a jail term. This was later overturned on appeal.

An alarming development has been the use of multiple personality disorder as an excuse by criminals to explain away their crimes. Mark Bianchi, the so-called 'Hillside Strangler', had raped and murdered ten women in the Los Angeles area before being caught. During his mental assessment he managed to convince one eminent psychiatrist that he was suffering from multiple personality disorder, and that it was another personality called Steve who had committed the murders without his everyday personality knowing anything about it. Other psychiatrists disagreed, and it later turned out that not only was Bianchi faking his multiple personality disorder but also he had for years had an interest in amateur psychology, which is where he got the idea from.

A similar defence was used in 1997 by lawyers defending 'vampire cult' members in Florida who had brutally murdered a couple. The defendants there all claimed to have multiple personality disorder and that their case was 'almost like' that of the famous 1970s book and subsequent television drama *Sybil*, which started the current wave of interest in multiple personality disorder.

As can be seen, multiple personality disorder, and in particular its link with sexual abuse, has caused almost as many problems as the Satanic ritual abuse scares, and there are indeed many similarities between the two. Multiple personality disorder is still virtually unheard of outside the USA, and the tight geographical distribution (which is also a feature of social panics) of this and other psychiatric disorders has been blamed on America's continuing love affair with every manner of psychological disturbance.

In the latest manual of mental disorders released by the American Psychiatric Association, clumsiness, coffee-drinking, poor handwriting, playing video games, jetlag and snobbery are all considered to be mental disorders. Such entries are not, however, fixed in stone, and it seems that the psychiatric fraternity is allowed to change its mind about what is and what is not a mental disorder. In the 1950s version of the manual of mental disorders, there is an entry which suggests that homosexuality is a mental disorder. In the modern version this has been replaced by a note saying that those who believe that homosexuality is a mental disorder are themselves deluded. Indeed, because of the controversy it has created, multiple personality disorder recently had its official title changed to 'dissociative identity disorder' in the hope that this would draw away some of the bad press attached to it. Perhaps, as the magazine *Harper's* has suggested, 'human life is a form of mental illness'.

# Part four

## EXTRATERRESTRIAL SEX

# 11

## AMOROUS ALIENS

Whereas many of the phenomena discussed in this book so far have roots that go back several centuries or more, reports of human sexual liaisons with beings from outer space is quite definitely a late-twentieth-century phenomenon. Although belief in extraterrestrial life forms stretches back to the early days of astronomy in the seventeenth century, the possibility that other life forms could be visiting Earth and making contact with the human race is barely more than 100 years old. The strange tales of sexually active extraterrestrials come much later than this, and are inextricably linked with the post-war rise of the UFO (unidentified flying object).

The sightings of UFOs and their occupants form one of the strongest and most enduring fascinations within the paranormal, the sexual element of which has grown steadily more important, and bizarre, over the years. In fact, the sexual motives of the extraterrestrial has changed somewhat and is broadly divisible into two main themes. In the early days of ufology, the aliens were simply after casual sex for pleasure or procreational purposes, but more recently there has been a far more sinister aspect to their sexual interest in humans. In this chapter, we shall hear of the aliens' more amorous intentions, but in order to understand both this and the more sinister contents of Chapter 12, it is necessary to know something of the UFO phenomenon from which both these trends have developed.

## The UFO phenomenon

Most textbooks date the start of the UFO phenomenon to Tuesday 24 June 1947, when light-aircraft pilot Kenneth Arnold saw nine crescent-shaped objects moving at speed through some mountains in Washington State, USA. A reporter interviewing Arnold soon afterwards coined the term 'flying saucer' to describe the strange objects, and the sighting generated a worldwide wave of publicity. Before long, hundreds of people came forward with their own stories of flying saucers. Although Arnold had assumed that what he was seeing was some kind of 'secret military aircraft', the press and the public quickly decided that the flying saucers were in fact piloted by visitors from another world – and so the UFO craze began. Although 1947 most certainly marks the beginning of the modern UFO era, the actual belief in life on other planets, and even in extraterrestrial craft, has a much older pedigree.

Since the discovery of the solar system in the sixteenth century, it has been a natural assumption that the other planets in it are inhabited. In common with religious convictions of the day, it was frequently written that all the known planets, from Mercury to Saturn, had thriving populations of Christian humans who had, as on Earth, been placed there by God. This view changed very little until the nineteenth century, when telescopes allowed us to see that many of the planets were actually very different from Earth. Belief in life on the other planets did, however, still persist and was particularly focused on Mars and Venus. In fact, until the early part of the twentieth century, many astronomers believed that they could see a network of canals on Mars that had been built by a dying civilization. The 'canals of Mars' later turned out to be an optical illusion caused by the poor optical quality of telescopes. There was actually still a strong popular belief in life on other planets in the solar system until the 1960s, when the first interplanetary probes actually visited some of our neighbours and found them all to be too hot, too cold, too dry or too gaseous to support life. Even now, there is still a strong movement advocating the existence of ancient relics on the Martian surface.

Although the belief in extraterrestrial life goes back to at least the sixteenth century, the possibility that 'aliens' might be able to build spaceships and visit us is a much more recent theory. The first thoughts that it might be possible for extraterrestrials to visit us come from late-nineteenth-century science-fiction writings, in which beings from another planet would arrive on Earth, usually with the intention of enslaving or eating us. One of the most influential books was H. G. Wells' *The War of the Worlds,* in which our desperate neighbours on Mars invaded us using tripod-like spaceships that could fire death rays. It is sometimes seen as being significant that the first real-life reports of extraterrestrial spacecraft came only a matter of years after the start of the science-fiction-writing tradition.

Between 1891 and 1898, a whole series of strange airship-shaped objects was reported from across the USA in what would later be known as 'The Great American Airship Scare'. These airships were inevitably large, and slow-moving, and often had strange beings piloting them. At least one was said to have crashed (in Aurora, Texas) and to have had its occupants buried in a local graveyard. Many assumed that the airships were piloted by extraterrestrials, especially Martians. Although the airships of the 1890s bear little resemblance to Arnold's sleek and fast-moving spacecraft, they nonetheless represent the start of mankind's sightings of interplanetary spacecraft and, more importantly, their occupants. From the time of the Great American Airship Scare, there is an almost continuous history of UFO sightings and of people meeting with the creatures that supposedly pilot them.

Although UFO sightings are themselves very interesting, what concerns us here are the tales that have emerged over the years of humans who have not only met up with extraterrestrials, but actually claim to have had sexual liaisons with them. These are the so-called 'Close Encounters of the Third Kind' – a term coined in 1972 by ufologist J. Allen Hynek. He defined them as being UFO stories '... in which the presence of animated creatures is present'.[134] In many of the cases that follow, the aliens are not just animated but positively rampant.

Sexual encounters with aliens can be broadly divided into two categories, each of which has a restricted time range. The first kind follows in the tradition of the straightforward alien contact where a UFO lands and an occupant gets out and interacts with a human. Sexual encounters of this kind are often portrayed as being enjoyable and to the benefit of both the alien and the human participant. These cases are mostly found between the 1950s and the late 1960s. The second type of contact is involuntary, with the victim being kidnapped against their will and then sexually examined on board a UFO before being returned to their original location. The memories of such encounters are often only recovered under hypnosis. Such encounters form the core of the modern 'alien abduction' movement and are by and large only found in the literature from 1985 onwards. Let us deal with the earlier and more spiritual sexual encounters first.

## Spiritual love and deep understanding

Within five years of Arnold's flying-saucer sighting, there was already an established and diverse UFO community in America, especially in the more liberated western coast states such as California. In this short time, a few charismatic individuals had already made a name for themselves by claiming to have been specially chosen by the extraterrestrials to be their representatives on Earth. Such people were known as 'contactees', and many of them would enthral their followers with tales of having met extraterrestrials, of being taken on board flying saucers and of visiting other planets. Minor cults developed around some contactees, most notably George Adamski and George King, and many would regularly meet with their followers in order to deliver messages given to them by the extraterrestrials.

One such contactee was Howard Menger, an ex-serviceman turned painter who lived in New Jersey. In 1956, Menger went public with his 24-year history of alien contact, which started when he met a voluptuous woman from Venus in 1932. Unfortunately, Menger was only aged ten at the time and did not understand the significance of the meeting, although he described the long-haired Venusian as emanating love and that he, even aged ten, felt physically attracted to her. The woman told him that she was contacting those of her own kind.

Menger's next encounter was in Hawaii during the second world war, when he encountered another slim, dark-haired woman from space, wearing a pink translucent ski-suit. Menger says of the encounter: '... this girl ... exuded the same expression of spiritual love and deep understanding. Standing in her presence I was filled with awe and humility, but not without a strong physical attraction one finds impossible to allay when in the presence of these women ... "Oh, Howard," she almost chided, "it's only a natural thing. I feel it myself. It flows from you to me as from me to you."'[135]

The woman explained that she was 500 years old and that her race had been shaping human civilization since the time of the Aztecs. Menger met the girl again after the war, at which time she said that he would not see her again but would instead one day encounter her sister, who was a Venusian in an Earth incarnation.

During this meeting, Menger offered the woman a bundle of bras as a present, but she rejected them, saying that her race did not wear bras!

Years later, when at a fellow contactee's lecture, Menger's eyes met with those of a beautiful and slim woman in the crowd. Menger '... knew at once who she was' and recognized her as the sister of the Venusian ufonaut with whom he had previously met. On talking with the woman, whose name was Connie Weber, both realized that they had been lovers in a previous life – when Menger was a Saturnian called Sol da Naro and Weber was a Venusian.

Menger left his wife and family to move in with Connie Weber and, by all accounts, the couple were very happy to be reunited after years of separation since their last incarnation. Weber was later to write about their affair (under the pseudonym Marla Baxter) in the book *My Saturnian Lover*. Of their lovemaking, Weber says: '[Menger] breathed in deeply, and I felt his chest expand greatly. It seemed as if he had grown a head taller. Not only did he grow taller and stronger, but his facial contour changed. His face seemed to get longer and triangular in shape, and his eyes grew larger and deeper. Even his voice was different – deeper and lower. He ceased to be [Menger] and had become a Saturnian ...'[136]

A similar tale to that of Menger was told by Elisabeth Klarer, who was a contactee from South Africa. Born in 1910, Klarer claimed to have first seen a UFO in 1917 and to have first contacted the 'space people' in December 1954 when in the Drakensberg Mountains of Natal. It was there in 1956 that she met with Akon, a tall and handsome being from Meton, one of seven inhabited planets around the star Proxima Centauri. Drawings of Akon depict him to be a smiling, silver-haired man with Scandinavian features who always seems to be wearing jumpsuits of the sort that used to be worn in the 1970s science-fiction series *Space 1999*. In fact, had he wanted a career in acting, Akon would have fitted well into the cast of this television programme.

Klarer went with Akon to Meton, which is described as being some form of Utopia with no money, politics or war, with the inhabitants all vegetarian. Klarer lived with Akon on Meton for some years before the atmosphere there started to cause her health problems and she was forced to return to Earth. While she was on Meton, however, Klarer had married Akon and even borne him a son, whom, regrettably, she had to leave behind. After returning to Earth, Klarer wrote up her extraterrestrial experiences in *Beyond the Light Barrier*. The book contained some graphic descriptions of sex with Akon: 'I surrendered in ecstasy to the magic of his lovemaking, our bodies merging in magnetic union as the divine essence of our spirits became one ... I found the true meaning of love in mating with a man from another planet.'[137] Elisabeth Klarer died in 1994, having spent a number of years in abject poverty.

Klarer's tale of intergalactic love has not been taken very seriously by many people, its content (and author) being a bit eccentric, to say the least. She does, however, still have her supporters, including the African shaman Credo Mutwa, who says of the case:

> There is a lady, Mrs Clarer [sic], who is known throughout the world as being a South African woman who not only communicated with, but mothered a child by a father from another world. There is nothing unusual about Madame Clarer's story. There have been many women throughout Africa in various centuries who have attested to the fact that they had been fertilized by strange creatures from somewhere. She's not alone. Last year I made a prayer with Elizabeth Clarer to the extraterrestrial beings, on behalf of the people of Africa.[138]

Menger's and Klarer's accounts of intergalactic sexual relations are both relatively rare examples of prolonged sexual relations between contactees and their contacters. Most close encounters involving sex are, like most UFO sightings, brief and isolated affairs that occur to a single individual without warning. The most famous case of extraterrestrial sex comes from near the town of São Francisco de Sales, Brazil.

The abduction concerns one Antonio Villas Boas, a 23-year-old farmer who was for years known to investigators only by the initials AVB. According to him, the strange events began on 5 October 1957, when he and his brother witnessed a UFO, in the form of a bright light, from their bedroom. On 14 October, the brothers again briefly saw a bright light while they were night-ploughing their fields. The next night, Villas Boas was ploughing on his own when the UFO returned and this time landed about 15m (50ft) away from him. The object was described as rounded with a distinct rim, purple lights and three legs. Villas Boas panicked and tried to drive away, but his tractor engine would not start, and as he left the cab he was grabbed by four humanoid beings who lifted him struggling into the UFO. He noted that his kidnappers, who wore tight-fitting suits with strange metallic helmets (drawings of them look a bit like the cybermen from *Doctor Who*), spoke to each other in barking sounds and that they were fascinated whenever he spoke.

Once inside the UFO, Villas Boas was moved around, stripped of his clothes and washed in a strange oily substance, until finally he was left alone in a metallic oval room. After some time a door opened and, to Villas Boas' complete surprise, a naked woman walked into the room. The woman was, according to Villas Boas, the most beautiful he had ever seen. She was shorter than him with long ash-blonde hair and a slim body. Unusually, he noted that her underarm and pubic hair were blood red. She approached Villas Boas and rubbed up against him; it was quite obvious that she was making sexual advances. They had sex twice, during which they did not kiss, although she did apparently bite him on the chin. The woman also never spoke, but made grunting noises that, according to Villas Boas, '... nearly ruined everything'.[139]

Before leaving the room, the woman pointed at her belly and then towards the sky. At the time Villas Boas thought that this meant he was going to be kidnapped and taken to another planet. An investigator later suggested that it probably meant that she was taking their baby into space. This led Villas Boas to claim later that the aliens were looking for 'a good stallion' to improve their stock. He was reclothed, given a tour of the spaceship and released back onto his field four hours after the ordeal started.

Villas Boas did not contact anybody about his experience until nearly four months after it had occurred, and then the people who did the investigating were so wary of the tale that it did not get published until 1965. One of the original investigators into the case, which was never fully resolved, later concluded: 'If this story be true, it may well be that, somewhere out there in the Universe, there is a strange child ... that maybe is being prepared to return here. Where does fantasy end? Where does reality begin?'[140]

A very similar tale to that of Villas Boas was published in a Bolivian magazine in 1976. A cowman named Liberato Anibal Quinterno also saw a round bright object land in his field. There are close similarities to the Villas Boas story, except that Quinterno found himself in a room being rubbed all over by three naked women. He had sex with one and noted: 'She seemed absolutely insatiable, very, very ardent.'[141] She, like the beings of Villas Boas, barked like a dog. After having sex with other beings, Quinterno was released again. The authenticity of this story has never been verified and most ufologists are cautious about it.

Another suspiciously close story to that of Villas Boas occurred in Heilongjiang, China, to the farmer Meng Zhaoguo. On 7 June 1994, a large white object landed on Meng's farm and paralysed him with a strong white beam. As his co-workers carried him to a shed, Meng started screaming that he could see a tall humanoid standing by a tree. Thinking their friend was mad, the workers put Meng onto a wagon where, according to Meng, a female alien forced herself upon him. Some weeks later, on 17 July, Mr Meng was taken from his bed and transported to a UFO. He again met the lady from Jupiter, who showed him pictures of her home planet. As before, she took full sexual advantage of him. A local UFO researcher said of the incident: 'Mr Meng said the first time he was forced to have sex he felt pain. The second time he felt much better, because he just submitted.' He added: 'I had a similar feeling to what Mr Meng described when I had my appendix out and they used a catheter.'[142]

There are several other examples of sexual intercourse with aliens, all of which involve human men having intercourse with alien women. The woman is invariably very pretty and most of the men, like Villas Boas and Quinterno, describe some form of foreplay before actual intercourse occurs. Arizona shopkeeper John Williams, who had an extraterrestrial sexual encounter in 1975, described his female alien as having '... produced a device about the size of a hand massager and went over my entire body with it'.[143]

Based on the descriptions given by the contactees, alien women all seem to be very dominant in the sexual act and most people, including the rare woman contactee Elisabeth Klarer, hint that they are being used, in one form or another, by the extraterrestrials as breeding stock.

Some contactees, on the other hand, have not been so lucky. Thruman Bethurum, a disciple of the great George Adamski, met with a female alien named Aura Rhanes in the Californian desert in 1954. Bethurum describes Aura, who came from the planet Clarion, as being 'tops in shapeliness and beauty'.[144] Despite Bethurum's obvious attraction to Aura, she ignored him and the potential interstellar relationship he desired went unfulfilled.

The above descriptions of extraterrestrial sex have never been taken very seriously by UFO investigators. The contactee cults of the 1950s and 1960s have been severely discredited after many of their claims turned out to be impossible or even hoaxes. In the Menger case, there is no way that either Venus or Saturn could have harboured life, let alone humanoids, and the length of time needed for Ms Klarer to travel to and from Proxima Centauri is far too long to achieve in one lifetime, although there are theories about wormholes in the space-time fabric being used to shorten the distances.

In the individual cases of Villas Boas, Quinterno, Meng and others, the sexual acts have all been criticized for being too much like a male fantasy. The attractive women, foreplay, dominance and the fact that the alien women leave and are never seen again all sound like the perfect one-night stand. There is also the very serious medical improbability of human sperm being capable of impregnating an alien. Even assuming they have the same reproductive system as us, our DNA is programmed only to fertilize other human beings. Our genetic make-up is sufficiently different to prevent us from being able to impregnate any other animal species on Earth successfully. It is therefore unlikely that we would be able to impregnate a life form that evolved on a different planet.

These tales of sexual excess are therefore often seen as a comic interlude in the otherwise serious study of ufology. They are not taken seriously and few people ever try to find rational explanations for them. The same cannot be said of our second category of alien sexual experience, which is far more real and frightening.

# 12

# *ALIENS STOLE MY VIRGINITY!*

In the late 1980s, firsthand reports of a sinister and frightening new type of close encounter of the third kind began to flood into UFO societies. These came from a variety of people, most of whom were describing the same terrifying experience. They were abducted from their beds (or occasionally cars) at night and awoke to find themselves strapped to a table in a strange room, surrounded by small grey beings with large black eyes. In the room the victim would then be examined medically, focusing particularly on the genitals and reproductive system, with sperm and egg samples commonly being taken. Most people only remember the experience after undergoing hypnosis, and some claim to have been abducted a number of times; sometimes women describe being made pregnant and then having the baby removed from their wombs. These reports were so consistent and common that the phenomenon received its own name within the wider sphere of ufology – alien abduction.

The alien-abduction phenomenon has now grown so large that, according to its promoters, over 3.7 million people from the USA alone are taken each year. The claims of abductees (as they are known) have been taken seriously by psychiatrists, psychologists and academics and the whole topic is a fiercely debated one both in and outside the UFO community.

The first celebrated case of alien abduction occurred in 1961, when Betty and Barney Hill were taken against their will aboard a UFO, and described being examined by alien beings. Under hypnosis, Betty Hill revealed that the aliens asked her to lie on a table, took various samples from her and then pushed a long needle into her navel. Barney revealed a similar story, except that he had a probe thrust up his rectum and a suction device placed over his genitals. The couple both remember a great amount of detail about the spaceship itself, including a detailed 'star map' that ufologists have interpreted as meaning that the aliens came from the Zeta Reticuli system. The aliens were described as being short with grey skin and large broad heads. Barney Hill was particularly disturbed by the aliens' large black eyes, which he described as, '... not connected to a body'.

In retrospect, the Hill abduction was a blueprint for the majority of modern alien-abduction cases. The key elements of being taken at night, being medically examined, having samples taken and then being dumped back on Earth with a period of missing time all form the basis of modern alien-abduction experiences. Even the description of the aliens as short, grey and with large black eyes fits with the common depiction of the 'grey' alien. The use of hypnosis to recover the lost memories also conforms to the modern ufology and psychiatric treatment of abductees.

Despite the close comparison between modern alien-abduction cases and that of the Hills' 1961 experience, however, there were surprisingly few similar accounts of alien abduction in the years following its publication. The huge publicity generated by this case turned the Hills into national celebrities and it seemed that everybody had an opinion about their experience. Despite this, the other abduction cases that it brought forward were mostly similar to the Villas Boas type, where the person is grabbed, taken aboard the UFO for a short while, sometimes medically examined, and then released. Examples of alien abduction of the type being described by modern victims were to come much later. Indeed, the next recognizable example of a modern case did not surface until 1968.

This case centred on a teenage girl named Shane Kurz, who was at the time living in the New York area. On 2 May, she witnessed a UFO sighting and, later that night, went missing from her bedroom; she was found asleep in her bed, but with muddy feet, the next morning. A few days later, she noticed reddish marks on her abdomen and suffered from a disrupted menstrual cycle. Six years later, and still disturbed by her experience, Kurz sought the help of ufologist Han Holzer, who hypnotized her in the hope of finding out what it was that had happened to her that night.

Under hypnosis Kurz recalled being drawn out into a nearby muddy field by a beam of light and from there being transported into an oval-shaped UFO. She was placed inside what has been described as a 'white hospital room' where there were many small humanoid beings with 'compelling eyes' and no noses. The beings asked her to remove her clothing and to lie down on a table, telling her that she was 'special' and 'a good breed'.

Kurz then described a needle being inserted through her navel. A humanoid wearing a scarf appeared, and calmly informed Kurz that she would be having his baby, causing Kurz to protest strongly. This was to no avail and the scarfed being removed his clothes, rubbed warm jelly over her, and then copulated with her. Kurz described his genitals as being similar to those of a human male. After struggling and even hitting the scarfed being, Kurz was returned to Earth, where she continued to have flashbacks of the event in her dreams for some months afterwards. No mention has ever been made about whether or not she was pregnant.

The next similar case occurred in October 1973 in the English county of Somerset. A woman was kidnapped from her car at night by a metallic humanoid. The next thing she remembers is being naked and tied to a table inside a cold room where three humanoids were examining her. They were particularly interested in her genitals and at one point placed a suction device over them. Then she was awake and standing fully clothed next to her car.

At the time, these two cases were not viewed as being part of a trend or even as having any similarities, either to each other or to other abduction cases. They are now recognized, however, as being very early examples of what would later be identified as classic examples of alien abduction. The trigger point for the popularization of the abduction phenomenon came in 1987, when two important pieces of literature on the subject were published. These were Whitley Strieber's *Communion* and Budd Hopkins' *Intruders*, both of which were on the bestseller lists for some time, bringing the alien-abduction phenomenon sharply into focus and, more importantly, to the attention of the public.

The effect that these books have had can be seen in a sudden jump in the number of reported cases of abduction that occurred at the end of the 1980s. An extensive survey of abductions found that there had been just under 300 reported cases of abduction between 1947 and 1985. A similar survey in 1992 found that between 1985 and 1991 there has been over 500 new cases reported; this was nearly double the number of cases reported in the previous 40 years.[145] That trend has continued, so that there is now an entire alien-abduction industry and support network in place in the USA.

Europe has seen a similar increase in the number of reported cases, although they are not nearly as widespread.

## A typical abduction

There are now hundreds of cases of alien abduction that have been collected by UFO organizations, individual researchers or psychiatrists. In fact, so many cases have been documented that it has been possible to do a great deal of meaningful study into the phenomenon, and the subject has firmly entered into the psychology fraternity's list of research topics. Unusually for a paranormal topic, some of the results of this research have come out strongly in favour of the reality of alien abduction, although, as would normally be expected from the scientific community, most of the conclusions are negative.

In general terms, those examples of alien abduction that occurred before 1987 were highly diverse, with the abductees' experiences varying greatly. Some people were abducted by robots, others by hairy monsters, still others by normal-looking, or even sexy, humanoids. Their experiences also varied. Although there are some common factors in the stories, most notably the medical examinations, each abduction tale essentially stands on its own, unrelated to the others.

The same cannot be said of the post-1987 alien abductions. These reports have everything in common. The abductors, the method of abduction, the spacecraft, the experiences when on board the spacecraft, and the physical and psychological after-effects as related by each abductee are very similar indeed. The following is a classic example from 'Wendy', a mother of two from Pennsylvania:

> ... I was lying asleep in bed when something woke me. I looked up and saw these grey beings with huge, shiny, liquid-black eyes. They had large heads and incredibly thin, small bodies with no real nose and just a slit for a mouth. I was terrified.
>
> ... I was drawn into a bright beam of light that led to a craft of some sort – a UFO I suppose.
>
> I was taken into a sterile metal room containing instruments and equipment like you might find in a hospital. My clothes were removed and I lay down on a metal table.
>
> Two of the beings touched me all over my body. Their fingers moved really fast, sort of like they were typing, and they checked my eyes, ears and nose – like a doctor. Then a taller being, who seemed to be in charge, came over and put its face close to mine ...

> ... I couldn't feel much, even when they gave me a gynaecological examination. My feet were in stirrups and I wondered if they were implanting an embryo inside me, as I felt that they had done on other occasions.
> 
> Then I caught sight of the foetus. It must have been growing inside me and they had just taken it out. Then a long needle-like instrument was inserted in my abdomen and some eggs were removed.
> 
> After a while I was taken along to the nursery where they keep the hybrid children created using human and alien eggs and sperm ... There were new-borns and toddlers. I could tell they were a mix between the two species ...
> 
> Then it was time to go. A beam of light appeared and the next thing I knew I was back in bed ... I glanced up at the clock – I'd been gone for two and half hours.[146]

The commonality between cases is so great that it is possible to create a typical modern alien-abduction experience by drawing together information from the hundreds of published examples. A typical modern (i.e. post-1987) alien abduction will take place at night and almost always in the abductee's bedroom, although some do occur at the wheel of a motorized vehicle. The abduction is sometimes preceded by the abductee having seen a UFO in the few days or weeks prior to the abduction. The abduction normally begins with the abductee awaking from sleep with a feeling of dread or a presence in the room. This will sometimes be accompanied by the room being flooded with light and sometimes also by a buzzing or humming noise. At this stage, the aliens will come to 'collect' the abductee or, alternatively, the abductee will be 'floated' out of the room and then find themselves inside a UFO. Few people actually remember entering the UFO.

The UFO is normally described as being a cross between a hospital operating theatre and the set from a *Star Trek* film. The rooms are large, with curved walls, little or no furniture and with consoles or computers around the edge. The atmosphere is commonly described as being highly air-conditioned, cold, clear and crisp. Two sorts of alien are to be found on the UFOs. One is described as a 'grey', after the colour of its skin, and the other as a 'doctor', as this is the type that often performs the medical examinations. The greys have become a common icon in western youth culture, with images of their large elliptical heads, slit-like mouths and disproportionally big black eyes being found on a great deal of merchandise. Aside from their distinctive head and eyes, the body of the grey is small (about 1.3m/4ft 4in tall), generally thin and spindly, with light, over-long arms and only four fingers on each hand. They are completely hairless and are only rarely observed to have external genitalia. This latter matter once led sceptical ufologist Peter Brookesmith to declare at a conference, 'Their groins are smooth and round – just like my teddy bear!'[147] The greys wear a one-piece, tight-fitting tunic that covers their entire body. It is the greys that are normally described in the bedroom encounters.

The doctors are similar to the greys, but are taller and older, and are often described as giving the appearance of being far more intelligent than the greys. The doctors are rarely reported outside the UFO, and it is they who are in charge of the medical examination that most abductees undergo. During the medical examination, the abductee will be naked or minimally clothed. They are commonly strapped to a table and paralysed or somehow disabled. The medical examination seems to concentrate on collecting samples of all kinds (hair, skin, mucus, sperm, etc.) and also on physical examination of the head and reproductive organs. In the case of men, sperm samples may be taken using a suction device placed over the penis or, more humiliatingly, by having a probe placed in the rectum which stimulates the prostate gland and causes involuntary ejaculation. Sperm samples have also been taken using surgical operations on the testes.

The medical examinations on women are much more invasive and traumatic. Eggs are forcibly taken from women via needles that penetrate their abdomens or by devices inserted into the vagina. There are also tales of women being deliberately implanted with alien-human hybrid foetuses. These may be surgically implanted directly into the uterus, left to gestate for a few months and then removed during another abduction. Rarely, one of the aliens will directly fertilize a woman abductee, normally by raping her.

Commonly reported items aboard the UFO are cabinets or cupboards that contain hundreds of jars full of developing foetuses. This has been used to invoke a theory that there is a alien genetic hybrid breeding programme taking place inside the UFOs, although its exact purpose is unclear.

Both sexes may be liable to other examinations, particularly of orifices such as the mouth, nose, ears, anus, penis and vagina. Sometimes painful drilling of the teeth or sinuses is reported, and many abductees believe that they have had electronic tracking devices deliberately planted in them. Such devices, know collectively as 'implants', have been reportedly seen on X-rays and one or two have even been recovered; but many are apparently reclaimed by the aliens before scientists can get their hands on them.

After the abduction has finished, the abductee will be returned to the place of abduction and will often be unaware of their experience for some time afterwards, as the aliens try to erase all memory of the experience. A person may be abducted more than once and many victims claim to have been abducted continually since their early childhood. Alien abduction is even said to run in families, with three or more generations sometimes being involved. The after-effects of the abduction can include headaches, nosebleeds, amnesia, mysterious cuts and bruises, enhanced psychic powers, a feeling of persecution or, conversely, a feeling of self-importance.

There really is very little difference between the details given by the hundreds of abductees that have come forward in the last decade or so. There is also little question that the majority of abductees are not attention-seekers, cult members or psychologically disturbed. There are as many white-collar as blue-collar workers being abducted, although, statistically, abductees are very unlikely to be from the more professional sectors such as the law, medicine, academia and so on.

There is also little question that these people genuinely believe in the experiences they describe. Anybody who has met with an alien abductee cannot doubt their sincerity, and time and time again the psychological assessment of abductees describes them as being mentally balanced and normal in every way possible. They are, like the victims of ghost rape and penis-snatching, utterly convinced of the experience which they claim to have had – but can this conviction be supported by physical evidence?

## The physical evidence

As with most areas of the paranormal, the stumbling block with alien abductions is the almost complete lack of physical evidence to support the claims of its victims. The search for such physical evidence has concentrated on three main areas:

1. finding witnesses to the abduction itself;
2. finding medical evidence on the victim themselves;
3. finding information or objects that could have originated only from beyond this world.

With regard to the search for witnesses, there have been a number of multiple abductions where two or more people have been kidnapped together, usually from a car at night. These cases are normally considered to be unreliable because by the time an independent investigator gets to interview the people, it may be several days, months or years after the original event, during which time the topic may have been widely discussed among its victims with details being shared between them.

In the case of Betty and Barney Hill, a classic example of a multiple abduction, Betty had discussed detailed dreams she had had about her abduction with Barney for some weeks before an investigator was called in. Moreover, the same psychiatrist hypnotized and questioned them both within minutes of each other. This, as we have seen in the Nottingham Satanic ritual abuse scare, is not necessarily a good thing, and leading questions have been seen to be used by over-eager ufologists in more than one alien-abduction case. For these reasons, multiple witness cases, while intriguing, are not accepted as a means of verifying an abduction experience. What are needed are truly independent witnesses who have seen the victim being kidnapped and taken to a UFO. Of all the hundreds of known alien-abduction cases, there is only one in which independent witnesses have come forward.

This case centres itself on Linda Cortile (a pseudonym), a New York resident who was allegedly abducted from her twelfth-floor Brooklyn apartment in November 1989. She claimed, under hypnotic regression with Budd Hopkins, that she was kidnapped and transported into a waiting UFO that then plunged into the river below. Hopkins wrote up the Cortile case in a book called *Witnessed* in he states that the case '... is easily the most important in recorded history'.[148]

Cortile contacted Hopkins in 1989 after reading his book *Intruders*. She had had episodes of paralysis all her life and had become convinced that she had been kidnapped by aliens after a doctor found a small scar inside her nose. Cortile and Hopkins corresponded for a while before, on 30 November 1989, she rang him to say that she had had a paralysis attack the night before and that she had 'felt a presence' in the room and then seen a black-eyed figure. She had vague memories of being floated out of her window into a UFO and then being on an examination table. The case seemed to be like any other alien abduction until, some time later, witnesses to the abduction started to come forward.

In the early spring of 1991, two policemen apparently contacted Hopkins to say that, on the same night as Cortile's reported abduction, they had seen a woman or small child being floated out of her building and into a UFO. The floating figure was in the foetal position and was accompanied by three 'small figures'. After meeting with the policemen and obtaining statements and drawings of what they had seen, Hopkins became convinced that they had witnessed the abduction of Linda Cortile. Much later (after the publication of *Witnessed*) another policeman came forward as a witness.

Hopkins also claimed that on Brooklyn Bridge there were cars containing the Pope, Mikhail Gorbachev and George Bush, all of whom must also have witnessed the abduction. He has also said that 30 November 1989 was a key date in human history and that, on that night, the General Secretary of the UN, Peres de Cuellar, was also abducted. In total, Hopkins believes that about 20 people would have witnessed the abduction and, at a conference at which I was present, declared that '... the abduction either happened or it was a hoax made with collaboration'.[149]

The Cortile case is an unusual one, both in terms of the rather outlandish claims that Hopkins has made for it and also because it provides the much-needed independent witnesses. Hopkins has refused to name any of the witnesses that night, or to allow anybody from the media, or UFO groups, access to them. In fact, we know nothing at all about these witnesses. We have no proof of their existence, let alone their credibility, their movements that day or, more importantly, any relationship they may have to Linda Cortile herself. Under these circumstances, the witness statements must be looked at with some suspicion, and the Cortile case is generally not considered to be of great value by the UFO fraternity.

Other than the Cortile case, the nearest we can come to independent witnesses are the parents or sleeping partners who wake to find the abductee missing from their bed, only to have them back in place by the morning. Students of alien abduction claim that the lack of witnesses is because the abductions take place at night and that immediate family members, friends and pets are all 'turned off' by the aliens during the abduction itself.

The search for medical evidence on the abductees themselves would seem to be a more promising avenue. Most abductees claim to have had skin, hair and other samples taken from them, and some to have had their sinuses, teeth and heads drilled. More promising still are the tales of internal examination, pregnancy and even rape that are commonly reported by women abductees. All of these procedures, when carried out by human doctors, would leave tell-tale signs on the body in the form of scar tissue or physical holes. There are again many problems with this.

One of the classic physical signs of abduction that many abductees notice is a small scar and/or bruising where they think that samples have been taken from them. Others reportedly suffer from nosebleeds, sinusitis, toothache, genital discharge or a disrupted menstrual cycle after their medical procedures. These physical symptoms are, however, all relatively common medical conditions that are suffered by a large proportion of the population at any one time, and can thus be caused by something other than being abducted by aliens. Even the very pro-abduction psychiatrist John Mack says:

> ... even though the abductees are certain that the cuts, scars, scoop marks, and small flesh ulcers that appear on their bodies after their experiences are related to the physical procedures performed on the ships, these lesions themselves are too trivial by themselves to be medically significant. Similarly, abductees will often experience that they have been pregnant and have had the pregnancy removed during an abduction, but there is not yet a case where a physician has documented that a fetus has disappeared in relation to an abduction.[150]

Unfortunately, until there is a medical side-effect that can be tied directly to the abduction experience and nothing else, any medical evidence presented is always capable of being explained in other terms. Other side-effects noticed by abductees, including increased clairvoyant powers and the association of poltergeist-type activity, are as yet unproved in any sphere of science, let alone as attachments to abduction cases.

With the lack of verifiable evidence from both independent witnesses and medical evidence, the best-documented physical evidence from abductees comes from those enigmatic objects that the aliens medically insert into the bodies of abductees known collectively as implants. Implants are commonly embedded in either the nose, particularly the sinuses, or under the skin in fleshy parts of the body, such as the neck, legs or buttocks. The role or function of the implants is not known, but it is generally assumed they are used by the aliens to keep track of the abductees or to take medical readings. In other words, implants are afforded the same role as the tags used by zoologists on animals, the implication being that we are the object of study by an alien race.

Alien implants have turned up as white objects on medical X-rays which, when the implants have been searched for or the X-rays have been duplicated, have invariably disappeared. Their absence, like the missing foetuses, is commonly blamed on the aliens having done a repeat abduction to reclaim what is rightfully theirs.

Nonetheless, a number of implants have been recovered by abductees, usually by accident. These objects are invariably small and normally wiry in appearance, although amorphous lumps of metal have also been found. Some of them have found their way into the hands of scientifically trained people and have been chemically analysed. Dr Susan Blackmore identified one implant as being made of an identical mix of elements as a tooth filling. All the others have been found to be made of known chemical compounds and none has had any moving parts or sign of advanced circuitry. At least one implant, however, has been identified as 'not a naturally occurring biological subject but [it] could be a manufactured fibre of some sort'.[151] Again, a major problem is that the abductee has, in every case, come forward with the implant already recovered, so it is difficult to know the exact location from and circumstances under which it was recovered.

The physical evidence supporting alien abductions is thus most unreliable, and even ardent supporters of the phenomenon do not believe that there is good independent evidence yet. But why should this be so?

The main theory used to explain this is that the aliens are following a secret agenda and do not wish their presence to be detecable by humans. Thus they are very careful not to leave any tell-tale medical after-effects and, if a pregnancy or implant is detected, they will reabduct the person and remove the evidence before any medics can document it. Whether this is true or not, the lack of any definable physical evidence in the several hundred documented cases of alien abduction (let alone the 3.7 million who are supposed to be abducted every year from the USA alone) leaves us solely with the testimonies of abductees that, for the most part, have been taken under hypnosis.

Ultimately, the alien-abduction experience is completely reliant upon the testimony of the victim, with no real independent evidence to back it up. Yet there is little question that abductees themselves are not, for the most part, deliberately lying about their experiences, which are very real and, more importantly, have many features in common with the experiences of other abductees worldwide. We have, however, encountered this situation with other phenomena in this book.

The victims of penis-snatching, ghost rape, Satanic ritual abuse and hysteria were all convinced that what they had experienced was absolutely real, and yet there was little physical evidence to suggest that this was so. Furthermore, in all these cases there was a psychological explanation that far better fitted their experiences than the supernatural one. Could the case of alien abduction be part of this same trend?

One problem that has really worried me about the whole alien-abduction scenario is the similarity it has to cases both of Satanic ritual abuse survivors and multiple personality disorders. In Chapter 8, I discussed how the pattern of diagnosis of these phenomena relied heavily on a two-stage process. The first stage is the initial self-diagnosis done by the 'victim', who becomes convinced that they have been the victim of Satanists or aliens or that they have multiple personalities within them. Having decided this, they then seek to have their self-diagnosis confirmed by a psychiatrist (or ufologist) who is sympathetic to their disorder (i.e. they believe in it). The one thing that Satanic survivors, multiple personality sufferers and alien-abduction victims want from their consultation with a psychiatrist (other than confirming their own self-diagnosis) is to be able to recover the memories that they think, from having read about similar cases, are missing. This second stage of the diagnosis is commonly done by the psychiatrist (or ufologist) using hypnosis.

In the case of alien abduction, it is the first stage of the diagnosis, where the person becomes convinced that they have been abducted by aliens, that is the most fascinating. Whereas people claiming to have missing memories of Satanic abuse or multiple personalities also generally have other psychological conditions, usually of a neurotic nature, the abductees do not. Their social range and number suggest that whatever it is that causes them to come forward in the first place goes far deeper than just a conventional psychological disorder. In fact, the psychological profiles that have been done on alien abductees find them to be, on the whole, well-balanced individuals (87 per cent were, however, found to be fantasy-prone and most had a prior interest in the paranormal). This, to my mind at least, makes it less likely that the initial self-diagnosis of the individual is based on a psychological desire to be an abductee (in the same way that a multiple personality sufferer wants to be recognized for their disorder) and more that their self-diagnosis is based on an actual event that could lead people to believe that they have been kidnapped by aliens. In other words, at the heart of most alien-abduction cases is a solid tangible experience of the sort that is missing from Satanic ritual abuse survivors and multiple personality sufferers. But what could this tangible experience be?

The more I read of individual alien-abduction experiences, the more I notice similarities between the core abduction experience and certain other phenomena discussed in this book. After a while, the abduction event itself begins to show remarkable similarities to other cases of nocturnal supernatural assault that involve mystical beings attacking people in their beds at night.

## Old hags and aliens

One of the greatest problems with studying any paranormal phenomena, including alien abductions, is a lack of good published firsthand witness accounts. The majority of books, articles and interviews lack the crucial details which can make the difference between understanding a phenomenon and it simply becoming another strange-but-true story.

In this respect, one of the best studies of the alien-abduction phenomenon available is that by John E. Mack, a Professor of Psychiatry at Harvard Medical School, who wrote the book *Abduction: Human Encounters with Aliens*. Mack is a firm believer, and a very vocal promoter, of the reality of alien abduction (much to the disgust of many of his peers) and, as a result, has had a great number of people come to him to have their suspicions of being abducted confirmed.

Unlike most books on the subject, *Abduction* provides very detailed transcripts from hypnosis sessions that Mack undertook with 13 abductees who sought his help. In contrast to the random quotes and summarized case histories that most books use, *Abduction* allows us to read the abductees' experiences in their own words. They are most revealing and enable us to understand the exact experience that each abductee undergoes. Most importantly for this study, there is also a great deal of information about the actual abduction experience itself. It is this event that drives people to diagnose themselves as abductees and thence to seek professional help, and so understanding what it is that is happening to people during this abduction is crucial.

Having read through many accounts of abductee experiences, and having even met some abductees themselves, I have been struck by the similarity between the descriptions of their initial stages of abduction and those of the old-hag, sleep-paralysis attacks and ghost rape described in Chapter 1. The trademarks of these experiences are waking up paralysed with a feeling of fear and that somebody is in the room, a feeling of pressure on the chest like a heavy weight being placed there, and hearing, seeing, smelling or feeling being(s) in the room. The old hag is explicable scientifically as a combination of two common sleep disorders, sleep paralysis and hypnopompic hallucinations, and has been induced in the laboratory by interfering with the body's REM (dream) cycles. In addition to sensing a presence in the room, many people report feelings of flying or floating, and anomalous noises and lights are also commonly reported.

The similarities between the bedroom abduction experience and the symptoms of old-hag attacks are quite remarkable. Before discussing them in detail, here are six examples to consider. The first two are descriptions of classic old-hag attacks, and the other four are from abductees.

1. Ron (old-hag victim): 'I was sleeping ... but the next thing I knew, I realized that I couldn't move. My eyes – I was able to look around the room. And I started to feel that pressure [on my chest]. And it increased, and it increased, and the next thing I knew I was like totally wiped out ... the next thing I knew, from one of the areas of the room this greyish, brownish murky presence was there. And it kind of swept down over the bed and I was terrified ... it was kind of like a – a surrealistic shape ... I felt it pressing down all over me. I couldn't breathe. I couldn't move ... I was wide awake, you know ... This was evil! You know, this was weird.'[152]

2. Sharon (old-hag victim): This woman was in traction in hospital when she awoke and found herself unable to move, with a pressure on her chest. She was aware of a presence in the room with her which manifested itself as a disembodied bearded face. It is what happened next that is of interest. 'Next she described the feeling of being lifted from her bed. She felt that she was at least two feet above the bed when she heard the door open again, and a nurse came in. The moment the door opened ... she felt herself dropped onto the bed with considerable force.'[153]

3. Jerry (abductee): 'She [Jerry] woke up terrified and remembered pressure in the abdomen and the genital area and that she could not move. "In my head I was screaming," Jerry remembers, but does not know if any sound came out. "Somebody was doing something," she recalled, but it was "something alien". Although she recalls wondering to herself, "Is that how sex is done?" she knew with great certainty that "it wasn't a person"... In the years that followed, Jerry had a number of "nightmares" in which she would awake paralysed, hear "buzzing and ringing and

whirring" noises in her head, and see humanoid beings in her room.'[154]

4. Catherine (abductee): 'In the session Catherine began to recall (actually relived) feeling numb, with pressure in the chest. Beginning to sob and pant Catherine said, "I'm starting to feel numbness in my face now. My arms are starting to feel real heavy. Numbness is moving down to my hands. I'm feeling a very heavy weight on my chest and stomach."'[155]

5. Karrin (abductee): 'The real [alien-abduction] experience started one night with the realization that something was on the end of my bed ... as it stepped its way up on either side of my legs, I began to panic, realizing that I was awake ... it paused and stopped with one knee on my chest, one knee on the other side of me, two arms straddled around my neck, and although my eyes were not open at the time, I was aware that it was very close to me."'[156]

6. Peter (abductee): '[Peter] was paralysed, conscious of "what's going on" but "not having any control of it". With his eyes closed Peter "felt a presence ... Then I looked up. There's a being standing on the other side of the couch ... He's the blue man. He's blue. He's very dark." The ship "looks like a sunset," and Peter floated up with one being "on my left and the big one's on my right," as his arms hung down by his side. After he was in the ship it "moved really fast. We're just going off. We're flying, zoom."'[157]

The similarity between the old-hag experiences and those of the abductees is very close indeed. The paralysis, pressure on the chest, feeling of a supernatural presence in the room and sensations of flying are found in both cases. If one reads back through the quoted examples of 'ghost rape', which are another form of old-hag attack, in Chapter 1, then one can also find a comparison to the claims of sexual interference and rape that have been made by abductees. Even the reports of loud buzzing noises and bright lights that fill the abductees' bedrooms have also been associated with old-hag-type experiences (for example, the case of Michael John Marshall in Chapter 1).

In every one of the 13 alien-abduction cases listed in John Mack's *Abduction* there are the classic symptoms of an old-hag attack and, once one knows what to look for, many of the well-documented cases of alien abduction worldwide become explicable in terms of this common sleep disorder. Linda Cortile, the subject of the Brooklyn Bridge abduction case discussed earlier, is noted to have suffered from bouts of night paralysis throughout her life. On the night of her witnessed abduction, she claims that she was falling asleep when she felt a presence in the room and felt herself being paralysed. She next saw a black-eyed figure in the room and tried to throw something at it but found that she was totally unable to move. To Budd Hopkins, who investigated this case, this was a classic abduction scenario. To myself (and others) it has all the classic hallmarks of an old-hag attack. Many other cases can be similarly explained.

In fact, one of the ways in which a ufologist can diagnose whether a person has been abducted is to ask them whether they have ever woken up paralysed. If they have, then, according to some alien-abduction researchers, that means that they have been abducted. In 1992, a Roper poll in America famously claimed that 3.7 million Americans had been abducted by aliens. This poll worked by asking 5,947 adults 11 so-called 'indicator questions' which, if four or more were answered 'yes', meant that the individual had probably been abducted by aliens. Several of these questions were directly related to the key symptoms of old-hag experiences: for example, 'Have you ever felt as though you left your body and could fly around without it?', 'Have you ever seen unusual lights or balls of light in a room without knowing what was causing them, or where they came from?', 'Have you ever woken up paralysed – that is, with the feeling that you could not move?' and 'Have you ever woken up with the sense that there was a strange person or presence or something else in the room?'

Of the 5,947 people surveyed, 119 (2 per cent) answered yes to four or more of the questions and were thus considered to be victims of alien abduction; when scaled up to the entire American population, this becomes 3.7 million people. Other polls put this figure higher, including one by David Jacobs which estimated that as many as 15 million Americans have undergone an abduction by aliens. The aliens must, like Santa Claus on Christmas Eve, be very busy, particularly if they are abducting people at the same rate in every country across the world.

Two of the questions quoted above in the 1992 Roper poll are particularly relevant to the old-hag experiences. These are the ones about waking up paralysed and feeling a presence in the room. Together, 18 per cent of those surveyed said that they had had these two experiences at some point in their life. This proportion equates very well indeed to David Hufford's own survey of old-hag experiences, taken a decade before alien abductions became popular, which found that 15 per cent of people have at some point in their lives undergone an old-hag-type experience as characterized by sleep paralysis and hypnopompic hallucinations producing a feeling of a presence in the room. The fact that approximately the same proportion of people in two separate surveys have undergone experiences that can be identified as being caused either by alien abduction or by a known and studied sleep disorder suggests that many abduction experiences are also explicable in terms of these sleep disorders. Thus, the core experience of alien abductions (the feeling of being paralysed, kidnapped and sexually interfered with) can be readily compared with almost identical descriptions that have come from old-hag, ghost-rape, succubus, incubus and Popobawa victims.

This comparison would seem to be backed up by the tendency for the old-hag experience to reflect the cultural beliefs of the community in which it occurs. In Chapter 1, we saw that people in Africa who wake up paralysed with a sense of something in the room believe that they are being sexually molested by demons. In Europe, however, the bedroom perpetrator is commonly said to be a ghost. In Thailand, it is the demon of a sexually frustrated widow; in Vietnam, it is a 'grey ghost'; in Hong Kong, it is an 'oppressing ghost'; in medieval Europe, it was a succubus or incubus; in Newfoundland, it is the old hag herself. Even though the core experience of sleep paralysis and hypnopompic hallucinations is identical in each region, the supernatural entity held responsible for the nocturnal assault is a direct reflection of the cultural beliefs of that society.

The alien-abduction nocturnal assaults in America and Europe are merely the latest cultural reflection of the old hag. Thanks to science fiction and the upsurge in paranormal interest, the western cultural belief in UFOs has grown so strong since the 1950s that the focus of the old hag has easily transformed itself into the cultural icon of the sexually abusive alien. A hundred years ago, the average European or American would expect a nocturnal supernatural visitor to be a ghost or demon. Nowadays, we expect them to be 'greys', come to remove us to their mother ship. To me, the similarities between sleep paralysis and the actual abduction experience are too great to be explained in any other way. I will readily admit that there are alien-abduction cases that cannot be explained in these terms, particularly those that take place in cars at night, and that there are many more where there is insufficient detail to draw any conclusions whatsoever. Nevertheless, most cases begin with what is clearly a bedroom-centred experience, in which the abductee wakes to find beings in the room who then float the abductee off to a UFO and physically abuse them. With or without exact descriptions of paralysis, weights on the chest and other classic old-hag symptoms, the two phenomena of alien abduction and old-hag attacks are very similar.

I am not the first person to notice the link between old-hag and alien-abduction experiences. The world expert on the old hag, Professor David Hufford, has commented on the link between aliens and the Newfoundland occurrences of sleep paralysis. The parapsychologist Dr Susan Blackmore has written extensively about a possible link, and in recent years there have been at least two TV programmes suggesting a link between them. In fact, the link has been so widely publicized that it quite surprises me that the leading academic who supports the reality of alien abduction, Professor John E. Mack, has not noticed it himself. Professor Mack, aside from writing about alien abduction, has written extensively about sleep disorders, and one of his most famous works is the book entitled *Nightmares and Human Conflict,* which recognizes that 'oppression and helplessness' can be a part of the nightmare experience.

## Experiences on board the mother ship

Although the old-hag experience can, in my opinion, explain the initial abduction, it cannot explain the wealth of detail given by abductees about their time on board the UFO. These descriptions are too far removed from those of typical old-hag experiences to be explicable in terms of sleep paralysis and hypnopompic hallucinations. Yet, if the initial abduction experience is, in most cases, attributable to a common sleep disorder, this suggests that the detailed descriptions of encounters with aliens and the medical experimentation that follows the abduction experience are also more down to earth in their origin.

When looking at the studied cases of alien abduction, one has to remember that there are two clear stages in the diagnosis of each case. The first is the independent self-diagnosis made by the alien-abduction victim. In this chapter, it has been suggested that this initial diagnosis has been based upon the misinterpretation of an old-hag experience. According to assessments of abductees, prior to their self-diagnosis all of them had an awareness of UFO topics, especially alien abduction, and of the paranormal in general. Many believed themselves to be psychic in some way, or had had earlier paranormal experiences, the most common of which were seeing a UFO or poltergeist-type phenomena. It is this predilection towards the paranormal, and UFOs in particular, that may give the abductees the cultural grounding to interpret their old-hag experience in terms of aliens. It also means that the majority of them, when they go looking for the help of a psychiatrist, ufologist or other professional, have a good knowledge of the typical alien-abduction experience as outlined at the beginning of this chapter.

In fact, thanks to the modern media, it is hard for anybody not to know something of the experience of a typical abductee. Aside from the writings of Hopkins, Jacobs, Mack and others, there are also, thanks to the Internet and specialist magazines, many lists of 'symptoms of alien abduction' available which can help people confirm their self-diagnosis. Like the 1992 Roper survey, these lists focus on symptoms that can be interpreted by most psychologists as being due to sleep disorders, phobias or other psychological problems. The list of symptoms can be very long (there are 52 warning signs on one Internet self-help guide alone), but generally include the following:

- The appearance of unusual and inexplicable scars or marks on the body which might have been caused by sample-taking or the insertion or removal of implants. Nosebleeds, headaches and toothache are also signs of medical interference.
- A tendency to suffer from sleep disorders, especially insomnia or bad dreams about kidnapping, UFOs or medical experiments. Waking up paralysed with a noise, blue light or feeling of a presence in the room.
- A fear of sex or intimacy with people. A general distrust of doctors and hospitals. Phobias about needles or medical procedures. Claustrophobia (or agoraphobia, according to some people) is also a sign.
- A feeling that you have periods of 'missing time' that you cannot account for, particularly when driving or at night.
- Signs of a phantom pregnancy or an unexplained feeling of pregnancy. Waking up having had nocturnal emissions of blood, sperm or other bodily fluids. Waking with a soreness around the genitals.
- Psychic experiences, or having an adverse effect on electronic equipment.

This list, which is much shorter than most published ones, covers a wide range of symptoms, and there can be few people who have not, at some time, experienced at least two of these criteria. I have had four of them, but I do not believe I have ever been kidnapped by aliens. The problem lies in the fact that, with the widespread promotion of these alien-abduction criteria, many people have mistaken perfectly normal and explicable experiences, especially the old hag, insomnia, wet dreams and nightmares, for evidence that they have been kidnapped by aliens. They do not, at first, remember much about their abduction, only the initial stages of it, and these are usually attributable to an old-hag experience. In order to confirm their self-diagnosis of having been abducted by aliens, and to try to recover their missing memories, would-be abductees then seek out a friendly psychiatrist to help them in their struggle to understand what has happened to them. In this way, most examples of alien abduction are not in fact diagnosed by a qualified professional but by the victim themselves.

Once the psychiatrist has agreed with the patient that they may well have been the victim of alien abduction, the next common move is to try to recover the patient's memories of the abduction itself. The most common method of doing this is to hypnotize the patient and then 'regress' their mind back to the moment of abduction. This is the second stage in the diagnosing of alien abduction. As we have seen with the Satanic ritual abuse survivors and multiple personality disorder victims, using hypnosis as a means of recovering lost memories is a controversial technique that has been at the centre of a war between those psychologists and psychiatrists who believe it is a useful tool and those who believe it is not. Hypnotically retrieved memories are not admissible as court evidence, and the association of hypnosis with false memory syndrome (see Chapter 8) has lessened the value of any information obtained in this way.

It is still not fully understood what hypnosis actually is, or what it does to the brain. Most studies seem to equate the trance-like state of hypnosis with that strange period of quasi-consciousness that we experience just before falling asleep or just after waking up. Some think it is a separate stage of consciousness into which we slip, while others believe that it is nothing more than a self-induced phase of hysteria. Regardless of its true nature, what is certain about hypnosis is that the person in the trance becomes very suggestible and is liable to provide the hypnotist with the information they are looking for, whether it is true or not. Equally, the hypnotic subject is just as liable to regurgitate information they have read or heard about as fact, often placing themselves in the centre of events. This is how Satanic survivors are able to provide stories about their own ritual abuse which is in fact based solely upon accounts that they have read.

For this reason, using hypnosis to try to recover hidden memories is a very uncertain technique that is liable to reflect the preconceived beliefs of both the psychiatrist and the patient rather than the truth.

Expert ufologist Jerome Clarke says:

> Hypnosis helps reconstruct rather than recover memories, according to experts, but in the process it distorts recollections and debases them with falsehoods until little semblance remains of what really happened. With abduction investigators largely untrained in hypnosis and committed to a specific agenda, they lead their subjects to combine suggestions, fantasies, and prior knowledge into pseudomemories of an abduction. Hypnosis seals the fantasy with a sense of conviction and creates trauma where none really existed.[158]

Thus, even under the care of a professional psychiatrist, the abduction experience as related under hypnosis is liable to be a mixture of the patient's and psychiatrist's own expectations and prior knowledge on the issue.

One of the few strengths of the modern alien-abduction phenomenon, however, is the extraordinary similarities in the stories given by abductees from different parts of the world at different times. These similarities, according to ufologists, are a sign that different people at different times are undergoing the same experience perpetrated by the same group of aliens. The odds against so many people independently coming up with the same stories are, according to ufologists, very high. This would be true if these people were coming up with the same stories completely independently of each other – but they are not.

The two-stage diagnosis involved in most alien-abduction cases means that patients come to the psychiatrist or UFO investigator already convinced that they are abductees. They will have read up extensively on the topic and already be well aware of other people's experiences. Indeed, one of the common signs of having been abducted is if the individual 'identifies with [Whitley Strieber's novel] *Communion*', and many people's ideas about abduction experiences come from reading accounts of modern abductees. The majority of the 13 abductees discussed in John Mack's *Abduction* show an awareness not only of other people's alien-abduction experiences but also of the paranormal in general, and often from an early age.

Once under hypnosis, the patient is able to repeat their own personalized version of the typical abduction story outlined at the beginning of this chapter. This tale may be enhanced by the hypnotist, who, like the social workers in Satanic ritual abuse cases, may ask leading questions to encourage the patient to conform to their notion of what an alien-abduction experience should be. It is this general adherence to the Hopkins/Strieber model of alien abduction that can explain how there was suddenly such a uniformity in the tales of abductees after the huge success of both Strieber's and Hopkins' books on the subject in 1987. Prior to this time there had been no standard model, and so tales were far more varied.

Yet another clue about the personalized, as opposed to the independent, nature of these experiences can be gained from the motives and actions that the abductees attribute to the aliens. While the perceived physical aspects of people's abduction experiences, such as the kidnapping, the type of alien, the sexual interference, the implants and so on, may be similar, the supposed ethos behind the aliens' motives is not, and varies wildly. Some believe that the aliens are cold, clinical beings that are there to conduct horrific medical experiments on humans. They are viewed very much in the same manner as the guards in Nazi concentration camps. Other abductees, however, believe that the aliens are here to help us, and that the medical experiments are nothing more than a means of preserving the human race against our own destructive abuse of the planet. Some individuals even believe that the aliens are there solely to help them as a person by enhancing their knowledge or intelligence, or by giving them psychic powers or glimpses of the future. The same grey aliens thus mean different things to different people and, more importantly, are thought to be kidnapping them for different reasons.

Having waded through hundreds of alien-abduction cases, it is clear that each person's perceived experience at the hands of aliens largely reflects their personality traits and personal beliefs. For example, Karrin, a frequent abductee who was interviewed on TV, says that '... since I was eight years old all I have wanted is to know everything there is to know as a human being'.[159] During her abduction experiences, the aliens 'reward her with knowledge' and give her 'special messages' and warnings about the future path of humanity. She is consequently convinced that she is a prophet chosen specially by the aliens, and indicates that she is a very special person as a result of her experiences. This clearly reflects her childhood ambition to be an intellectual, something that, judging by her job in a bar, has been unfulfilled in her everyday life.

The belief among abductees that they are special or chosen in some way is a common one. Many think that they have reached a higher level of consciousness or that they have in some way evolved as a result of their abductions. One abductee said of himself: 'I am a shaman/artist/teacher ... what the shaman is doing is playing with the emotional discourse between ... the person who travels and the person who remains or who lives a life here. I teach by emotion and experience.'[160] The belief that one is special in some way or, indeed, a leader or teacher, was also a vital part of the psychological make-up of the 1950s and 1960s contactees, who similarly thought themselves to be ambassadors for the extraterrestrials. With abductees, as with contactees, this appears to be a reflection of the unfulfilled ambitions or minor superiority complexes of the individuals.

Other abductees, however, appear to transfer other aspects of their personalities to the aliens. Jerry, one of John Mack's patients, had a phobia about intimacy and sex. Her aliens were seen as being rapists and abusers who were artificially inseminating her. Another abductee, an English woman called Ros, had a pre-existing fear not only of sex but also of pregnancy. Her aliens were intent on raping and impregnating her against her will.

Contrast these experiences with those of abductees who enjoy their time with the aliens and even get sexual pleasure out of it. Liz Murphy from Yorkshire, England, described her encounter with a grey as '... the best sex I had ever had'.[161] Could these be the same beings that, according to Maria Ward, raped her and left her feeling '... guilty and disgusted – just like a rape victim'?[162]

Some psychiatrists and ufologists believe that the fact that an individual's personality can be reflected in their abduction experience shows that it is their alien-abduction experience that is responsible for shaping their personalities. Most psychologists, however, argue the reverse, saying that the inclusion of people's personality traits in their abduction experience actually shows that these stories are by and large made up by the abductee. Further problems arose when a survey of 152 abductees showed 87 per cent of them to be strongly fantasy-prone.

## The alien-abduction 'survivor'

This pattern of self-diagnosis and then seeking the help of a friendly professional psychiatrist is something that we have seen before in this book with both the adult survivors of Satanic ritual abuse and the victims of multiple personality disorder. When looked at side by side, the alien-abduction phenomenon has an extraordinary amount in common with these other two experiences.

Victims of Satanic ritual abuse, multiple personality disorder and alien abduction all seek out psychiatrists with two goals in mind. The first is to have the self-diagnosis of their problem confirmed. The second is to be allowed to remember the trauma of the experience(s). This act of remembering is almost exclusively achieved through hypnotic regression techniques. The similarity does not, however, stop there. In the analysis of both Satanic ritual abuse and multiple personality disorder in Chapters 8 and 10, it was shown that nearly all examples of these phenomena were reported in the USA, and that both had definite start dates and peaks in the number of reports. With both Satanic ritual abuse and multiple personality disorder, there was a huge increase in the number of reported cases in the early 1980s, peaking in the early 1990s and then tailing off again. Although small increases in reported cases occurred in Europe and Australasia, these came a couple of years after the start of the American wave of interest (which suggests that, like the penis-snatching panics, belief in the conditions was being exported from one continent to another). Most significantly, cases would only be diagnosed by those psychiatrists and psychologists who believed in the reality of the phenomenon.

Alien abduction shows exactly the same pattern, and is still essentially an American phenomenon, the start of which can be dated precisely to 1987. Its peak, however, has, at the time of writing, yet to be reached. With the popularization of alien abduction in many television programmes, the most important of which is *The X Files*, the phenomenon jumped the Atlantic and Pacific in the early 1990s, leading to an increased number of reported cases of alien abduction, all identical to the Hopkins/Strieber model, in Australasia and Europe. Tellingly, cases of Satanic ritual abuse, multiple personality disorder and alien abduction are almost non-existent in sub-Saharan Africa, Russia, China and southeast Asia, where the culture is not predisposed to such beliefs.

All of the few African abduction cases that I know of show strong signs of cultural influence from more western traditions. For example, the South African shaman Credo Mutwa claims that in 1959 he was digging for herbs when he fell unconscious:

> When I came to I was in a small, unfamiliar place lying on a table. There were five little fellows around me ... They were sticking things in me, up my nostrils, other places, and I was in terrible pain, but could not cry out or do anything ... [Next this alien woman] made love to me ... it was awful, indescribable. When you are with a human woman there is this sharing, this give and take ... there was nothing like this here.[163]

The author relating Mutwa's experience notes its similarity to that of modern alien abduction but swears that the shaman has no detailed knowledge of this phenomenon. It is, however, obvious from Mutwa's other writings that he is very clued up on western ufology, and it is made clear that he has met both John Mack and Elisabeth Klarer (see Chapter 11). It is clear that Mutwa's supposedly traditional tribal folklore stories are a deliberate blend of western paranormal and native African traditions. I have not yet seen an African abduction case that has been uninfluenced by western ufology tradition. Are the aliens purposefully ignoring the Africans, Asians and Russians or do they, unlike the western world, not recognize that they are being abducted?

Aside from the geographical comparisons of Satanic ritual abuse and alien abduction, there are also strong similarities to the stories of the Satanic ritual abuse 'survivors', as discussed in Chapter 8. Satanic ritual abuse survivors show the same two-stage diagnosis pattern that alien abductees do. They are commonly adults who, having read other Satanic ritual abuse survivor tales, become convinced that they have been the victims of Satanists themselves. Having made this self-diagnosis, they then seek out a sympathetic psychiatrist or Christian counsellor who will inevitably hypnotize them to recover their lost memories.

Satanic ritual abuse recovered memories normally involve the 'survivor' telling a tale whereby they have been kidnapped (or duped) by Satanists, taken to an underground cavern (or some other foreign place like a crypt, empty house, cellar or similar) and ritually abused. Common themes in the stories are descriptions of 'brood mares' (women kept in captivity specifically to breed foetuses or babies for sacrifice), baby sacrifices, ritual sexual abuse, people locked in cages and being tied to sacrificial altars. These stories themselves go back to religious persecutions in Roman times.

Many of these themes are also reflected in stories of alien abduction. Tales of women made pregnant by aliens, only to have their babies reclaimed, are common, as are stories of sexual abuse (in the form of rape or intrusive medicals), seeing people restrained in glass capsules and, of course, being strapped to a medical table, which replaces the Satanic altar. In common with alien abduction, victims of Satanic ritual abuse will often have their memories of the events erased using drugs or magic and subsequently remember them in bits and pieces through their dreams.

Many alien-abduction survivors have, like Satanic ritual abuse survivors, set down their experiences in the form of books and, as with Satanic ritual abuse, there are now many self-help and support groups for victims of alien abduction. The two phenomena closely parallel each other (as indeed do many aspects of multiple personality disorder) and, considering that both rely heavily on self-diagnosis, hypnosis and very little physical evidence, it is easy to see why.

## The ultimate phenomenon?

Alien abduction was left to this last chapter because I believe that it is the ultimate expression of many of the themes that have been discussed during the course of this book. It reflects the psychology of the sleep-paralysis disorders that have so commonly been mistaken for supernatural sexual assault. It reflects the strange cases of the Satanic ritual abuse survivors whose self-diagnosis and hypnotic regression treatment by psychiatrists have led to the recovery of memories that were never there. It also, in its geographical origins within the USA and subsequent spread to Europe, reflects the unusual way in which the penis-snatching panics spread from east Asia to west Africa.

For the moment, alien abduction remains the number-one sexual assault tradition in the world, and is certainly one of the most visible and talked about. Indeed the term 'kidnapped by aliens' has entered common usage to describe why somebody or something is unexpectedly missing. Although the phenomenon may be common now, as with Satanic ritual abuse, multiple personality disorder and penis-snatching, the odds are that interest in alien abductions will peak after a few more years and then the number of reported cases will begin to decline. For now, alien abduction, with its blend of psychology and supernatural sexual assault traditions, can be considered to be the ultimate paranormal phenomenon for the twenty-first century and is a more than fitting topic on which to end this book.

I hope that, with these stories of penis-snatching, supernatural rape, Satanic ritual abuse and much more that have been covered in this book, the reader has learned something of the incredible way in which apparently unrelated paranormal phenomena can suddenly be found to have complex links with each other. Charles Fort, a pioneer in the study of strange phenomena, famously wrote that one measures a circle beginning anywhere. By this, he meant that whichever section of the paranormal world you begin to look at you very soon find that what was an apparently independent phenomenon becomes inextricably linked to other equally strange goings-on. Part of the Fortean tradition, which I consider myself to come from, is to help to find these links. Most Forteans do this by not only having an interest in any one part of the paranormal but also being interested in all of it. This is no small task, but it is ultimately very satisfying when patterns do start to emerge from the seemingly random mass of unusual events that surround human society.

In this book, we have seen how it is possible to link a variety of nocturnal sexual assaults both to each other and to a studied sleep disorder. Beyond this, there are also links based on hypnotic techniques, traditions of diabolic orgies and religious sexual worship and persecution. Some of these links can be traced back several millennia; others are only a few years old. Some can possibly explain the phenomena that they are centred on; others just beg more questions.

Furthermore, the Fortean tradition compels us to treat the strange stories and weird experiences that we encounter with reverence and interest. Science has a bad habit of immediately dismissing the inexplicable or unusual as being fraud, mistake or coincidence, but without offering up any reason why. Fortunately, the titbits that science ignores are readily received by Forteans, parapsychologists, ufologists and others who wander the imaginary land that Mike Dash has called '… the borderlands, an almost enigmatic world where anything seems possible'.[164]

It has turned out that most of the sexually orientated titbits in this book would appear not only to have had very close links with each other but also to have probable explanations that are not necessarily paranormal in nature. I must say that this, in my experience, is a relatively rare situation, as even the most mundane paranormal topics usually leave some room for doubt. Even in the topics we have discussed here, however, there is still a hint of the inexplicable. Not every case of alien abduction or demon sexual assault is, or will be, explained by sleep paralysis, and no doubt somebody will someday turn up with their penis fully retracted into their body. Who knows – in 20 years' time entire cities could be powered by William Reich's orgone energy. There is as yet no theory of everything, and however good the explanations there are always exceptions to any rule. It is this struggle against a constantly moving target that keeps me, and many others, interested in the weird, the strange, the unusual and, ultimately, the inexplicable phenomena that, for whatever reason, have intertwined themselves into the fabric of human existence.

# Notes

1. McGreal, C., 'Zanzibar Diary', article in *The Guardian*, 2 October 1995.
2. Hufford, D.J., *The Terror that Comes in the Night – An Experience-Centered Study of Supernatural Assault Traditions*, University of Pennsylvania Press, 1982, p.2.
3. Hufford, *op. cit.*, p.11.
4. Hufford, *op. cit.*, p.73.
5. Hufford, *op. cit.*, p.185.
6. *Spectral!*, Issue 5, p.15.
7. Huston, P., 'Night Terrors, Sleep Paralysis, and Devil Stricken Demonic Telephone Cords from Hell', *Skeptical Inquirer*, 17(3), 1992, p.65.
8. Summers, M., *The Vampire in Europe*, Kegan Paul, Trench, Trubner & Co., 1929 (reprinted in 1995 by Bracken Books), p.163.
9. Ey, A., *Harzmärchenbuch; oder, Sagen und Märchen aus dem Oberharze*, 1862, p.47.
10. Roper, L., *Oedipus and the Devil*, Routledge, 1994, p.209.
11. *Ghostwatch*, 1(5), p.20.
12. Huston, *op. cit.*, p.66.
13. Spence, L. *The Encyclopaedia of the Occult*, Routledge & Sons, 1929 (reprinted in 1994 by Bracken Books), p.297.
14. *Ibid*.
15. Spence, *op. cit.*, p.251.
16. Zohar 3:76, in Patai, R., *Gates to the Old City*, Wayne State University, 1981, p.456.
17. Augustine (St Augustine), edited by Welldon, J. E. C., *De Civitate Dei (The City of God)*, London, 1924, Book 15, Chapter 23.
18. Olliver, C. W., *Handbook of Magic and Witchcraft*, Rider & Co., 1928, p.163.

19. Kramer, H., and Sprenger, J., translated into English by Summers, M., and Rodker, J., *Malleus Maleficarum*, 1928, p.28.
20. Kramer and Sprenger, *op. cit.*, p.114.
21. Kramer and Sprenger, *op. cit.*, p.164.
22. Kramer and Sprenger, *op. cit.*, p.114.
23. Kramer and Sprenger, *op. cit.*, p.166.
24. *Ibid.*
25. Sinistrari, L. M., *Démonialité ou Incubes et Succubes*, Scientia Duce, 1882 (originally published in Latin in 1709).
26. Internet web site is: www.demonbuster.com (The End-time Deliverance Center).
27. Olliver, *op. cit.*
28. Ladurie, E. Le Roy, translated into English by Bray, B., *Montaillou*, Penguin Books, 1980, p.291.
29. Ladurie, E. Le Roy, *op. cit.*, p.292.
30. Tawney, C.H., *The Ocean of Story*, Chas. J. Sawyer Ltd., 1924, Appendix IV.
31. Genesis 1:27.
32. Genesis 2:18.
33. *The Alphabet of Ben Sira*, Question 5. Quoted in Stern, D., and Mirsky, M., *Rabbinic Fantasies: Imaginative Narratives from Classical Hebrew Literature*, Jewish Publication Society, 1990, p.183.
34. Zohar 3:76. Quoted in Patai, *op. cit.*, p.456.
35. *Ibid.*
36. *Ibid.*
37. Bacharach, 'Emeq haMelekh, 19c. Quoted in Patai, *op. cit.*, p.463.
38. Isaiah 34:14.
39. Erubin, 18b. Quoted in Epstein, I., *The Babylonian Talmud*, Socino Press, 1978.
40. Erubin, 100b. Quoted in Epstein, *op. cit.*
41. Nidda, 24b. Quoted in Epstein, *op. cit.*
42. Shab, b. Quoted in Epstein, *op. cit.*
43. Patai, R., *The Hebrew Goddess*, Wayne State University Press, 1990, p.226.
44. Schwartz, H., *Lilith's Cave: Jewish Tales of the Supernatural*, Oxford University Press, 1989.
45. Scott, G. R., *Phallic Worship*, Luxor Press, 1966, p.107.
46. Kings 17:9–10.
47. Genesis 24:2.
48. Genesis 47:29.
49. *Encyclopaedia Biblica*, vol. 8, p.3453.
50. Augustine, *op. cit.* Book 6, Chapter 9.
51. Rosenbaum, J. *The Plague of Lust, being a History of Venereal Disease in Classical Antiquity, and including Detailed Investigations into the Cult of Venus, and Phallic Worship, etc.*, Carrington Ltd, 1901.
52. *Ibid.*
53. Ezekiel 16:7.
54. Baruch 6:43 (Epistle of Jeremy)

55. More, H., *Grand Mystery of Godliness*, 1660, Book 3, p.83.
56. Leviticus 19:29.
57. Deuteronomy 23:18.
58. Jude, verse 7.
59. Kramer and Sprenger, *op. cit.*, p.xiii.
60. Kramer and Sprenger, *op. cit.*, p.xi.
61. Translation taken from Kramer and Sprenger, *op. cit.*
62. Translation from Summers, M., *The History of Witchcraft*, Routledge and Kegan Paul, 1926 (reprinted in 1994 by Senate), p.121 (original listed as being Minge, *Patres Latini*, CXXXII, p.352).
63. Delrio, M., *Disquitiones magicae*, Book 2.
64. Boguet, H., *Discours des sorciers*, Lyon, 1590.
65. Summers, M., *The History of Witchcraft*, p.171.
66. *Ibid*.
67. Summers, M. *The History of Witchcraft*, p.119.
68. Evans, E. P., *The Criminal Prosecution and Capital Punishment of Animals*, London, 1906, p.152.
69. Evans, *op. cit.*, p.157.
70. Stanford, P., *The Devil – A Biography*, Arrow, 1996, p.165.
71. Olliver, *op. cit.*, p.145.
72. Summers, *The History of Witchcraft*, p.98.
73. Hopkins, M., *The Discovery of Witches*, The Cayne Press, 1928 (original edition published in 1647).
74. More, H., *Antidote against Atheism*, London, 1665.
75. Kramer and Sprenger, *op. cit.*, pp.41–2.
76. *Ibid*.
77. *Ibid*.
78. Quoted in Roper, *op. cit.*, p.19.
79. Statistics from Levack, B. P., *The Witch-hunt in Early Modern Europe*, Longman Group UK Ltd, 1992.
80. Quoted in Wedeck, H. E., *A Treasury of Witchcraft: A Sourcebook of the Magic Arts*, Gramercy Books, 1961.
81. Roper, *op. cit.*, p.208.
82. Kramer and Sprenger, *op. cit.*, p.46.
83. Masello, R., *Raising Hell: A Concise History of the Black Arts – and Those who Dared to Practice Them*, Berkeley Publishing Group, 1996, p.148.
84. Playfair, G. L., *This House is Haunted!*, Souvenir Press, 1980.
85. *The Unexplained*, vol. 12, p.2642.
86. Reich, *op. cit.*
87. King, F., 'Sex, Sin and Sacrament', *The Unexplained*, vol. 12, p.2641.
88. Reich, W., *The Sexual Revolution*, Vision Press, 1952.
89. Kings 1:1–3.
90. Shirer, W. L., *The Rise and Fall of the Third Reich*, Pan, 1964.
91. Dash, M., *Borderlands*, Arrow, 1997, p.379.
92. *JET Report*; unpublished, but available on the Internet.
93. 'Child Sexual Abuse, Assault, and Molest Issues', 1991–92 San Diego County Grand Jury, Report #8, San Diego County, USA.

94. See, for example, La Fontaine, J.S., *Speak of the Devil – Tales of Satanic Abuse in Contemporary England*, Cambridge University Press, 1998.
95. A widely used and popular quote. This version is from Scott, G.R., *op. cit.*, pp.129–30.
96. Hosea 3:13.
97. *Fortean Times*, 57, p.62.
98. Green, V., *A New History of Christianity*, Sutton, 1996, p.17.
99. Green, *op. cit.*, p.18.
100. Chadwick, H., *The Early Church* (revised edition), Penguin Books, 1993, p.29.
101. *Fortean Times*, 57, p.62.
102. Stanford, *op. cit.*, p.122.
103. Benson, L. D. (ed), *The Riverside Chaucer*, Oxford University Press, 1987, p.210 ('The Prioress's Tale' from *The Canterbury Tales*).
104. Shirer, *op. cit.*, p.42.
105. Stanford, *op. cit.*, p.134.
106. Baigent, M., Leigh, R., and Lincoln, H., *The Holy Blood and the Holy Grail*, Corgi Books, 1983, p.73.
107. Summers, *op. cit.*, p.139.
108. *Ibid*.
109. *Ibid*.
110. Summers, *The History of Witchcraft*, p.145.
111. *Ibid*.
112. Wickwar, J. W., *Witchcraft and the Black Arts*, Herbert Jenkins Ltd, 1925.
113. Kramer and Sprenger, *op. cit.*, p.45.
114. Summers, *The History of Witchcraft*, p.160.
115. Summers, *The History of Witchcraft*, p. 136.
116. Summers, *The History of Witchcraft*, p.162.
117. Norris, D., *Fetichism in West Africa*, New York, 1904.
118. Kerekes, D., and Slater, D., *Killing for Culture – An Illustrated History of Death Film from Mondo to Snuff*, Creation Books, 1994.
119. Campbell, P., *Back to Front*, London, 1919.
120. Brittain, V., *Testament of Youth*, Penguin Books, 1994.
121. 'Funny Old World', *Private Eye*, 28 October 1998.
122. *Electronic Telegraph* [www.telegraph.co.uk], Issue 457, 22 August 1996.
123. Quoted in Rubin, R. T., 'Koro (Shook Yang) – A Culture-bound Psychogenic Syndrome' in Friedmann, C. T., and Faguet, F. A. (eds), *Extraordinary Disorders of Human Behaviour*, Plenum Press, 1989, pp.155–73.
124. *Hong Kong Sunday Post*, 28 November 1993.
125. Rubin, R.T., 'Koro (Shook Yang) – A Culture-Bound Psychogenic Syndrome' in Friedmann and Faguet, *op cit.*, p. 170.
126. Kramer and Sprenger, *op. cit.*, p.59.
127. Kramer and Sprenger, *op. cit.*, p.119.
128. *Ibid*.
129. Scot, R., *The Discoverie of Witchcraft*, Da Capo Press, 1971 (original edition published in 1584).
130. Stafford, C. D., *What Freud Really Said*, Penguin Books, 1967.

131. Stanford, *op. cit.*, p.170.
132. Piper, A., 'Multiple Personality Disorder: Witchcraft Survives in the Twentieth Century', *Skeptical Enquirer*, May/June issue, 1988, p.49.
133. Merskey, H., 'The Manufacture of Personalities', *British Journal of Psychiatry*, 160, pp.327–40, 1993.
134. Hynek, J. A., *The Hynek UFO Report*, Sphere Books, 1978.
135. Menger, H., *From Outer Space to You*, Vantage Press, 1959.
136. Baxter, M., *My Saturnian Lover*, California, 1958.
137. Klarer, E., *Beyond the Light Barrier*, Howard Timmins, 1980.
138. Credo, M., *Song of the Stars – The Lore of a Zulu Shaman*, Barrytown Ltd, 1996, p.152.
139. Bowen, C., 'The Closest Encounter Ever', *The Unexplained*, vol. 5, p.1067.
140. Bowen, *op. cit.*, p.1068.
141. Clarke, J., *The UFO Book – Encyclopedia of the Extraterrestrial*, Visible Ink, 1998, p.538.
142. *The Independent*, 17 March 1995.
143. Clarke, *op,. cit.*, p.537.
144. Spencer, J., *The UFO Encyclopedia*, Headline, 1997, p.51.
145. For statistics see Bullard, T. E., *UFO Abductions: The Measure of a Mystery*, vols. 1 and 2, Fund for UFO Research,1987, and see Clark, J., *UFOs in the 1980s*, Apogee Books, 1990.
146. *TV Quick*, 26 November 1994.
147. Personal notes taken at the *Fortean Times* Unconvention, London, 1997.
148. Hopkins, B., *Witnessed: The True Story of the Brooklyn Bridge Abductions*, Pocket Books, 1996.
149. Personal notes taken at the *Fortean Times* Unconvention, London, 1997.
150. Mack, J. E., *Abduction: Human Encounters with Aliens*, Charles Scribner and Sons, 1994, p.41.
151. Mack, J. E., *op. cit.*, p.42.
152. Hufford, D., *op. cit.*, p.58.
153. Hufford, D., *op. cit.*, p.69.
154. Mack, J. E., *op. cit.*, p.118.
155. Mack, J. E., *op. cit.*, p.151.
156. Transcribed from *Everyman* BBC1 television programme, spring 1998.
157. Mack, J. E., *op. cit.*, p.299.
158. Clarke, J. *op. cit.*, p.14.
159. Transcribed from *Everyman* BBC1 television programme, spring 1998.
160. Mack, *op. cit.*, p.363.
161. *Options* magazine, June 1995.
162. *Options* magazine, June 1995.
163. Credo, M., *op. cit.*, pp.141–2.
164. Dash, M., *op. cit.*, Preface.

# BIBLIOGRAPHY

**Chapter 1**

*Sexual demons and spectral sex*

Anderson, J., 1995, Real-life Ghostly Encounters. *Spectral!* 5, p.15.
Anonymous, 1994, Amazing Psychic Children. *News of the World* (UK), 4 September.
Anonymous, 1996, Dwarf Batman Terrorises Zanzibar. *Fortean Times* 86, p.11.
Anonymous and untitled (Gill Philipson Case), 1996, *The People* (UK) 12 June.
Anonymous and untitled (Jill Cook Case), 1996, *The People* (UK), 5 June.
Blackmore, S., 1994, Alien Abduction – The Inside Story. *New Scientist* 19 November, pp.4–6.
De Felitta, F., 1978, *The Entity*. Warner Books.
McGreal, C., 1995, Zanzibar Diary. *Guardian* (UK), 2 October.
Sieveking, P., 1990, Sleep's Deadly Widows. *Fortean Times* 55, p.15.

*Old hags*

Hufford, D.J., 1982, *The Terror that Comes in the Night – An Experience-Centered Study of Supernatural Assault Traditions*. University of Pennsylvania Press.

*Sleep paralysis and hypnagogic hallucinations*

Bell, C.C., Dixiebell, D. and Thompson, B., 1986, Panic Attacks – Relationship to Isolated Sleep Paralysis. *American Journal of Psychiatry* 143(11), p.1484.
Conesa, J., 1997, Isolated Sleep Paralysis, Vivid Dreams and Geomagnetic Influences. *Perceptual and Motor Skills* 85(2), pp.579–84.

Dement, W. and Kleitman, N., 1957, The Relation of Eye Movements during Sleep to Dream Activity, an Objective Method for the Study of Dreaming. *Journal of Experimental Psychology* 53, pp.339–46.

Fukuda, K., Inamatsu, N., Kuroiwa, M. and Miyasita, A., 1991, Personality of Healthy Young Adults with Sleep Paralysis. *Perceptual and Motor Skills* 73(3), pp.955–62.

Hudson, J.I., Manoach, D.S., Sabo, A.N. and Sternbach, S.E., 1991, Recurrent Nightmares in Post-traumatic-Stress-Disorder – Association with Sleep Paralysis, Hypnopompic Hallucinations, and REM-Sleep. *Journal of Nervous and Mental Disease* 179(9), pp.572–3.

Huston, P., 1992, Night Terrors, Sleep Paralysis, and Devil Stricken Demonic Telephone Cords from Hell. *Skeptical Inquirer* 17(3), pp.64–9.

Kettlewell, N., Lipscomb, S. and Evans, E., 1993, Differences in Neuropsychological Correlates Between Normals and Those Experiencing Old Hag Attacks. *Perceptual and Motor Skills* 76(3), pp.839–46.

McNulty, S., Decurtis, E. and Spanos, N., 1995, Imagery, Dissociative Experiences and Reports of Abuse in Sleep Paralysis. *Canadian Psychology-Psychologie Canadienne* 36, p.114.

Sobanski, T., Sieb, J., Laux, G. and Moller, H., 1997, Auditory Hallucinations in REM Sleep Associated Parasomnia. *Psychiatrische Praxis* 24(6), pp.302–3.

Spanos, N.P., Mcnulty, S.A., Dubreuil, S.C., Pires, M. and Burgess, M., 1995, The Frequency and Correlates of Sleep Paralysis in a University Sample. *Journal of Research in Personality* 29(3), pp.285–305.

Takeuchi, T., Miyasita, A., Inugami, M., Sasaki, Y. and Fukuda, K., 1994, Laboratory-Documented Hallucination During Sleep-Onset REM Period in a Normal Subject. *Perceptual and Motor Skills* 78(3), pp.979–85.

Takeuchi, T., Miyasita, A., Sasaki, Y., Inugami, M. and Fukuda, K., 1992, Isolated Sleep Paralysis Elicited by Sleep Interruption. *Sleep* 15(3), pp.217–25.

Wing, Y., Lee, S. and Chen, C., 1994, Sleep Paralysis in Chinese – Ghost Oppression Phenomenon in Hong Kong. *Sleep* 17(7), pp.609–13.

*Explaining the impossible*

Marshall, M.J., 1995, Humming in Bed. *Ghostwatch* 1(5), p.20.

Roper, L., 1994, *Oedipus and the Devil*. Routledge.

Spence, L., 1929, *The Encyclopedia of the Occult*. Routledge & Sons (reprinted in 1994 by Bracken Books).

Summers, M., 1929, *The Vampire in Europe*. Kegan Paul, Trench, Trubner & Co. (reprinted in 1995 by Bracken Books).

## Chapter 2

Augustine (St Augustine), edited by Welldon, J.E.C., 1924, *De Civitate Dei (The City of God)*. Volumes I and II. London.

Briffault, R., 1927, *The Mother: A Study of the Origins of Sentiments and Institutions*. Allen and Unwin.
Delassus, J., 1897, *Les Incubes et Succubes*. Paris.
Gougenot des Mousseau, H.R., 1854, *Moeurs et Practiques des Démons*. Paris.
Kramer, H. and Sprenger, J., translated into English by Summers, M. and Rodker, J., 1928, *Malleus Maleficarum* (reprinted with 1946 introduction in 1996 by Bracken Books).
Ladurie, E. Le Roy, translated into English by Bray, B., 1980, *Montaillou*. Penguin Books.
Lea, H.C., 1938, *Materials Towards a History of Witchcraft*. Thomas Yoseloff.
L'Estange, Ewen, 1935, *Witchcraft and Demonianism*. Heath Cranton Ltd.
Maple, M., 1966, *The Complete Book of Witchcraft and Demonology*. A.S. Barnes & Co.
Olliver, C.W., 1928, *Handbook of Magic and Witchcraft*. Rider & Co.
Scot, R., 1971, *The Discoverie of Witchcraft*. Da Capo Press.
Sergeant, P.W., 1936, *Witches and Warlocks*. Hutchinson and Co. Ltd.
Sinistrari, L.M., 1882, *Démonialité ou Incubes et Succubes*. Scientia Duce (originally published in Latin in 1709).
Summers, M., 1926, *The History of Witchcraft*. Routledge and Kegan Paul (reprinted in 1994 by Senate).
Summers, M., 1929, *The Geography of Witchcraft*. Routledge and Kegan Paul.
Tawney, C.H., 1924, *The Ocean of Story*. Chas. J. Sawyer Ltd.
Wickwar, J.W., 1925, *Witchcraft and the Black Arts*. Herbert Jenkins Ltd.
Williams, C., 1941, *Witchcraft*. Faber and Faber.

## Chapter 3

Colonna, M.T., 1980, Lilith, or the Black Moon. *Journal of Analaytical Psychology*, October, pp.325–50.
Gaster, M., 1900, Two Thousand Years of a Charm Against the Child-Stealing Witch. *Folklore* 11, pp.129–61.
Graves, R., and Patai, R., 1964, *Hebrew Myths: The Book of Genesis*. Doubleday.
Koltuv, B.B., 1986, *The Book of Lilith*. Nicolas-Hays.
Matt, D.C., 1983, *Zohar: The Book of Enlightenment*. Paulist Press.
Schwartz, H., 1989, *Lilith's Cave: Jewish Tales of the Supernatural*. Oxford University Press.
Schwartz, H., 1992, Mermaid and Siren: The Polar Roles of Lilith and Eve in Jewish Lore. *The Sagarin Review* 2, pp.105–16.

## Chapters 4 and 5

Augustine (St Augustine), edited by Welldon, J.E.C., 1924, *De Civitate Dei (The City of God)*. Volumes I and II. London.
Buckley, E., 1895, *Phallicism in Japan*. University of Chicago Press.

Carroll, R. and Prickett, S., 1997, *The Bible – Authorised King James version with Apocrypha*. Oxford University Press.
Chadwick, H., 1993, *The Early Church* (revised edition). Penguin Books.
Cohen, C., 1919, *Religion and Sex*. Foulis.
Cutner, H., 1940, *A Short History of Sex Worship*. Watts.
Howard, C., 1925, *Sex and Religion*. Williams and Norgate.
Layton, B., 1987, *The Gnostic Scriptures*.
Scott, G.R., 1966, *Phallic Worship*. Luxor Press.
Scott, G.R., 1968, *Ladies of Vice*. Tallis Press Ltd.
Westermarck, E.A., 1891, *The History of Human Marriage*. Macmillan.

## Chapter 6

*General witchcraft*

Chambers, P., 1998, *Paranormal People*. Blandford Press.
Cohen, N., 1975, *Europe's Inner Demons*. Sussex University Press.
Kramer, H. and Sprenger, J., translated into English by Summers, M. and Rodker, J., 1928, *Malleus Maleficarum* (reprinted with 1946 introduction in 1996 by Bracken Books).
L'Estange, Ewen, 1935, *Witchcraft and Demonianism*. Heath Cranton Ltd.
Maple, M., 1966, *The Complete Book of Witchcraft and Demonology*. A.S. Barnes & Co.
Olliver, C.W., 1928, *Handbook of Magic and Witchcraft*. Rider & Co.
Scott, R., 1971, *The Discoverie of Witchcraft*. Da Capo Press.
Sergeant, P.W., 1936, *Witches and Warlocks*. Hutchinson and Co. Ltd.
Stanford, P., 1996, *The Devil – A Biography*. Arrow.
Summers, M., 1926, *The History of Witchcraft*. Routledge and Kegan Paul (reprinted in 1994 by Senate).
Summers, M., 1929, *The Geography of Witchcraft*. Routledge and Kegan Paul.
Wickwar, J.W., 1925, *Witchcraft and the Black Arts*. Herbert Jenkins Ltd.
Williams, C., 1941, *Witchcraft*. Faber and Faber.

*Witchcraft, sexuality and gender*

Banner, L.W., 1992, *In Full Flower: Aging Women, Power, and Sexuality*. Alfred A. Knopf.
Levack, B.P., 1992, *The Witch-Hunt in Early Modern Europe*. Longman Group UK Limited.
Masello, R., 1994, *Fallen Angels ... And Spirits of the Dark*. Berkeley Publishing Group.
Masello, R., 1996, *Raising Hell: A Concise History of the Black Arts – and Those Who Dared to Practice Them*. Berkeley Publishing Group.
Roper, L., 1995, *Oedipus and the Devil: Witchcraft, Sexuality and Religion in Early Modern Europe*. Routledge.

Wedeck, H.E., 1961, *A Treasury of Witchcraft: A Sourcebook of the Magic Arts*. Gramercy Books.

## Chapter 7

*Poltergeists, spiritualism and sex*

Fodor, N., 1958, *On the Trail of the Poltergeist*. The Citadel Press.
Green, A., 1982, Sex and the Mischievous Spirit. *The Unexplained* 2, pp.314–17.
Hubbell, W., 1882, *The Great Amherst Mystery*. New York.
King, F., 1982, Sex, Sin and Sacrament. *The Unexplained* 12, pp.2641–5.
King, F., 1982, Sex, Sorcery and Seances. *The Unexplained* 12, pp.2674–7.
Owen, A., 1992, *The Darkened Room*. Routledge.
Playfair, G.L., 1980, *This House is Haunted*. Souvenir Press.
Rickard, B., 1977, Spectral Spoilsports. *Fortean Times* 22, pp.4–5.
Rogo, S.D., 1986, *On the Trail of the Poltergeist*. Prentice-Hall.
Wilson, C., 1978, *Mysteries*. Granada Publishing.
Wilson, C., 1981, *Poltergeist! A Study in Destructive Haunting*. New English Library.

*Wilhelm Reich*

King, F., 1982, The Cosmic Orgasm. *The Unexplained* 11, pp.2554–7.
Mortimer, N., 1998, Wilhelm Reich – Guru of the Orgasm. *Fortean Times* 107, pp.26–30.
Reich, W., 1952, *The Sexual Revolution*. Vision Press.
Wilson, C., 1971, *The Occult*. Panther Books.

*Shunamitism*

King, F., 1971, *Sexuality, Magic and Perversion*. Spearman.
Shirer, W.L., 1964, *The Rise and Fall of the Third Reich*. Pan.
Walker, B., 1971, *Sex and the Supernatural*. Macdonald.

## Chapter 8

*General Satanic ritual abuse*

Dash, M., 1991, Satan and the Social Workers. *Fortean Times* 57, pp.46–52.
Harper, A. and Pugh, H., 1990. *Dance with the Devil*. Kingsway.
Hicks, R.D., 1990, Police Pursuit of Satanic Crime. Part 1. *Skeptical Enquirer* 14(3), pp.276–86.
Hicks, R.D., 1990, Police Pursuit of Satanic Crime. Part 2. *Skeptical Enquirer* 14(4), pp.378–89.
La Fontaine, J.S., 1994, *The Extent and Nature of Organised and Ritual Abuse: Research Findings*. HMSO.

La Fontaine, J.S., 1998, *Speak of the Devil – Tales of Satanic Abuse in Contemporary England*. Cambridge University Press.
McClure, K., 1991, Front Line Against Satan. *Fortean Times* 57, p.53.
Pazder, L. and Smith, M., 1980, *Michelle Remembers*. Pocket Books.
Richardson, J., Best, J. and Bromley, D., 1990, *The Satanism Scare*. Aldine de Gruyter.
Rickard, B., 1991, Satanic Child Abuse Mania. *Fortean Times* 57, pp.54–8.
Rickard, B., 1991, The Fantasy of Satanic Conspiracy. *Fortean Times* 57, pp.58–61.
Rickard, B., 1992, Satanic Round-Up. *Fortean Times* 64, p.52.
Sandell, R., 1995, Desperately Seeking Satan. *The Skeptic* 9(1), pp.11–8.
Sinason, V., 1994, *Treating Survivors of Satanic Ritual Abuse*. Routledge.
Stratford, L., 1988, *Satan's Underground*. Harvest House.
Victor, J.S., 1991, The Spread of Satanic Cult Rumors. *Skeptical Enquirer* 15(3), pp.274–80.

### Individual cases

Chapman, A., 1996, Six Years On, Rochdale's Last Victims Can Go Home. *Daily Mail* (UK), 29 December.
Eberle, P. and Eberle, S., 1993, *The Abuse of Innocence: The McMartin Preschool Trial*. Prometheus Books.
Fukurai, E., 1994, Sociologists in Action: The McMartin Sexual Abuse Case, Litigation, Justice and Mass Hysteria. *American Sociologist* 25, p.44.
Joint Enquiry Team (JET) Report, completed in 1989, but kept secret. It is currently freely available on the internet.
San Diego County, California, 1992, *Child Sexual Abuse, Assault and Molest Issues*. San Diego County Grand Jury Report No. 8 (available on the Internet).
Summitt, R.C., 1994, The Dark Tunnels of McMartin. *Journal of Psychohistory* 21(4), pp.5–13.
Tate, T., 1991, *Children for the Devil: Ritual Abuse and Satanic Crime*. Octopus Group.

### False memory syndrome

Wright, L., 1994, *Remembering Satan: Recovered Memory and the Shattering of a Family*. Serpent's Tail.

### Parallel stories

Brittain, V., 1994, *Testament of Youth*. Penguin Books.
Campbell, P., 1919, *Back to the Front*. London.
Dash, M., 1997, *Borderlands*. Arrow.
Harris, M., 1982, Where Angels Fear ... *The Unexplained* 12, pp.2846–9.

Kerekes, D. and Slater, D., 1994, *Killing for Culture – An Illustrated History of Death Film from Mondo to Snuff*. Creation Books.
Lewis-Smith, V., 1998, Funny Old World. *Private Eye* issue 962, 30 October, p.16 (original article cited as *Hong Kong Eastern Express*, September 1998).
Monk, M., 1836, *The Awful Disclosures of Maria Monk of the Hotel Dieu Nunnery*, Montreal, Canada. Howe and Bates.
Morin, E., 1971, *Rumour in Orléans*. Blond.
O'Gorman, E., 1871, *Convent Life Unveiled*. Connecticut Publishing Co.
Regal, B., 1996, Nuns on the Run. *Fortean Times* 87, pp.34–40.

## Chapter 9

Baigent, M., Leigh, R. and Lincoln, H., 1983, *The Holy Blood and the Holy Grail*. Corgi Books.
Baigent, M., Leigh, R. and Lincoln, H., 1987, *The Messianic Legacy*. Corgi Books.
Chadwick, H., 1993, *The Early Church* (revised edition). Penguin Books.
Daraul, A., 1969, *A History of Secret Societies*. New York.
Fowler, W.W., 1899, *The Roman Festivals*. London.
Green, V., 1996, *A New History of Christianity*. Sutton.
Mackay, C., 1995, *Extraordinary Popular Delusions and the Madness of Crowds*. Wordsworth Editions (originally published in 1852 as *Memoirs of Extraordinary Popular Delusions*, Volumes I and II).
Rickard, B., 1991, Cannibalistic Infanticide. *Fortean Times* 57, p.62.
Rolle, P.N., 1824, *Recherches sur le Cult de Bacchus*. Paris.
Runciman, S., 1978, *A History of the Crusades*. Volumes I, II and III. Penguin.
Scott, G.R., 1966, *Phallic Worship*. Luxor Press.
Shirer, W.L., 1964, *The Rise and Fall of the Third Reich*. Pan.
Stanford, P., 1996, *The Devil – A Biography*. Arrow.
Summers, M., 1926, *The History of Witchcraft*. Routledge and Kegan Paul (reprinted in 1994 by Senate).

## Chapter 10

*African penis-snatching*

Anonymous, 1984, Smurfs on the Rampage. *Fortean Times* 42, p.14.
Anonymous, 1996, Three Hanged over 'Missing Manhood'. *Electronic Telegraph*, issue 457, 22 August.
Dzisah, M., 1997, Ethnic Witch-hunts Spark Ivory Coast Riots. *Electronic Mail and Guardian*, 11 March.
Sieveking, P., 1997, Witchcraft. *Electronic Telegraph*, issue 659, 15 March.

*Asian penis-snatching (koro)*

Adityanjee, H., Zain, A.M. and Subramaniam, M., 1991, Sporadic Koro and Marital Disharmony. *Psychopathology* 24, pp.49–52.

Gwee, A.L., 1963, Koro – a Cultural Disease. *Singapore Medical Journal* 4, pp.119–23.

Gwee, A.L., 1968, Koro – Its Origin and Nature as a Disease Entity. *Singapore Medical Journal* 9, pp.3–5.

Illman, J., 1998, Warning: Smoking Can Seriously Shrink Your Manhood. *Observer*, 26 July.

Koro Study Team, 1968, The Koro 'Epidemic' in Singapore. *Singapore Medical Journal* 10, pp.234–43.

Nandi, D.N., Banerjee, G., Saha, H. et al., 1983, Epidemic Koro in West Bengal, India. *Indian International Journal of Social Psychiatry* 29, pp.265–8.

Ngui, P.W., 1969, The Koro Epidemic in Singapore. *Australian and New Zealand Journal of Psychiatry* 3, pp.263–6.

Rubin, R.T., 1989, Koro (Shook Yang) – A Culture-Bound Psychogenic Syndrome. In Friedmann, C.T. and Faguet, R.A., eds., *Extraordinary Disorders of Human Behaviour*, Plenum Press, pp.155–73.

Scott, R., 1971, *The Discoverie of Witchcraft*. Da Capo Press.

Tseng, W.S., Kan-Ming, M. Hsu, J. et al., 1988, A Sociocultural Study of Koro Epidemics in Guangdong, China. *American Journal of Psychiatry* 145, pp.1538–43.

Yap, P.M., 1965, Koro – a Culture-bound Depersonalization Syndrome. *British Journal of Psychiatry* 111, pp.43–50.

*Mass hysteria*

Chambers, P., 1998, *Paranormal People*. Blandford Press.

Dash, M., 1997, *Borderlands*. Arrow.

Gregory, R.L., 1987, *The Oxford Companion to the Mind*. Oxford University Press.

Huxley, A., 1952, *The Devils of Loudon*. Chatto and Windus.

Inglis, B., 1982, All in the Mind. *The Unexplained* 3, pp.670–73.

Spence, L., 1929, *The Encyclopedia of the Occult*. Routledge & Sons (reprinted in 1994 by Bracken Books).

Stafford, C.D., 1967, *What Freud Really Said*. Penguin Books.

Stanford, P., 1996, *The Devil – A Biography*. Arrow.

*Multiple personality disorder*

Chambers, P., 1998, *Paranormal People*. Blandford Press.

Mayer, R.S., 1991, *Satan's Children: Shocking True Accounts of Satanism, Abuse, and Multiple Personality Disorder*. Avon Books.

Merskey, H., 1993, The Manufacture of Personalities. *British Journal of Psychiatry* 160, pp.327–40.

Ofshe, R. and Watters, E., 1994, *Making Monsters: False Memories, Psychotherapy and Sexual Hysteria*. Scribner's.

Piper, A., 1988, Multiple Personality Disorder: Witchcraft Survives in the Twentieth Century. *Skeptical Enquirer*, May/June issue, pp.44–50.

Roy, A., 1982, Squatters in the Mind. *The Unexplained* 10, pp.2370–73.

## Chapter 11

*The UFO phenomenon*

Chambers, P., 1999, *Life on Mars – The Complete Story*. Blandford Press.
Clarke, J., 1998, *The UFO Book – Encyclopedia of the Extraterrestrial*. Visible Ink.
Spencer, J., 1997, *The UFO Encyclopedia*. Headline.
Stacy, D. and Evans, H., 1997, *UFO 1947–1997*. John Brown.

*Spiritual love and deep understanding*

Baxter, M., 1958, *My Saturnian Lover*. California.
Clarke, J., 1998, *The UFO Book – Encyclopedia of the Extraterrestrial*. Visible Ink.
Credo, M., 1996, *Song of the Stars – The Lore of a Zulu Shaman*. Barrytown Ltd.
Klarer, E., 1980, *Beyond the Light Barrier*. Howard Timmins.
Menger, H., 1959, *From Outer Space to You*. Vantage Press.

## Chapter 12

*Alien abductions*

Brookesmith, P., 1995, Do Aliens Dream of Jacobs' Sheep? *Fortean Times* 83, pp.22–9.
Holzer, H., 1976, *The Ufonauts: New Facts on Extraterrestrial Landings*. Fawcett Gold Medal.
Hopkins, B., 1981, *Missing Time: A Documented Study of UFO Abductions*. Random House.
Hopkins, B., 1987, *Intruders: The Incredible Visitations at Copley Woods*. Random House.
Hopkins, B., 1996, *Witnessed: The True Story of the Brooklyn Bridge Abductions*. Pocket Books.
Klass, P., 1988, *UFO Abductions: A Dangerous Game*. Prometheus Books.
Mack, J.E., 1994, *Abduction: Human Encounters with Aliens*. Charles Scribner and Sons.
Rimmer, J., 1984, *The Evidence for Alien Abductions*. Aquarian Press.
Strieber, W., 1987, *Communion: A True Story*. William Morrow and Co.

*Individual cases*

Anonymous, 1994, Kidnapped by Sex-mad Aliens. *Eva* (UK), 7 December.
Anonymous, 1994, Sex Was Out of This World. *Daily Star* (UK), 16 September.
Anonymous, 1994, The Real X Files. *TV Quick*, 26 November.

Davies, M., 1993, I Was Snatched by a UFO ... Then I Had an Alien's Baby. *Sunday People* (UK), 15 August, p.9.
Poole, T., 1995, Close Encounters of an Intimate Kind. *Independent* (UK), 17 March.
Shakespeare, J., 1995, The Sex Files. *Options* (UK), June , p.15.

*Alien abduction and sleep paralysis (see also entries for Chapter 1)*

Blackmore, S., 1994, Alien Abduction – The Inside Story. *New Scientist* 19 November, pp.4–6.
Blackmore, S., 1994, Alien Abductions. *The Skeptic* 8(4), p.10.
Blackmore, S., 1996, Jackie and the Aliens. *The Skeptic* 11(1), pp.13–14.
Kennedy, A., 1996, Little Grey Men. *The Skeptic* 10(3), pp.10–12.
Rose, N., 1996, Abduction Theory. *The Skeptic* 10(4), pp.12–14.

# ACKNOWLEDGEMENTS

There is not the room to thank everybody who has in some way contributed to the writing and publication of this manuscript, but the following have particularly helped and without them the book would never have made it into print.

I would especially like to thank the librarians at the Society for Psychical Research, University College London, the Natural History Museum (London), the Royal Astronomical Society, Senate House and Imperial College. I am also grateful to the following colleagues and friends for their discussions and comments: Neil Dubé, Dr Mark Biddiss, Simon Butler, Karen Pulford, Karen Ings and John, Sarah and Elizabeth Baxter. Many thanks must also go to the staff at Cassell, most especially Stuart Booth, Jane Birch and Miranda Stonor, whose patience and professionalism ensured that all went smoothly in the production of this book.

Finally, I reserve my greatest thanks and gratitude to Rachel Baxter, for her patience and for the number of times she had to read this manuscript, and to my mother, father, brother and sister-in-law for their help and encouragement over the years.

# INDEX

*Italics* refer to publications and TV programmes.

abductees 184, 187–8, 198, 200–3
*Abduction: Human Encounters with Aliens* 190, 192, 198
abstention from sex 71
Adam, son of God 30, 49, 50
Adamski, George 172, 176
adolescence, poltergeist activity 95–9
Africa 149–50, 202
Akon (alien) 173–4
alien abduction 27, 171–2, 175, 178–204
    examples 180–4
    symptoms 196–7
aliens, amorous 169–77
*Alphabet of Ben Sira, The* 48–9
de Ameno, Father L. M. Sinistrari 41
ancient religions 58–61
angels, fallen 37
anxiety, sleep paralysis 20, 24
Aratus (occultist) 103
Arnold, Kenneth 170, 171
artificial phalluses 85
Asia, penis-snatching 152
attacks, sleep paralysis 17–18, 24
Aura Rhanes (alien) 176

babies, Lilith 49
Bacchanalia 130–1
*Back to the Front* 145
baptism, demons 33–4
belief of abductees 184
bestiality 41, 46, 83, 83–4

*Beyond the Light Barrier* 173
bions (matter) 101–2
Blackmore, Susan 188, 195
Boas, Antonio Villas 174–5, 176
Bouget, Henry 138–9
brain inhibitors 22
Broxtowe Estate case 111–13

Campbell, Phyllis 145
Canada, old hags 16–19
cannibalism 112, 132, 134, 146
Cathars 45–6, 136–7
celibacy, temptation 52
chastity 72, 103–5
children
    Lilith 49–53
    as sacrifice 109, 134, 136, 139–40
    sexual abuse 115
    witnesses 120
China, Christian persecution 142–3
chosen people 199–200
Christianity 70–2, 132–8
    demons 31–2
    devil worship 75
    evangelical 42, 119, 159
    Internet 43
    pre-marital sex 34
    Satanic ritual abuse 126
Mrs Clarer *see* Klarer, Elizabeth
Clarke, Elizabeth (witch) 36
Clarke, Jerome 198
close encounters, third kind 171, 178
*Communion* 180, 198
contactees 172

*convulsionnaires, les* 161–2
Cortile, Linda (abductee) 185–6, 192
crime, multiple personality disorder 165–6
Crowley, Aleister (occultist) 62
cultural causes 18
cultural fear 19, 24–5
cultural-based phenomena 13, 15

*De Demonialitate, et Incubis, et Succubis* 41
demons 29–41, 43, 50, 73
  belief 42
  exorcism 39
  offspring 44
  perceptions of victims 33
  physical form 37–8
  pregnancy 44–6
  reincarnation 45
  theology 47
devil, the 48, 74
Devils of Loudon 160–1
digestion, sleep paralysis 27
*Discours des Sorciers* 138–9
*Discoverie of Witchcraft, The* 157–8
dissociation hysteria 162–3
*Doctor Who* 174
doctors, alien 182–3
dreaming 22–5
dusii (demons) 31

Egyptian gods 61
energy 94–5, 101, 102, 104–5
*Epic of Gilgamesh* 52–3
Eucharist 132
Europe, penis-snatching 156–7
evidence, physical 184–90
evil, personified 48
extraterrestrial sex 167–204

fairies 118–24
false memory syndrome 120
fantasy proneness 189
fashion 89
fear, cultural 19, 24–5
female gentalia worship 59–60
films 14–15, 144–5
flying saucers 170
folk tales, sleep paralysis 26–7
Fort, Charles 203–4
Freud, Sigmund 94

gender, sexual appetite 89
Genesis, book of 30, 48–9
genetics 177
ghosts, rape 7–8, 14–16
Gnostic Christianity 69–72
Goats, the 142
gods 47–8, 58, 61, 64–72

Gollom Report 112
Grandier, Father Urbain 160–1
The Great American Airship Scare 171
Greek gods 61

hags 16–19, 27–8, 190–5
hair, demons' 39
hallucinations 23–4, 191
  sleep paralysis 19–26
Hausa tribe, penis-snatching 150
Hill, Betty and Barney 178–9, 185
Hispala Fecenia 130
Hitler, Jewish persecution 136
homosexuality 69, 81, 82
Hopkins, Budd 180, 185–6, 193, 198–9
hormones, penis-snatching 152
Hosea (prophet) 131
Hufford, David 16–19, 193–4, 195
Hume, Grace 146
hymen, breaking 65–6
Hynek, J. Allen 171
hypnopompic hallucinations 23–4, 191
hypnosis 123, 190
  memories 114, 121, 164, 197–9
hysteria 158–66

implants 183, 187–8
incubi 29–36
  *see also* demons
Internet 43, 196
*Intruders* 180, 185
Isaiah, book of 52

Jeffries, Anne (witch) 40
Jews, persecution 135
Judaism 49–50, 58–60, 69
Jung, Carl 54

*Kabbala* 30, 50, 51
Karrin (abductee) 199
kidnapping *see* alien abduction
King, George 172
Klarer, Elisabeth 173–4, 176
Knights Templar 75–6, 137
koro (panic) 152–8
Kurz, Shane 179–80

Liberalia 131
life forces 103
Lilith 30, 48–54
literature, effect of 180
love, spiritual 172–7
lust, power of 94–105
Luther, Martin 79, 87

Mack, John E. 187, 190, 192, 195, 198
McMartin Case 115–17
magicians, penis-snatching 151–2

# Index

*Malleus Maleficarum* 36–40, 76–9, 157
Manhattan Beach 115–17
Mars 170, 171
mass executions, witches 76
mass hysteria 158–62
masturbation 51
media scares 118
medical evidence 183, 186–8
memories 114, 120–1, 164, 197–9
Meng Zhaoguo (abductee) 175–7
Menger, Howard 172–3, 174
menopause 90
menstruation 66–7, 90
mental balance 184, 189
mental illness, demonic possession 42
*Michelle Remembers* 114, 118
midwives 92
Minucius Felix 132
misogyny 36, 86–8
morality, demonic intercourse 35
mother-ship experiences 195–200
multiple personality disorder 163–6
Murphy, Liz 200
Mutwa, Credo (shaman) 174, 201–2
*My Saturnian Lover* 173

Naamah (demon) 51–2
Nazi experiments, virgins 105
*Nightmare, The* 28
*Nightmares and Human Conflict* 195
Nuns, ritual abuse 144
offspring, demons 44
Ordo Templi Orientis 62
orgasmic power 100–3
orgies 80–3, 111–12, 128–46
orgone energy 102, 204
Orléans, sexual slavery 129

paedophilia 118
pagan rituals, Christianity 32
panic attacks 20, 148, 191
Papal Bull 77–8
paralysis 192, 203
Passover, child sacrifice 136
Pazder, Lawrence 114, 118
penis-snatching 7–8, 147–58
persecution 143
   Cathars 136–7
   Christians 132–3
   Jews 134–6
   Knights Templar 137
   witches 138–9, 141
Persia, Lilith 53
personal hysteria 159–61
phallus 57, 60, 65, 131
phantom pregnancy 44–6
physical evidence 124, 126, 184–90
Pi (Buddhist spirit) 12

pillar worship 59–60
poltergeist activity 95–9
Popobawa, Zanzibar 11, 18
posterior kissing 139
pre-marital sex 34
pregnancy, phantom 44–6
Priapus (god) 58, 65
Psellos, Michael Constantine 134
psychiatry 124, 125, 164–5, 189
psychic phenomena, adolescents 95–9
psychicism 195
psychokinesis 97
psychology 154–5, 189, 203
puberty 88–9

questioning techniques 121–2

rape, ghosts 7–8, 14–16
recurrent spontaneous psychokinesis (RSPK) 97
regression 197
Reich, Wilhelm 100–3, 204
reincarnation 45
religions, modern 62–3
REM sleep 21–2, 25, 191
ritual abuse 110–13, 124–6, 132–3
robot zombies 149
Rochdale case 109
Roman Empire 129–33
Roper poll 193, 196
RSPK *see* recurrent spontaneous psychokinesis

sabbats 38–9, 80–6, 138–42
sacrifice, children 109, 136, 139–40
St Augustine 31–2, 74
St Paul 133–4
St Thomas 33
satanism 109–27, 202
*Satan's Underground* 114
science fiction 171, 194–5
Scott, George Ryley 59
Scott, Reginald 157–8
self-diagnosis 189, 197
semen 50, 91
sensory perception, sleep paralysis 18
sexual
   abuse 115, 129–31
   appetite, gender 89
   assault 9–54
      demons 29–36
      ghosts 14–16
   energy 94–5, 101, 104–5
   frustration 98
   intercourse 64, 72, 95–9
      animal spirits 46
      demons 38–9
      feasts 39

ghosts 8
Lilith 49
*Malleus Maleficarum* 37–8
spectral 13–16
witches 38–9
practice, diversity 142
Shaver, Richard 128
Shunamitism 103–5
Sian-Ow, Pao 153
SIDS *see* Sudden Infant Death Syndrome
sin, intercourse 72
Sinistrari de Ameno, Father Ludovicus Maria 41
sleep
deprivation 21
disorders 24–6, 203
links 204
paralysis 11–13, 17–18
attacks 190–1
causes 17, 18–19
folk tales 26–7
hallucinations 19–26
psychology 19–20
Smurfs, Texas 147
Smurl poltergeist haunting 14
snuff movies 144–5
social panic 148
social workers 109, 111
Spanish Inquisition 137–8
special people 199–200
spiritual love 172–7
star maps 179
stories, common themes 198, 202
Stratford, Lauren 114
Strieber, Whitley 180, 198–9
succubi 29–36, 38
*see also* demons
Sudden Infant Death Syndrome (SIDS) 50
Sudden Unexpected Nocturnal Death Syndrome (SUNDS) 12
suffocation 14, 31
suggestion, child witnesses 120
Summers, Montague 140
SUNDS *see* Sudden Unexpected Nocturnal Death Syndrome
surveys 193–4
survivors of abduction 200–3

*Sybil* 166
symptoms, abduction 196–7
talk shows 117
Talmud (Babylonian) 53
Tantra 62
temple prostitutes 67–8, 69
theology, demons 47
therapy 113, 125
trucken practice 27

UFOs *see* unidentified flying objects
unidentified flying objects (UFOs) 169–72, 182–3
United States of America (USA) 172, 188

vampires 26
Venus 170, 173
victims, self-diagnosis 189
virginity 38, 65–7, 178–204

war propaganda 145–6
*The War of the Worlds* 171
Weber, Connic 173
Wells, H. G. 171
Wendy (abductee) 181–2
white magic 141
white slavery 129
wine 131
witchcraft 86–8
witches 78, 88, 90–1
demons 35, 38, 40, 45
Elizabeth Clarke 36
mass executions 76
persecution 138–9, 141, 142–3
sleep paralysis 27
trials 40–2, 73–5, 92–3
*Witnessed* 185, 186
witnesses 185
women
hatred 86–7
witches 88

*The X Files* 201
X-rays, implants 187

Yaweh 59